The WBT Briarhoppers

Eight Decades of a Bluegrass Band Made for Radio

Tom Warlick and
Lucy Warlick

Foreword by Robert Inman

McFarland & Company, Inc., Publishers
Jefferson, North Carolina, and London

LIBRARY OF CONGRESS CATALOGUING-IN-PUBLICATION DATA

Warlick, Tom.
The WBT Briarhoppers : eight decades of a bluegrass band
made for radio / Tom Warlick and Lucy Warlick ; foreword by
Robert Inman.
p.   cm.
Includes bibliographical references, discography, and index.

ISBN-13: 978-0-7864-3144-1
softcover : 50# alkaline paper ∞

1. Briarhoppers (Musical group)   2. Bluegrass musicians —
United States.   3. WBT (Radio station : Charlotte, N.C.)
I. Warlick, Lucy.   II. Title.
ML421.B75W37   2008
781.642092'2 — dc22   2007031414
[B]

British Library cataloguing data are available

Cover images: Briarhoppers on stage, courtesy of author; fiddle
and guitar, courtesy Kate Irwin; microphone and banjo, ©2008
PhotoSpin

Manufactured in the United States of America

McFarland & Company, Inc., Publishers
Box 611, Jefferson, North Carolina 28640
www.mcfarlandpub.com

This book is dedicated:

To the WBT Briarhoppers, past and present, those who are listed in this book and those whose names have vanished from the records;

To the families of each and every Briarhopper, who supported their loved ones so that several generations of music lovers could enjoy "Briarhopper Time";

To Billie Burton Daniel, Martin Schopp, and Newell Hathcock, the last known surviving members of the "Briarhopper Family" radio show of the 1930s;

To Roy "Whitey" Grant and Eleanor Bryan Fields, the last surviving members of the original WBT Briarhopper String Band, Roy's wife, Polly, and their daughters;

To Dwight Moody and David Deese for their support and encouragement in this endeavor;

To Leslie Crutchfield Tompkins and Richard Crutchfield, for their trust in sharing the files of their father, Charles Crutchfield, with us, and for sharing poetry, art, ghosts, and water-witching;

To the Country Music Hall of Fame's John Rumble, Gasoline Alley's Jim "Fiddlin' Scank" Scancarelli, and the Levine Museum of the New South's Tom Hanchett;

To the members of the BT Lunch Club, who regale us with stories once a quarter at the Charlotte Café;

And to our family and friends.

Contents

Foreword

It was 1970, and I was arriving in Charlotte to begin a newscasting career at what everybody in my business knew was a giant in broadcasting — the powerhouse Jefferson-Pilot flagship stations of WBTV and WBT radio. It was home to some of the best-known names in American media — TV stars like Doug Mayes, Clyde McLean, Jim Patterson and Betty Feezor, and radio folks such as Ty Boyd and the recently retired Grady Cole.

The stations, and their people, were the stuff of legend. But they were also a warm-hearted family who welcomed me, made me feel at home, and nurtured my life on the air through twenty-three years of newscasts.

One of my stops that first day on the job was the basement studio of Hank Warren, the company photographer, to have my official picture made. Hank was the kind of guy you liked right off, and liked more the more you knew him. It wasn't long before somebody mentioned that Hank was part of the Briarhoppers. The what? And there I was, into the fascinating story of a group of guys and gals who had transformed radio years before.

Radio in its early days — from infancy to the 1930s — was pretty much a stuffed-shirt affair. Announcers spoke in stentorian tones and the language they used was pretentious and fatuous. Music on the radio was staid and sedate, too. Radio, it seems, took itself pretty seriously.

And then, along came the Briarhoppers.

The late Charles Crutchfield, the longtime president of Jefferson-Pilot Broadcasting, and the man many credit with bringing the Briarhoppers to life, told me a story a few years ago about the moment of creation. It began with a phone call to station manager Harry Schudt from a businessman in Chicago who wanted to know if WBT had a hillbilly radio program to showcase his products. The story goes that Schudt turned to Crutchfield,

1

his program director, and asked, "Do we have a hillbilly band?" "Yes, sir," Crutchfield fibbed. And then he ran down the hallway and told an associate to get together some hillbilly musicians. They soon went on the air, calling themselves "The Briarhoppers," with Crutchfield as announcer.

It was a different kind of radio than anyone had heard before. It featured lots of down-home music and lots of humor, much of it at the expense of the sponsors' products. It was intimate, personal radio, bringing a ray of sunshine into the bleak Depression-era lives of Americans all up and down the East Coast. When you tuned in the Briarhoppers' show in the afternoon, you could laugh, tap your foot, and forget your troubles for a while. It was also immensely successful radio. It sold a huge amount of products such as Peruna iron tonic and Kolor-Bak hair dye. It made household names of the men and women who appeared on the show during its long and happy life — both on the air and in hundreds of performances before live audiences. And it did a great deal to take the stuffed-shirtiness out of radio in general.

The show finally went off the air in 1951, but when I arrived in Charlotte in 1970, the Briarhoppers were enjoying a revival. Some of the guys got together and began picking and singing, just like old times, and then they began to appear in public. Generations of fans still remembered them and welcomed them back. And new generations discovered some incredibly nice people who had great fun making music. I became a huge fan, and the Briarhoppers became my friends.

Now, years later, through the meticulous research and appreciative writing of Tom Warlick and Lucy Warlick, we're able to recapture the special time and place the Briarhoppers created, and to hear the echoes of their music. It's a rich legacy, a vital part of Americana, a story worth repeating. Tom and Lucy have done us all a favor by preserving it and passing it on. Read and enjoy.

— Robert Inman

Alabama native Robert Inman left journalism after a 31-year career, the majority of which was spent as news anchor at WBTV-Charlotte, to become an author, screenwriter, and playwright. He is the author of four novels, two plays, six screenplays for television and a collection of short stories.

Inman and his wife, Paulette, reside in Charlotte, North Carolina, and have two daughters. Robert Inman's website can be found at http://www.robert-inman.com

Preface

In 1934, WBT radio announcer Charles Crutchfield formed a musical group to satisfy Consolidated Drug Trade Company of Chicago, a potential sponsor that wanted to advertise on the radio station. The first Briarhoppers was basically a Tin-Pan Alley group that lasted from 1934 to 1940. The group's theme song was "Wait Till the Sun Shines, Nellie."

A paradigm shift in country music took place when Roy "Whitey" Grant, Arval Hogan, Claude Casey, Fred Kirby, and Shannon Grayson joined original band members Don White and Big Bill Davis to create a string band that was a precursor to many bluegrass bands and became, according to the Country Music Hall of Fame, one of the longest-lasting bluegrass/country bands in America.

Now, the WBT Briarhoppers are in the waning years of existence. Since our time with them, Briarhopper family members Arval Hogan, Cathy Moody, and Don White have passed away. Roy Grant, Dwight Moody (who replaced the late Fiddlin' Hank Warren), and David Deese (who replaced the late Shannon Grayson) are the only ones left to hold up the mantle of "The Briarhoppers."

The remaining Briarhoppers asked us to compile this record of one of the greatest musical groups in our country. We were able to go through thousands of pages of what we believe represent the advent of bluegrass and country music, and tried to exhaust all avenues available to us; those included conducting interviews with members of the Briarhoppers from the 1930s through the present day (and interviews with their family members we tracked down through files held by the Country Music Hall of Fame and the Internet), reading newspaper articles from all over the Southeast, scouring files at the Country Music Hall of Fame and various museums and libraries, consulting books and articles in scholarly journals, and looking at photographs documenting nearly 80 years of the band's existence.

To study the WBT Briarhoppers is to study the growth of Charlotte, North Carolina, the development of American country music, the beginning of radio and television in the Southeast, mill life in small towns, and the full-circle nature of music: string band; rock and roll; and acoustic Americana. The WBT Briarhoppers are intertwined with some of the best-known bluegrass and country bands this country has seen: The Tennessee Ramblers; Arthur Smith and the Crackerjacks; The Johnson Family; The Swingbillies; and others. The WBT Briarhoppers have played side-by-side with the original Carter Family, Mainer's Mountaineers, Bill and Charlie Monroe, The Delmore Brothers, The Hired Hands, Flatt & Scruggs, even the great violinist David Rubinoff and pianist Jose Iturbi. One of the common threads of traditional American music has to be the WBT Briarhoppers in all its incarnations.

We have relied on many people's memories of who were Briarhoppers and who were guests, which apparently is a very thin line. Roy "Whitey" Grant supplied much of this information through several interviews during 2005. Information pertaining to Johnny McAllister, Clarence Etters, Jane Bartlett (of the first batch of Briarhoppers), Homer Christopher and Sam Poplin (of the string band Briarhoppers beginning in 1941) was difficult to find, either due to their brief stays at WBT or the lack of written materials about them.

We did get invaluable data from "the forgotten Briarhopper," Billie Burton Daniel, one of the last two original members of the pre–1940 Briarhopper family. Through her, we were able to bring life to those original Briarhoppers of 1934, who were all basically forgotten. Tim Drye, son of the late Briarhopper Homer Drye, supplied data on his father, from Homer's time as a youngster on WBT radio through his successful music, TV and radio career in Raleigh, North Carolina. Thorpe Westerfield's story was told by his daughter, Terry Marshall.

Also, through Daniel's help, we were able to describe a typical radio show and stage show of the original Briarhopper family, of which no recordings or transcripts, to our knowledge, remain.

"Wait Till the Sun Shines, Nellie"
music by Harry Von Tilzer,
lyrics by Andrew B. Sterling

The WBT Briarhoppers' Theme Song

Wait till the sun shines, Nellie,
As the clouds go drifting by.
We will be happy, Nellie,
Don't you sigh.
Down Lovers' Lane we'll wander,
Sweethearts, you and I.
Wait till the sun shines, Nellie,
By and by.

1

The 1920s: The Big Bang of Country Music

Do Y'all Know What Hit Is?
No, Crutch!
Hit's Briarhopper Time!

Long before radio, music was a family and a community affair. In the South, fiddles, guitars, and banjos echoed off old farmhouse porches into the night, bringing those neighbors interested enough from miles around to sit and hear the songs of their youth.

Some of the music came from the mountains of Appalachia, as mountain farmers ventured into the cities to find work. As they came down from the hills, they brought their instruments and their memories of the old songs of their Irish ancestors.

Life was hard for the majority of U.S. residents. Backbreaking labor in the fields, dangerous mill life, horrifying coal mining, and segregation of the races were par for America's course. Rural electricity was uncommon. Folks still read by oil lamps and cooked with wood stoves. Outhouses were part of the family vocabulary.

Up to this point, working-class people received information from newspapers and by word-of-mouth. With the advent of battery-operated radio, folks could begin to get real-time information. "Radio was the lifeline to the world," one mill worker said.[1] Another mill worker continued that thought, saying:

> In the summertime, Daddy'd open up the window there and turn that (radio) horn around to the outside and the whole neighborhood would come around. Old folks would sit in chairs, right there in the yard. Those kids

would lay on quilts and those babies would be laying around out there in the yard and listen to the Grand Ole Opry or some local bands.[2]

American radio entertainment changed forever on November 28, 1925, when WSM radio announcer George D. Hay featured an aged fiddler, Uncle Jimmy Thompson, after a national broadcast of *The Grand Opera*. Hay's scheduled act apparently did not show. Thompson's niece, who worked at the radio station, said her uncle was waiting in the car outside and he knew one thousand songs on his fiddle. The old man was dragged up the stairs to the studio, and Uncle Jimmy Thompson's legacy was born. Cards and letters flooded WSM, the radio station in Nashville, Tennessee. On December 28, 1925, Hay featured Thompson and Uncle Dave Macon, and the *Grand Ole Opry* was born.[3]

WBT Radio

WBT radio got its start in a chicken coop in the Dilworth Community in Charlotte, North Carolina, thanks to a bill passed in Congress in the previous decade. "The Radio Act of 1912" allowed any citizen to apply for a radio license to open and operate a radio station.[4]

This bill allowed tinkerers like Fred Laxton, Earle Gluck, and Fred Buckner in the Charlotte chicken coop to get their start. The three men met at a local amateur radio parts shop in 1920 and bought the components to make a small radio. The small radio was operated out of Laxton's home at the corner of Mecklenburg and Belvedere Avenues in what is now the Midwood section of Charlotte. The telephone-microphone was in the dining room, the transmitter in an adjoining room, and the receiver in the chicken house.[5] In 1921, the group received an "experimental" radio license from the United States Department of Commerce with the call letters 4XD.[6] In 1922, the group applied for a commercial radio license and moved the equipment to the eighth floor of the Independence Building in Charlotte. The new license gave the radio station owners the call letters WBT.[7]

C.C. Coddington, the owner of a Buick dealership, purchased the radio station and claimed the call letters WBT, advertising the letters to mean "Watch Buick Travel."[8]

WBT historian David Eades records that in 1927 WBT increased its power to 1,000 watts and joined the NBC Radio Network. Johnny Long made his debut at WBT as a big band leader. In 1928, WBT's power increased to 5,000 watts. Bands such as Jimmie Purcell and his Dixonians, the Hawaiian Serenaders, the Woodlawn String Band, Joe Nesbit and his Pennsylvanians, Fisher Hendley, and the Carolina Tarheels began broadcasting over the airwaves.[9]

Up to this point, WBT stressed classical music, "reflecting an obsession with European culture and a focus on modernization on the region and its population."[10] Pam Grundy wrote in her article "From *Il Trovatore* to the Crazy Mountaineers: The Rise and Fall of Elevated Culture on WBT-Charlotte, 1922–1930" that the first music heard over WBT was on April 27, 1922, with "the sweet, romantic tones of Jules Massenet's 'Pleurez, mes yeux,' sung by Miss Kathleen Culbertson of the Carolina Concert Club ... from the Chamber of Commerce assembly hall in Charlotte, North Carolina, and spread out across the country."

However, as Grundy wrote, "The city's [Charlotte's] most influential musicians would turn out to belong not to the Carolina Concert Club but to working-class string bands with names such as the Briarhoppers and the Crazy Mountaineers."[11]

The Big Bang

American music changed in 1927 when Ralph Peer advertised for rural musicians to meet him in Bristol, on the Tennessee-Virginia border, to record a genre made famous by Vernon Dalhart and others. Many have called this year the "Big Bang of Country Music." From this book's perspective, it is the starting date of the germination of a band called the WBT Briarhoppers.

The Bristol story is a simple one to understand now, but was a major leap of faith at the time. The following text comes from Barry McCloud's *Definitive Country: The Ultimate Encyclopedia of Country Music and Its Performers:*

> Former Okeh record executive Ralph Peer joined Victor Talking Machine Company to help the company grow in the area of country music. Peer went to Bristol to find fresh, unrecorded talent. With his wife Anita and two engineers named Eckhart and Lynch, Peer packed recording equipment into a car and traveled to Bristol where they had rented an empty storefront located at 408 State Street near the state line between Virginia and Tennessee. Although Peer had arranged in advance for performers to record, he also invited newspaper reporters to the first recording session to hype the event in the local newspapers. Soon, many telephone calls came from the Virginia and Tennessee mountain folk wanting to know how they could be recorded.
>
> The first major act to be recorded was the already well-known Stoneman Family from Galax, Virginia, headed by Ernest "Pop" Stoneman. Others to be

recorded included the West Virginia Coon Hunters, the Shelor Family, and the Tenneva Ramblers, which was the group headed by Jimmie Rodgers. During the last week, Peer recorded The Carter Family and Jimmie Rodgers. These recordings were the most important of these sessions. The records produced under Victor's "New Southern Series" were a hit, and caused many people to purchase "talking machines" to play these records. Many budding musicians listened to these records, learning the songs and dreaming of being music stars. Corporations began to realize that this type of music touched a segment of the country ripe to tap for purchasing products. With the growth of radio, country music began to take over the airwaves.[12]

Hillbilly music performers began to drift to Charlotte to recording studios quickly placed by RCA Victor and their budget-priced label, Bluebird. According to Tom Hanchett, formerly of the Charlotte-Mecklenburg (County) Historic Properties Commission and now with the Levine Museum of the South, "The Original Carter Family ... the teenaged Arthur Smith (of 'Dueling Banjos' fame) ... Uncle Dave Macon ... Jimmie Davis ... and the Blue Sky Boys" came to Charlotte to record.[13]

Eventually, the recording side of the music business would interact with the radio side of the music business, and musicians would start performing on the radio to sell their records, to sell their sponsors' products, and to tell the audience where that certain musician would be playing a concert. These two entities, plus the addition of advertisers and rural listeners who came from the country to work, would gel into a growth medium which would germinate local string bands performing on the radio.

It would be another seven years before a group of people from WBT radio in Charlotte, North Carolina, would be called "Briarhoppers."

Timeline*—1920s

1920— Fred Laxton, Earle Gluck, and Fred Buckner set up an amateur radio station in a chicken house in the Plaza Midwood area of Charlotte.

1921— Experimental license was given to station 4XD, precursor to WBT.

1922— Radio station moved and was assigned the call letters WBT (Watch Buick Travel).

1923— First *Barn Dance* held on WBAP-Fort Worth, Texas.

1924— WLS-Chicago was on the air.

1925— Freeman Gosden and Charlie Correll broadcast over WBT as the

*Sources for the timelines in this book come from http://www.wbt.com, *The Grand Ole Opry History of Country Music*, and http://www.pbs.org.

"Black Crows," and later moved to Chicago to become "Amos and Andy." WSM started at 1,000 watts. Dr. Humphrey Bates was the first country act on WSM. George D. Hay became WSM announcer. WSM *Barn Dance* began. *Barn Dance* name changed to *Grand Ole Opry.*

1926— WBT increased to 500 watts.

1927— WBT increased to 1,000 watts and was bought by NBC and went to 5,000 watts. Bristol Sessions with the Carter Family and Jimmie Rodgers were held. Herbert Hoover was elected president.

1928— WBT increased to 5,000 watts. Local musical groups began to broadcast. The Carter Family recorded "Wildwood Flower."

1929— CBS purchased WBT and increased to 25,000 watts. The stock market crashed.

America's Musical Taste:*

The top record of this decade was Louis Armstrong's "When the Saints Go Marching In."

*Information at the end of each chapter under "America's Musical Taste" comes from the website "Octopus's Garden," found at http://www.rareexception.com/Garden/Best/Decade.php.

2

The 1930s:
Charles Crutchfield Goes
Rabbit Hunting

Through the inspiration of the *Grand Ole Opry*, string and jug bands began to spring up, performing at community gatherings and on the radio. Companies began hiring these bands to hawk their wares. These companies would produce local radio shows where the bands would entertain the families while slipping in a little information on whatever product they wanted to sell.

According to Grundy, "A group of advertisers sparked a revival of local talent on WBT in the mid–1930s. It was not the violins of the city's concert societies that filled the station's air time. Rather, the representatives of a laxative called Crazy Water Crystals and the makers of the highly alcoholic tonic with the mysterious name 'Peruna' found that the sounds of fiddles and banjos, played by young men from the region's farms and textile mills, attracted enormous audiences and enthusiastic responses."[1]

Created in Mineral Springs, Texas, Crazy Water Crystals was the remains of evaporated spring water. A whole city gained a national reputation solely on the mineral extracts from their springs, similar to today's Epsom salts.

Crazy Water Crystals at WBT

Crazy Water Crystals knew of WBT and its growing radio audience. In 1933, Crazy Water Crystals dispatched J.W. Fincher and his son, Herbert, to the Carolinas, and to Charlotte, North Carolina. The setup was quick, starting an office in town and advertising in the *Charlotte Observer*, inviting readers to drop by and try some of the "electrically cooled" Crazy Water.[2]

Crazy Water Crystals began sponsoring not only daily radio shows on WBT, but also the *Crazy Barn Dance*, featuring regional string bands on Saturday nights, emulating the *Grand Ole Opry* and the *National Barn Dance*.[3]

This program aired from March 1934 to the fall of 1935, according to Grundy's doctoral thesis cited above. Groups like Mainer's Mountaineers, Bill and Earl Bolick (The Blue Sky Boys), the Monroe Brothers, Homer "Pappy" Sherrill's Crazy Blue Ridge Hillbillies (comprised of Sherrill and the Blue Sky Boys), the Crazy Tennessee Ramblers, and others changed their names slightly to reflect the sponsorship of Crazy Water Crystals.

The bands were gathered by Fisher Hendley, a local musician and banjo player, who had a successful band called the Aristocratic Pigs, that name also based on a sponsor. (Hendley would go down in fame as the person who purchased a new Gibson Granada banjo in 1934, and that banjo would eventually be owned by DeWitt "Snuffy" Jenkins, Don Reno, and, finally, Earl Scruggs).

The *Crazy Barn Dance* lasted until 1935, after financial disputes ended the radio show. The Charlotte office closed soon after the Atlanta Crazy Water Crystals office closed in 1937.[4] However, string band music had embedded itself into WBT and its listeners. As Grundy cited, "Charlotte

Crazy Water Crystals box, circa 1930s (author's collection).

had become a major center for the recording and broadcast of 'hillbilly' music, and the talent assembled in the city could compete with any in the world."[5]

Fred Kirby remembered Crazy Water Crystals fondly: "It'd become part of your daily thing. In (other) words, you go by the Crazy Water Crystals place in Charlotte before you went out on a personal appearance and you represented Crazy Water Crystals out there, too, and before you left there, you got some Crazy Water Crystals right out of the cooler. They had a big glass cooler that you just get you a cup or two of Crazy Water Crystals before you left town."[6]

Though the *Crazy Barn Dance* ended, and the Crazy Water Crystals product would soon cease production due to governmental interference, their style of combining string bands and advertising would ignite a new genre of radio programming, transforming many radio stations, including WBT, into national powerhouses.

Charles Crutchfield and the Birth of the WBT Briarhoppers

When Charles Crutchfield was hired as an announcer at WBT in 1933, he decided to take a chance in 1934 and change the "high-brow programming of the station to music from the country and mountains. A major part of that plan was a hillbilly music show called *The Briarhoppers.*"[7]

Author and former WBTV television news anchor Robert Inman, in a 1997 self-published biography on Charles Crutchfield, recorded how and why the Briarhoppers were formed. Inman writes, "'Crutch' was in station manager Bill Schudt's office when the call came in from Harry O'Neal of the Consolidated Drug Trade Company wanting to schedule a hillbilly music show, an hour a day, six days a week, to showcase his products. Schudt turned to Crutch and asked, 'Do we have a hillbilly band?' The answer was 'Yes, sir.'"

Inman continues: "No such band existed at WBT, but this was an opportunity that was too good to pass up. He [Crutchfield] found an associate, Johnny McAllister, in the hallway and told him to get together some hillbilly musicians. They named the band 'The Briarhoppers,' and went on the air with Crutch as the announcer...."[8]

According to Joe DePriest, writer for the *Charlotte Observer*, Crutchfield coined the Briarhoppers' name from a tale about a rabbit chase through a briar patch.[9]

Ivan Tribe, in the March 1978 edition of *Bluegrass Unlimited*, wrote, "In the mid-thirties when the Drug Trade Products Company of Chicago wanted to sponsor a country music program at WBT, [they] got some boys together and started a program but they didn't have a name. One day, Charles Crutchfield, the announcer, was out hunting with some fellows. When they jumped a rabbit, one of the party said, 'Look at that rabbit jump those briars.' Crutchfield hit upon 'Briarhoppers' as the name of the band."[10]

Another theory of the band's name came from musicians Cecil Campbell and Harry Blair, who were off-and-on members of the WBT Briarhopper radio show in the 1940s. They remember that their main band, the Tennessee Ramblers, had used the pseudonym "Briarhoppers" whenever they needed to avoid contractual conflicts in their pre–Charlotte days.[11]

Scholars point out that the term "Briarhoppers" was also slang for Kentucky migrants at the time.[12] Barry Willis writes in his book, *America's Music: Bluegrass*, that radio listeners who moved from eastern Kentucky were known as "Briars," or "Briarhoppers."[13] Paul F. Braden, who began broadcasting on WPFB in Middletown, Ohio, said the station's call letters became synonymous for "We Play For Briars."[14]

Claude Casey, a member of the WBT Briarhoppers, told the Country Music Hall of Fame's John Rumble on October 3, 1983, that he remembered a "fellow up around Cincinnati, up in that section of the country, or Chicago, somewhere, he called hisself [*sic*] 'The Old Briarhopper,' Bill Briarhopper. John, I don't know if you are aware of this or not, but the people that live in Kentucky, they're called briarhoppers...."[15]

When Rumble asked Casey about the story of Crutchfield coming up with the name while rabbit hunting, and whether or not that was more of a publicity stunt, Casey responded, "Yeah, I think so."[16]

Billie Burton Daniel, a member of the Briarhopper Family from 1936 to 1940, told the authors that when she was with the group, the name was "Briar Hopper." "If I'm not mistaken, we spelled it 'Briar Hoppers.' I always signed autographs as 'Billie Burton Briar Hopper.'"[17]

In 1934, Crutchfield organized the first group of Briarhoppers, as noted by McCloud: John McAllister; Clarence Etters; Jane Bartlett; Billie Burton; Thorpe Westerfield; Homer Drye; and Bill Davis.[18]

Probably the most important member of the WBT Briarhoppers, "Charlie Briarhopper" Crutchfield, was not only the announcer of the WBT Briarhoppers and the birth parent of this musical clan, but was also the father of Charlotte/North Carolina/United States' radio and television broadcasting, news reporting, and advertising.

Crutchfield was born in Hope, Arkansas, on July 27, 1912. The family moved to Spartanburg, South Carolina, where he attended Wofford College. One night in 1930, he went to WSPA to look for a job, and the announcer's booth was empty. Crutchfield answered a telephone and took a listener's recording request. The station owner called Crutchfield in immediately and offered him a job on the spot. Crutchfield's pay at the time was a ten-dollar meal ticket for the restaurant next door.[19]

Crutchfield recollected more on how he got his first radio job: "The owner called me one night and asked me if I'd like to try to announce. He said I had a deep voice. Back in those days, you didn't have to have any sense. You just had to have a deep voice to announce on the radio. So that's the way I got started."[20]

In 1933, Crutchfield and his wife hopped a bus to Charlotte, where he took an announcing job at $20 per week, Crutchfield said in "The Crutchfield Chronicle" (a handout presented at Crutchfield's retirement from WBTV). "FDR [U.S. president Franklin Delano Roosevelt] had told us that the only thing we had to fear was fear itself, but those of us with families knew better. We feared an empty belly, and the thought that the federal government owed us a living had just never crossed our minds."[21]

Charles Crutchfield at the WBT microphone, 1938. Courtesy Leslie Crutchfield Tompkins and Richard Crutchfield.

Crutchfield recalled being low man on the seniority list at WBT. "Well, I was a junior announcer, of course, when I arrived [at WBT]. They had three other announcers then who'd been around for a good while, so I got all the bad shifts. I signed on in the morning, and then I was off about noon for the afternoon and then came back on at six o'clock and worked till midnight. This was usually six days a week, but quite often, since I had all these senior guys around, three of them, why, sometimes it was seven days a week. But I loved it."[22]

Through Charles Crutchfield's imagination, the WBT Briarhoppers were born. Betty Johnson would write that she thought "the Briarhopper program was a relaxation for him at the end of the day."[23] As an announcer, Crutchfield spent 60 hours a week at the station. WBT, which NBC sold to CBS, billed itself "The Pioneer Voice of the South." At night, gin rummy kept Crutchfield awake for station breaks.[24]

There were announcers at WBT who became famous. Rumble notes, "Charles Kuralt ... was an announcer on WBT before he went up into big time.... Eddy [Arnold] did quite a bit of broadcasting from WBT."[25]

The WBT Briarhoppers

Crutchfield's new musical family was comprised of many talented staff musicians and youngsters: Johnny McAllister was "Dad Briarhopper," Jane Bartlett was "Minnie Briarhopper," Big Bill Davis was "Bill Briarhopper," Clarence Etters was "Elmer Briarhopper," Thorpe Westerfield was "Zeb Briarhopper," youngster Homer Drye was "Homer Briarhopper," and little Billie Burton was "Billie Briarhopper."

Johnny McAllister

Johnny McAllister, or "Dad Briarhopper," joined the original group coming from New York. "He was a very up-beat, very intelligent, extremely creative and sophisticated man," Billie Burton Daniel remembers in an email to the authors:

He was a devout Catholic. He possessed a clear, beautiful voice. He sang tenor and rendered many Irish ballads. I loved to hear him sing "Danny Boy" and "I'll Take You Home Again, Kathleen" and he did a great "My Rosary," but he did many other songs as well ... "Wagon Wheels," "Going Home," and "Harbor Lights." When he portrayed the part of "Dad," he genuinely sounded like an old, country, feisty character, not only in the way that he spoke, but also in the way he sang.

The show was his, pure and simple. He ruled with an iron hand. Not everyone liked him, but those of us who did were very loyal to him and had the utmost respect for him. We started the show with the song, "Wait Till the Sun Shines, Nellie," and we ended the show with "Wait for Me at the Close of a Long, Long Day." Apparently, these were determined by McAllister.

Lots of people thought that he was my real father, because we both had blonde hair. He was married to a woman named Dotty and she worked at

The Original WBT Briarhoppers. From left to right: Clarence Etters (at piano); Don White; Bill Davis (bass); Billie Burton (holding microphone stand); Thorpe Westerfield (harmonica and banjo); Jane Bartlett; Johnny McAllister, Homer Drye (with mandolin); Charles Crutchfield (inset), 1936. Courtesy Tom Hanchett.

WBT. They were from New York City and after he left the show, they went back to New York. I don't believe that anybody really knows what became of them.[26]

Charles Crutchfield remembered McAllister:

[He was] a tenor singer, falsetto singer, and ukulele player, a friend of Bill Shute, the first manager that CBS sent down to run WBT.... Bill brought him [McAllister] down [from the Bronx] and told me to put him on the air. McAllister played ukulele and Bill Davis played the upright bass in the staff orchestra. They started to look for other people. They found Thorpe Westerfield ... Jane Bartlett ... Homer Briarhopper [Drye] and Billie [Burton].

"[Johnny McAllister] was quite an actor, quite a comedian, a hillbilly actor. He had a high, squeaky voice he used on the air.[27] Johnny was a natural. He put in false teeth and put some tar stuff on the teeth. We dressed him like a farmer and he talked in this high squeaky voice like a hillbilly with a little Yankee accent thrown in it. He was great. He gave a lot of class to the show."[28]

Newell Hathcock, a fiddler from North Carolina, met up with Homer Drye and Johnny McAllister towards the end of this decade and played a few dates with the Briarhoppers. According to Hathcock, McAllister had a college degree from a northern university and was from a wealthy family in New York. He was also a shrewd businessman.[29]

Homer Drye

Homer Drye was hired as a young boy to be on the Briarhoppers' radio show. Taking on the name of "Homer Briarhopper," the young man sang songs and played an A-style mandolin. Tim Drye, Homer Drye's son, and Larry Mangum, a nephew of Drye, supplied much information about his uncle for this book.

In a *Raleigh Magazine* article, dated Summer 1969, Grady Jefferys wrote "A Musician Who Is All Heart and Soul," of which a copy was supplied by Mangum. The article states that Homer Drye was born in Union County, North Carolina, in 1924, the son of a "poor one-horse farmer." Drye's father taught Homer how to play the guitar and mandolin when Homer was still a toddler. When Homer was six years old, he won the first prize at the Annual Fiddlers Convention in Fairfield, North Carolina.[30]

In 1936, at the age of twelve, Homer learned that WBT was looking for a young boy to sing on the Briarhoppers' radio show. Homer tried out and was hired along with Billie Burton. In the Saturday, October 30, 1971, edition of the *Raleigh Times,* reporter A.C. Snow wrote that Homer won the audition and was asked if he could be there every day for the show. "I didn't know," Snow reported Drye recalling the event. "After all, I was 12 and lived quite a piece away up the country but my brother Slim said, 'You won and you're going to be here somehow.' Mom was awfully reluctant but Dad finally said I could, so I left home at 12."

Homer's sister, Kate Mangum (who taught country and gospel music star Randy Travis how to play the guitar), recalled the audition in an October 31, 2005, telephone interview:

We were all listenin' to the radio ... about six of us were crowded around the radio. We heard Homer perform and then we heard a little girl named Billie perform. Then they announced that Homer and Billie had won the amateur contest and would be on the Briarhopper Show. Now Mama didn't approve of this and did not want Homer to go away. He was 12 or 13 at the time. We had some friends across the creek, Faye and DeWitt Simpson.... They had a daughter named Sarah and Homer liked Sarah a lot.... Anyway, they had moved to Charlotte. The Simpsons told Mama that Homer could stay with them. That was the only way that she would let Homer go to Charlotte and be on the radio.[31]

In the Snow article, Homer told the writer about his trip to Charlotte: "They put me on a bus and Dad told me that I was to get off the bus and walk down Tryon Street till I came to Mr. Williams' grocery store. Mr. Williams had been to our farm a lot rabbit hunting. It was a mighty

Homer "Homer Briarhoppper" Drye at WPTF in Raleigh, North Carolina, early 1940s. Courtesy Tim Drye.

long walk."[32] According to Snow, Drye moved in with the Williams family and lived there several years before moving to another family friend's home (the Simpsons) in Charlotte.

In Charlotte, Drye was suddenly rich, earning $12 per week at the show, according to Snow. Drye stayed on until 1941 when the Briarhopper Family disbanded, according to Jefferys. Roy "Whitey" Grant said Drye was fired from the show because Drye's voice had changed. "They hired him as a boy, but his voice changed and he didn't sound like a boy anymore."[33]

Even after being fired from the show, Drye still considered Charles Crutchfield a friend. Mangum says, "Homer loved that man to death ... even after the Briarhopper show ended and after he moved with Johnny McAllister to Raleigh. McAllister didn't stay too long, but that is where Homer remained."[34] Homer Drye would keep the professional name Homer Briarhopper and would make a name for himself in the Raleigh-Durham area of North Carolina as an entertainer.

Billie Burton

Billie Burton Daniel, currently residing in Wilmington, North Carolina, is one of the last living members of the original WBT *Briarhopper Variety Show*. She was a member of the show from 1936 until 1941. At the age of 81, her memories of the show are still vivid.

In the draft of her upcoming book, "Whatever Happened to Billie Briarhopper?" Daniel writes that her father worked for a drug company and that she and her mother traveled with him as he made customer calls. One day, while in Charlotte and listening to the car radio, an announcement came on the Briarhoppers show that the station was looking for a little boy and a little girl to sing on the show. "Well, this was my golden opportunity. I cried and carried on something awful, before I got Daddy to write an excuse so I could get out of school early and go try out. (I overheard Mama tell Daddy it wouldn't hurt to let me go, because they probably wouldn't choose me, anyway.)"[35]

"I was with Father and Billie in the car," Daniel's sister, Kingsland Loughlin, said in a telephone interview with the authors. "I was the one who wanted to audition, but I knew that I couldn't sing as well as Billie. Anyway, I went to our mother and begged her to let me audition. She said, 'No, you can't sing, but Billie can. Let her audition.' Mother really wanted Billie to get the job. You see, our mother was a great singer and had the chance to go to the Boston Conservatory, but she got married and that was the end of that."[36]

To Daniel, it seemed that "a million children" were there to try out. She says, "I went up to the reception desk and they gave me a number and told me to wait. To tell you the truth, I was scared to death. Some of those children were dressed up in cowboy boots and had on makeup and looked just beautiful. I just looked like a little girl."

When Daniel was called up to audition, she went into a big studio. "I nearly fainted when I saw the piano player. He was the same one [Clarence Etters] who used to play for the *Popeye Club* on the radio that I used to attend. Well, for some reason, he seemed to like me. He told me to sing 'Bill Bailey,' and that's what I did. There was nobody else in that big studio but Clarence, the piano player, and me, but this voice came out of the nowhere and asked me what my name was, and I said, just as plain as I could, Billie Burton (I wasn't about to tell them it was Willie), then the voice asked me if I knew twenty songs.... I crossed my fingers and said, 'Yes, sir, I do.'"

According to Daniel's book draft, the voice told her to go sit down in the lobby and wait. After a while, she wrote, there was nobody waiting but her and a little boy. Still later, both children were told to come back tomorrow and sing on the program. The boy was Homer Drye.

Daniel makes it clear that the radio show was nothing like the well-known Briarhopper shows during the 1940s and 1950s. "In the first place, the original show was in no way a country show, it was a variety show, and it appealed to people from all walks of life," Daniel says in an email to the authors on June 2, 2005. "The musicians were top notch, highly trained and adept at playing all kinds of music. Some of the members were, indeed, members of the North Carolina Symphony."

In an email to the authors dated June 26, 2005, Daniel states that at the time of her hire, Johnny McAllister, Don White, Clarence Etters, Jane Bartlett, Thorpe Westerfield, Bill Davis, Judge Davis, and Charles Crutchfield were on the show:

> I was hired for the show in the fall of 1936, as was Homer Drye. Johnny McAllister was the manager and producer of the show. Homer and I called him "Dad" from the very beginning and we obeyed him. His [McAllister's] role was a dual role, as he played "Dad" and "Ham." Don White was "Sam." Ham and Sam were a duo, but they sang individually as well. Clarence Etters played the piano and they called him "Elmer." When Elmer, Ham and Sam sang together, they were the Trio. Jane Bartlett was "Minnie." She had a beautiful voice, and she played the violin beautifully. Thorpe Westerfield was "Zeb." He played guitar and harmonica, and he sang as well, mostly novelty songs. Bill Davis was "Big Bill." He played bass fiddle and violin. He also was a comic. Bill was the oldest member of the cast. His son was "Judge." If he

had another name I never heard it. He [Judge] was on the show as well, played the bass fiddle. Charlie Crutchfield was the announcer.[37]

In her book draft, Daniel remembers that her father taught her the song "Let the Rest of the World Go By," and that was what she sang on her first show the next day. "After we [Daniel and Drye] had been on the program a week, when I got off the elevator, the boy, Homer, was waiting. He told me to go back to the payroll department and get my check.... When I got there they gave me a check for ten dollars. I was flabbergasted, this was too good to be true, and that was more than my mama even made."[38]

Daniel was enjoying her new-found stardom:

They called me the "Sweetheart of the Carolinas" and the "Carolina Sunshine Girl," and, what I liked best of all, "The Youngest and the Last of the Blues Singers."[39]

The Briarhoppers was the most popular radio show in North Carolina, and we got mail from Maine, and even Cuba. WBT was a powerful station, made even more powerful because its tower was on top of Mount Mitchell (the highest mountain peak east of the Rockies). In those days there were not all that many radio stations, in fact, there were very few, especially big ones. They didn't play records then. Every station had its own staff of musicians, and every show was live. WBT could afford the very best musicians and the best announcers. Every studio was equipped with a Steinway Grand (piano).[40]

Daniel loved being on the show: "It came on every day at four o'clock (P.M.) and lasted an hour. It was on six days a week, Monday through Saturday. I never tired of it and it consumed most of my time, for by the second year we had begun going on 'personal appearances.'"

Daniel and Drye became almost more popular than the rest of the cast, according to Daniel:

Homer soon became a (teenaged) idol.... The girls went wild for him, and the mail poured in. We were sponsored by Drug Trade Products, and they seemed pleased with the show. I got lots of mail as well. I didn't see much of it [because the letters were] sent to the sponsor, but Grady Cole (an announcer for WBT) told Daddy that I got 2,500 letters one day.

When I was on stage, it was okay to flirt; in fact, Clarence [Etters] showed me how. I'd pick out some little boy in the front row and "make eyes" at him and everybody would laugh, and the little boy would turn red ... but when I wasn't on stage, I just pretended not to see boys; that's the way that Clarence liked it, and "Dad," Johnny McAllister, too."[41]

The show's popularity seemed to grow as the stars did personal appearances outside of the radio station: "The second year, my salary went up to

Top: Early WBT radio control panel, circa 1930s. *Bottom:* WBT radio station, 1930s. Courtesy Tom Hanchett.

fifteen dollars a week, plus whatever I made on personal appearances. We always played to a packed house, but you have to remember, tickets ranged from twenty-five to seventy-five cents, so nobody got rich. I averaged, though, about thirty-five dollars a week, and that was very good for those days."[42]

BEING THE BRIARHOPPER CHILDREN

Being a child radio star was one of Daniel's life joys, and being able to share it with another child, Homer Drye, made it better. Even though they were expected to act and perform as professionals, they were still children.

In Daniel's book draft, she remembers some of the antics that she and Drye experienced while being Briarhopper children. (As a reminder, when Daniel refers to "Dad," she is referring to Johnny McAllister, who played "Dad Briarhopper."):

Homer and I waited in the wings while the show was going on until Dad would call us out to do our songs. We never got tired of watching, and we'd laugh at the same jokes we'd heard so many times before. Sometimes we'd play games. We loved hide and seek. One time I was hiding up in a sort of loft, you had to climb a ladder to get up there, and Homer moved the ladder and when Dad called me out to sing, I couldn't get down.

One time we were playing "Tag," running behind the stage, and we knocked the scenery down on top of everybody. Dad didn't think that was very funny.

We had a show up in the mountains, in Boone (North Carolina). Boone was just a small town then. It was the worst weather imaginable, snowing hard and ice everywhere. It took us a long time to get there. We didn't even have time to stop and eat. The show was in the Courthouse, and Homer and I waited in the Judge's office. There was a big burlap bag full of apples, and Homer and I were hungry. We had a race to see who could eat the most apples. I got the worst stomach ache, and when Dad called me out to sing, I was almost doubled-over with pain.[43]

Daniel also remembers when Homer Drye bought a car at age 16: "He bought a little two-seater. I was about thirteen then, and he'd pick me up from school and off we'd go to the Wilder Building. He wouldn't pay to park in the parking lot across the street, and we didn't have much time to look for a parking space, so he'd just pull in an alley and park behind some near building. At least once a week somebody would steal his (car) heater. He'd really get upset, but he still wouldn't pay to park it."[44]

Daniel became a jazz singer who traveled the nation entertaining. She is currently writing a book on her life, tentatively titled "Whatever Happened to Billie Briarhopper?"

Thorpe Westerfield

Thorpe Westerfield was another member of the first Briarhoppers' group. His wife and children still live in the Charlotte area.

Westerfield was born on April 27, 1911, in New Orleans, Louisiana. Not a lot of information is known about him, according to Terry Marshall, Westerfield's daughter. In an email to the authors, Marshall writes that her mother met Westerfield in 1937 when she and some friends went to WBT to see the Briarhoppers radio show. "She was 16 and he was 25 years old," Marshall points out. The couple was married in 1940. Westerfield's wife did not know how long he was on the radio show, but she knew that he was on staff as a WBT musician and "that must have led (him) to become a member of the Briarhoppers."[45]

Billie Burton Daniel remembers Westerfield in an August 11, 2005, email to the authors:

The first WBT Briarhopper picture. Standing left to right: Thorpe Westerfield; Clarence Etters; Jane Bartlett; Bill Davis; Charles Crutchfield; Johnny McAllister. Kneeling at left: Don White: Seated left to right: Billie Burton; Homer Drye, 1936. Courtesy Leslie Crutchfield Tompkins and Richard Crutchfield.

I don't know much about Thorpe. He was extremely nice looking and always gave me a box of candy for my birthday and Christmas. He was funny, too. Homer [Drye] and I would ride in the back seat with him when we were traveling and we were always mad at him because he took up too much room (he did it on purpose, to make us mad). He teased us a lot. I liked his mother very much, and I remember Nan, the girl that he later married. She was pretty and came often to watch the show.... Thorpe played the guitar and harmonica at the same time, and I always thought that to be an amazing feat.[46]

Billie Ann Newman Carson, a singer on WBT, remembers Westerfield as one of the best guitarists that she had ever heard: "Have you heard [Django] Rinehardt [famous jazz guitarist]? That was exactly how Thorpe played."[47]

Westerfield left the Briarhoppers radio show in 1940 to join the air force. When he got out of the service, he joined a family business called Carolina Wholesale Building Materials as a salesman, where he worked the rest of his life. Marshall wrote that her father was a member of the Musicians Union and played in dance bands as often as he could ... playing quite a few instruments [like the] piano, guitar, banjo, accordion, and tuba [in the air force band].

Thorpe Westerfield's mother was born in Norway, according to Marshall, and Marshall could never understand what she was saying due to her accent: "Her name was Martha Dahl Westerfield but she was called 'Speedy' because she played the piano so fast and the name just stuck.... My cousin, Linda Westerfield, and I both remember being told that we were somehow related to the actress Arlene Dahl but we don't know any details."[48]

When Westerfield left the Briarhoppers, he apparently did not stay in touch with his former cast mates, Marshall said.

Jane Bartlett

Jane Bartlett was brought in as the mother of the group. "She had a beautiful voice, and everybody thought that she was my real mother," Daniel remembers. "I don't know what happened to her. I know that she had a daughter, and that she was on stage many times performing after the Briarhoppers, but I don't know any more about her."

Daniel also said that Bartlett had a deep voice, but that she was very short, "about my size when I was six years old."

Billie Ann Carson, a member of the 1930s WBT radio show, *The Dixie Jamboree*, says that even though Bartlett was married, "she had a thing for some of the higher ups at WBT. One time, she was caught *in the act* in the WBT observation room. After that happened, she sort of disappeared and we never heard from her again."[49]

Clarence Etters

Etters was hired as a piano player for WBT and was a natural fit for the Briarhoppers radio show. "He was one of the most talented people that we had on the show," Daniel said in an email to the authors. Billie Ann Carson remembers, "He was a great player. He would do the radio show and then play, I think, for the Charlotte Symphony, and then play at churches."

According to Carson, Etters never married: "He was as sweet as he could be with the youngsters on the Briarhoppers show. But he never married and never had his own kids. He lived with his father."[50] In the same telephone interview, Carson says that there were many newspaper articles on Etters, with one reporting that he was the best dressed man in Charlotte and that he had eighty pairs of shoes.

Daniel's sister, Kingsland Loughlin, said in a telephone interview with the authors on February 28, 2006, "Clarence was very prissy ... but he wanted the best from Billie and would push her very hard. He probably made her a better singer."

Daniel compared Etters to a father figure: "He treated me like I was his daughter. When I met the man that I married, he was dead-set against it. When I married that man, Clarence never talked to me again."

"Clarence was the one that I knew best," Daniel said in a September 10, 2005, email to the authors:

> I was his protégé, and I did everything that he told me to do. He told me what to sing, how to sing, when to breathe, what to say and how to dress. He would call my Mother and tell her if he saw a dress that I should have. He had big plans for me. I tried very hard to please him. I got to know his family very well, liked his father and his sisters and his grandmother and other relatives. [I] [h]ad Thanksgiving Dinner with them many times and had many meals with them. We would go to Thackers Restaurant nearly every night if we were going on a personal appearance.... Clarence would tell me what to eat.
>
> Every year he went to New York several times and saw all of the shows on Broadway. [He] [h]ad lots of girl friends up there and was invited to all of the right places. He was in the Army during the war and was stationed in Fort Jackson in South Carolina.... After he was discharged, he went back to Charlotte and became Music Director for WBT.
>
> Clarence was the organist for First Baptist Church in Charlotte. We had our own Sunday morning program. He played the piano and organ at the same time.... I watched him the whole time when I sang. He mouthed the words, told me when to breathe, how to stand, everything....

Daniel also remembers that Etters and McAllister had a second radio show on WBT that came on in the morning. McAllister was called "Philco Phil" and they started the show with the song "Roll Out of Bed in the Morning with a Big, Big Smile and a Good, Good Morning."

Betty Johnson, of the Johnson Family Singers who performed on WBT from 1938 to 1951, said in an article on the Website http://www.btmemories.com, "Clarence Etters had a wonderful, happy disposition. He played for my first solo Bendix-sponsored radio show. I was a freshman at Queens College (in Charlotte, North Carolina) then."[51]

Big Bill Davis and His Sons
Judge and Charlie

Of this band of original WBT Briarhoppers, "Big" Bill Davis is another important band member. A bass player, Davis was a classically trained violinist with the Charlotte Symphony who doubled as a country fiddle player and upright bassist.[52] Davis formed a string band called the Clover Blossoms in the late 1920s, which was one of the first bands to broadcast on WBT.[53]

Davis would become the dean of the Briarhoppers in the next five decades as he would become the longest-serving WBT Briarhopper.

"I received a letter from Bill Davis' family a few years ago," Levine Museum of the New South historian Tom Hanchett said to the authors. "The museum had a show or something about the Briarhoppers and some of the advertisements said that these were the 'Original WBT Briarhoppers.'"

Flyer for Bill Davis and his Clover Blossoms, early 1930s. Courtesy Dwight Moody.

The letter went on to tell me that the current group was not the originals, that Big Bill Davis and Don White were the only original Briarhoppers. They were slightly upset about it all."[54]

Davis' sons Charlie and Roger (Judge) would appear with their father on the Briarhopper show from time to time.

Gibb Young

According to Daniel, Young was a fine guitar player who was briefly on the WBT Briarhopper radio show: "We had a duet ... we would sing ... 'Frankie and Johnny.' We also did hymns together. He was very handsome, quite tall ... and very, very nice. In retrospect, I may have had a crush on him, but I was certainly not aware of it. I do know, though, that when I first saw the man that I would later marry, he reminded me so much of Gibb. When America went to war, Gibb joined the service ... in the Air Corps, stationed in Denver."[55]

Daniel commented on Young's photograph, saying that "it was a bad photo of him ... he was really handsome!"

Don Whytesell, aka Don White

Don Whytesell, known professionally as Don White, was a guitarist and bassist who joined the group in 1935 and played the role of "Sam Briarhopper" and, on several programs, that of "Pappy Briarhopper" until 1939.

Don White was a western-style singer who would make a name for himself on the WLS *National Barn Dance*, WLW in Cincinnati, and as part of the duo the Carolina Boys with Fred Kirby, who would also become a Briarhopper. He arrived in Charlotte as a musician in 1933 with the Blue Ridge Mountaineers, performing on WBT's competitor, WSOC.[56] Born in 1909 near Sutton, West Virginia, as Walden Don Whytesell, he adopted the stage name of Don White in the early 1930s.[57]

White left the Charlotte area but returned soon after as a member of the Crazy Bucklebusters, a band whose name reflected Crazy Water Crystals, which would sponsor the *Crazy Water Crystals Radio Show* on WBT and other stations. White joined the WBT Briarhoppers in 1935 and remained until 1939.[58]

"Dad (McAllister) called him 'Square Head,'" Daniel remembers. "I knew him before the Briarhopper program. We lived next door to Mrs. Peterson's boarding house, and Curly [Don White] boarded there. Mrs. Peterson, whom I called 'Pete,' had a daughter named Mary.

Don White as Pappy Briarhopper, 1934-35. Courtesy Dwight Moody.

Mary was just as sweet and as nice as she could be. She and Curly fell in love and were married.... Curly was the perfect gentleman, but then all of them were."[59]

Fred Kirby

White met Fred Kirby in 1935. Kirby was born in Charlotte, North Carolina, on July 19, 1910. His mother taught him how to play music on a $7.50 guitar.[60] When he was 17, Kirby's family moved to Florence, South

Carolina. Soon afterwards, Kirby got his first radio job at WIS in Columbia, South Carolina.

Kirby told John Rumble of the Country Music Hall of Fame that he got into professional music when he went to see his cousin on his cousin's fifteenth birthday:

> I got a guitar with the strings, bridge, and tuning keys missing. My cousin took me to a place where a musician fixed it up. WIS radio station was across the road. My cousin asked me if I'd like to see it.... No one was there. A microphone was standing there and I said, "Well, this is a time that I can pretend I'm on the radio." I sang every song that I could think of. Here comes Charles Crutchfield and the program director, who said, "You did fine. We want you to come to work tomorrow." I was a part of the station for eight months with no pay. I was living with my cousin.[61]

About a year later, Kirby moved to Charlotte and to WBT:

> Before I went to WBT, I talked to a "handwriting expert" that Crutchfield had on the radio at WIS. He would tell the listeners to send in their signature and he would read your future for a dollar. He saw me in the hallway at the station and asked for my signature. I thought that it would be okay to do that and I did. He said that he would talk to me the next day. When he saw me the next day, he said, "You are gonna leave this station for WBT in Charlotte, but before that, you will get the measles." I thought that it was something that he told me that I was going to WBT because I hadn't told a soul. But the measles part, I thought was wrong. But guess what? I got the measles before leaving! After I got over the measles, I left for WBT![62] Pete Lauderman hired me, he was the program director, and offered me $10 per week. I said, "Well now ... I can't do that. I'm gonna have to have $15." So he paid my room and board at $5 per week and I had it made.[63]

According to Pat Gubbins of the *Charlotte Observer*, Kirby noted that he tried to be like Jimmie Rodgers:

> I tried to emulate his [Rodgers] Blue Yodel. Somebody told me, "Fred, why don't you stop emulating Jimmie Rodgers and start emulating yourself?" So I changed, and I started writing my own songs.
> I started with Big Bill Davis and the Clover Blossoms. Crutchfield came about a year after I did as an announcer. Well, he created the Briarhoppers and I was a part of it.... And then Don White ... he and I decided that we wanted to go out into the world and spread our wings. So we went to WLW in Cincinnati and stayed there a year. Then we got an offer from WLS in Chicago and we went there to better our situation. We were on the *National Barn Dance* at the 8th Street Theater.[64]

Calumet Company published sheet music (for ukulele) for the Kirby song, "I Wish I Was Single Again." The cover had a picture of Kirby and the following description: "Fred Kirby — KMOX — CBS St. Louis Singer and Philosopher." This shows the extent of Kirby's travels throughout the United States.

KIRBY AND WHITE AS A DUET

During this time in Charlotte, White made numerous recordings for RCA. On June 19, 1936, White recorded "Mexicali Rose," "What a Friend We Have in Mother," and a duet with Kirby, as The Smiling Cowboys, "My Old Saddle Horse Is Missing."[65] In 1939, they changed their names to The Carolina Boys.[66] "We did sing-through-our-nose country," White said in 1996 interview for the *Charlotte Observer*. "Fred was a nice guy to work with. He had a good sense of humor."[67]

In 1939, White and Kirby moved to WLW in Cincinnati, Ohio to perform. White left Cincinnati and moved back to Charlotte, in 1942, where he rejoined the WBT Briarhoppers. Soon after, White filled a vacant spot with the Tennessee Ramblers.[68] The Tennessee Ramblers, of which many of the WBT Briarhoppers had been members, were veterans of the silver screen, especially in cowboy movies. The Tennessee Ramblers, with Don White, were called to be a part of the movie *Swing Your Partner* starring Lula Belle and Scotty. This was the first movie in which Dale Evans, wife of Roy Rogers appeared.[69] White also appeared in several other western movies with the Durango Kid and Jimmy Wakely.[70]

Fred Kirby got a call from Charles Crutchfield when Kirby was at WLS: "Crutchfield said, 'Fred, don't you think it's about time you come back home? Come on back and join the Briarhoppers.' So I came back and joined the Briarhoppers."[71] Kirby also got a letter from Johnny McAllister, asking him to come back to Charlotte, "but only as an instrumentalist," inferring that McAllister wanted to remain the main singer of the WBT Briarhoppers.[72]

In 1946, White moved back to WLS in Chicago where he and his band, the WLS Sage Riders, had a fifteen-minute radio show and were regulars on the WLS *National Barn Dance*.[73] This period of White's career, 1946 to 1952, would be his most prolific. White returned many times to the Briarhoppers throughout the rest of his life. Kirby would return to Charlotte and would become a household name in his own right with the advent of television.

Hank Warren

"Fiddlin'" Hank Warren was a professional musician before joining the Briarhoppers. He was born in Mt. Airy, North Carolina, on April 1, 1909.

As a young fiddle player, he formed Warren's Four Aces, and then was a member of the Blue Ridge Mountaineers and the Tennessee Ramblers.[74]

According to *The Charlotte Country Music Story*, "[Warren] recorded with the Ramblers and appeared with them on the 1936 film, *Ride Ranger Ride* with Gene Autry. He joined the Briarhoppers ... and became not only their fiddler, but also their baggy-pants comedian."[75]

In an interview with Ray Thigpen in the *Carolina Bluegrass Review*, Warren said that he did the movie because he "needed the money ... because [his] wife was expecting."[76]

According to Roy "Whitey" Grant, "Hank was the only one of us who could read music.... We would get a new piece of music and he would help us through it. Not only could he play hoe-downs, but he could play concert pieces, he was that good."[77] Warren learned to play the fiddle in Mt. Airy, where he received his first violin as a gift from his parents.[78]

During school, Warren played violin in the school orchestra.[79] The authors were also told by Grant that the Warren family's newspaper boy was Andy Griffith.[80]

In 1931, Warren married his childhood sweetheart, Inez Turney. He then joined the Blue Ridge Mountaineers, a band that played in West Virginia, Virginia, and the Carolinas.[81] In 1936, Warren joined the Tennessee

Hank Warren at the WBT/CBS microphone, early 1930s Courtesy Jim Scancarelli.

Ramblers, who played on WBT and appeared in the movie mentioned earlier. "Hank played with the Tennessee Ramblers on WBT and Charles Crutchfield heard him and liked his fiddle playin'," Grant said as he remembered how Warren became a Briarhopper.[82] In 1938, WBT offered Warren a spot on the WBT Briarhoppers.

As "Elmer Briarhopper," Warren not only played fiddle, but also played songs on a saw. According to *The Charlotte Country Music Story*, "Photos from that decade feature Hank ... made up with freckles, fake glasses, and blacked-out teeth ... cutting capers with his fiddle or even standing on his head. Few listeners realized that he had enough formal training to play with the Charlotte Symphony, or that his skill at sight reading allowed him to act as the Briarhopper musical director during the busy days...."[83]

Claude Casey, a future Briarhopper, noted that Warren "used to be over in Raleigh, North Carolina, with [legendary banjo player] Charlie Poole's son, Doug Poole.... [Warren] was a Swing [fiddler]— he was with a group called the 'Swing Billies' over there and he played a hot fiddle. [Warren] studied the violin, but he didn't let it interfere with his playing.... He reads music and all of that stuff."[84]

The Tennessee Ramblers

The Tennessee Ramblers were very influential in the growth of country/western and string band music during the 1930s and 1940s. The band traveled from Rochester, New York, to Charlotte in 1934 under the sponsorship of Crazy Water Crystals.[85] Dick Hartman was the recognized leader of the group, as he organized the Tennessee Ramblers in 1928 at KDKA in Pittsburgh.

According to Barry McCloud's *Definitive Country*, the Tennessee Ramblers did not hit their stride until 1933, with the addition of Kenneth Wolfe, Harry Blair, and Cecil Campbell while in Rochester. When the group arrived in Charlotte, Hank Warren and Jack Gillette joined the band.

Hartman left the group in 1938 and Gillette took over as leader. Warren went with the WBT Briarhoppers. Don White, Tex Martin (Martin Schopp) and Claude Casey joined the Tennessee Ramblers at various times. Don White, Claude Casey, Cecil Campbell, Harry Blair, Jack Gillette, and Tex Martin would fill roles with the WBT Briarhoppers in the late 1930s through the 1940s.[86] As mentioned earlier in this chapter, this is the same group that played on the Crazy Barn Dance under the name the Crazy Tennessee Ramblers.

Cecil Campbell

Born in 1911, Campbell was raised on a farm in Stokes County, North Carolina, and became interested in music as a young child.[87] While a youngster, Campbell was determined to make a living as a country musician, learning hundreds of songs while learning to play various stringed instruments. He was given his first chance to perform in Winston-Salem, North Carolina, on radio station WSJS.[88]

In an interview with John Rumble, historian for the Country Music Hall of Fame in Nashville, Tennessee, Campbell remembers when he started playing his most famous instrument, the steel guitar: "I used the Rickenbacker. The first electric that I had was in 1940. Before that, why, I used a dobro, and I had an old Regal guitar.... When I first started playing the old steel was, I'd say, about 1923."[89]

Bored, Campbell moved to Pittsburgh to live with his brother. It was there he met Dick Hartman and joined the Tennessee Ramblers.[90] He says, "I first left home in 1932, I hitchhiked from Winston-Salem to Pittsburgh. I just knew a little music back then. I [had] never played professionally or anything like that. I was doing strictly country. I first joined the Tennessee Ramblers in Pittsburgh on WWSW; then we were on KDKA and KQV in Pittsburgh. I was just getting started yet, before I was playing professionally on the old dobro."[91]

Campbell got a job with the Crazy Water Crystals as a performer after a glowing letter from WGST-Atlanta's assistant manager, Charles A. Smithgall in 1935, writing that "Mr. Campbell possesses moral, sober habits, and I am glad to say that he has shown himself to be a gentleman in every sense of the word during his stay here."[92]

J.W. Fincher notes in a similar letter, "[Campbell's] energy and punctual observance of engagements and duties impressed me very much.... [Campbell's] habits of energy, thrift, and principles of honesty make [him] worthy of consideration...."[93]

Campbell describes his singing style to Rumble during his interview: "Of course, my voice has always just been country — and lively. It's in between — jammed in the cracks, you know — too lousy to be good and too [good to be lousy]. It's not good enough to be good. That's what I tell people, you know. There could be a lot of truth in that, because it's possible to be in between the cracks. You're not corny enough to do what you call real country, and not good enough to do the pop country. I don't know whether I'm considered that or not, but I just tell people that."[94]

Through his association with Hank Warren and Don White, Campbell and the rest of the Tennessee Ramblers would be on the Briarhoppers show and would serve as band members.

Harry Blair

William "Horse Thief Harry" Blair was born in 1912 in New Martinsville, West Virginia. As a teenager, he worked at Wierton Steel where his uncle worked. Sometimes his uncle would bring a guitar to work, which Harry began to learn to play. He joined Dick Hartman in Pittsburgh after being rejected at a prior audition. Blair heard Hartman dedicate a song to him on a radio show, and Blair went back to Pittsburgh and joined the group.[95]

According to Campbell, the Tennessee Ramblers started to do more western swing music due to Blair. "Yes, Harry Blair. He'd do the singing of these tunes [western swing] like that, because we used to do a lot of western stuff— the old Bob Nolan stuff, you know, with the harmony yodel.... Up 'til then, we had just done regular country — they call it country-western now."[96] When the Tennessee Ramblers moved to Charlotte, the group performed on the WBT Briarhoppers show and would eventually serve as Briarhoppers when needed.

Jack Gillette

Raised in Rhode Island, Gillette was a novelty musician who would play music on tire pumps and balloons. He joined the Tennessee Ramblers in 1938 and was in several films with the band. "Montana Jack" Gillette, while based in Charlotte, joined the rest of his band performing on the WBT Briarhopper show.

Tex Martin

Tex Martin, whose real name was Martin Schopp, was born in Chenoa, Illinois, in 1918. He got his first shot on the radio when he was in his second year of high school on WDZ in Illinois.[97]

Martin/Schopp joined the Tennessee Ramblers and WBT in 1938. During a telephone interview on September 15, 2006, Martin /Schopp said that he was playing a bass for a jazz band when Dick Hartman heard him. It seems that Hartman was looking for a bass player and Martin/Schopp was looking for another job. It was that day Martin/Schopp became both a Tennessee Rambler and a WBT Briarhopper at the same time.[98]

One of the First Briarhopper News Articles

Tim Drye, son of Homer Drye, supplied the authors a copy of a framed, matted newspaper article that Drye could only describe as being in "a Charlotte paper." The article was written by Adam Street, and is titled "How The Briarhoppers Hop." Since there was more than one major newspaper in Charlotte during the 1930s, the authors cannot assume that the article came from the *Charlotte Observer*.

Due to the article's poor reproduction quality, the following is written verbatim. Please remember that there was no political correctness in the press during the 1930s, and racism was part of the norm, especially in Southern newspapers.

HOW THE BRIARHOPPERS HOP!
BY ADAM STREET

To see the Briarhopper band coming into the WBT studios in Charlotte, North Carolina, with all of their instruments, you might think the New York Symphony was to play a concert. But there are only six members of Dad Briarhopper's family.

Chief of the outfit is Dad Briarhopper, known to his mother and father as Johnny McAllister, or "Mac." Johnny doesn't care which instrument he picks up when, without looking, he plunges his hand into the pile and takes one.

If it's a fiddle, he begins sawing with all the assurance of a Kreisler; a banjo, he picks with the delight of a darky on a cabin porch; a guitar, he strums with the ease and soulfulness of a South Sea native; if it's a mandolin, he plucks it like a Cossack on a balalaika. But the part he likes best in his role as Dad Briarhopper is when he steps before the mike and sings hillbilly with that nasal twang. However, Johnny can and does sing tenor of a quality to please even the most fastidious music lover, and his repertoire ranges from opera arias to "horse opry" ditties.

Minnie Briarhopper, nee Jane Bartlett, is a mite of talent. She, too, changes from instrument to instrument with precision gears, never missing a beat or mussing the music. And when she sings solo, her low notes add distinction to any program. Jane and Johnny team frequently on old favorites requested by listeners.

Bill Briarhopper, sometimes known as Bill Davis, gets a kick out of his fiddle, as well as good music period. Standing before the microphone with one foot patting and his whole body bubbling in tune, he rolls his eyes then (Dad Briarhopper says Bill flirts with the audience!) and keeps time with his whole body. Even his buttons shimmy rhythmically. And every once in a while Bill "calls the figgers," lending a barn-dance atmosphere to the show.

Don Briarhopper, alias White, is a musician. Further than that, it is difficult to classify him. Don is another who plays whatever instrument he can find and plays it well. He is the mainstay when it comes to singing too; for anything from a solo to a quartet contains his tenor.

Thorpe Westerfield is the silent member of the Briarhopper group, except for the sounds he makes with a guitar, violin, mandolin, banjo and harmonica. Silence, in Thorpe's case, means he hardly ever sings in more than two songs a day. He has a wicked-looking contraption which he swings around his neck to hold his harmonica, which he plays with the abandon of a Minnevitch and the ease of an artist, at the same time strumming away on one of the group's many stringed instruments.

Elmer Briarhopper, who occasionally plays the piano as Clarence Etters, doesn't do much either. When he isn't playing the piano or violin, he is singing. Otherwise, he rests.

Two new additions to the Briarhopper family promise to gain a huge following among listeners to the popular show. Homer Drye, fourteen years old, is what "Chock" Crutchfield, WBT's program director, termed a "natural." When Dad Briarhopper announced on the show one day that he wanted a boy and girl to join the cast, dozens of applicants came for an audition.

Homer, as naively fresh as a pound of country butter, was instant choice for the place and his first performance drew praise from everybody who heard it — his first appearance on any radio station.

Billie Burton, twelve years old, was the choice for the new girl member of the Briarhoppers. Billie is a blonde with blue eyes and a shy smile. She has been singing ever since she can remember and when Dad Briarhopper heard her sullen but smooth tones, he threw away his lantern and, like Diogenes, retired to his "studio tub and put her name on the payroll."

"She's got what it takes," the chief Briarhopper announced. "Our search is ended."

The Briarhoppers are a lively set, and if challenges were in order, WBT would challenge any group to match versatilities, if nothing more.

Bob Wilbur, popular young announcer, whose duties have brought his voice to Central New Yorkers and listeners in New England, has joined the announcing staff of WSUN, NBC's outlet for west-coast Florida, St. Petersburg. Wilbur will assist in the production department.

Bob has been in radio for the past three years, having begun his broadcasting career at his college station in Canton, New York. Prior to his journey into the Sunny South to WSUN, he was with WIBX in Utica, New York.

Pre–1940 Briarhopper Show Description

Daniel describes the show and its characters: "Johnny McAllister, a master showman, devised and managed this show and it was extremely good. The format of the show was a crotchety old man ['Dad' portrayed by McAllister], and his family of five grown sons and a daughter and two children, a little girl named Billie and a young teen-aged boy, Homer. Charles Crutchfield was the announcer and he was great. The banter between 'Dad' and 'Charlie' was a scream. Certainly, 'Dad' acted like an old hillbilly man, but it was all an act.... His voice was beautiful."

On the type of music played on the show during the 1930s, Daniel recalled, "There was no bluegrass, although Big Bill Davis could play some hoedowns. This was a group of extremely talented performers. The music was beautiful at times; tinny and twangy at other times ... but it was all in fun."[99]

The authors asked Daniel to describe the radio show and their stage show, since there are no tapes extant for this period for the WBT Briarhoppers. Daniel described these in an email to us dated January 21, 2006:

[On the radio show] Mr. Crutchfield would come rushing into the studio when the little hand on the clock got to 4 and just before the big hand got to 12. I used to wonder if he'd make it, but he always did. The light would come on the studio clock and Mr. Crutchfield would say, "Pappy, what time is it?" and Dad (Johnny McAllister) would say as only he could, "Why, Crutch, hit's Briarhopper Time!" Then the band would start playing "Wait Till the Sun Shines, Nellie." Then we'd all start "yipeeing" and applauding and then the show would start. We had a live studio audience, and they'd be laughing and applauding as well. Homer [Drye] and I sang two songs each. The trio, Ham [also McAllister], Elmer [Clarence Etters], and Sam [Don White], sang one song. Sam would sing one, Thorpe [Westerfield] sang one, usually a novelty, Dad sang one, as Dad, and then he'd do a beautiful one as Ham. Bill Davis would play a hoedown. Sam would play the steel guitar, and that was so pretty. When Minnie [Jane Bartlett] was on the show she'd also sing a solo. She had the prettiest voice.

We didn't dress up like "Briarhoppers" for radio. The men wore nice looking suits and Homer and I wore what we had worn to school that day. And on Saturdays, the same.

Our closing theme was "Wait for Me at the Close of a Long, Long Day."

When asked to provide a typical program, Daniel supplied the following information to the authors on January 21, 2006:

Briarhopper program, Wednesday, November 6, 1936,

Opening: Wait Till the Sun Shines Nellie
Hoedown: Buffalo Girls
Trio: Beautiful Isle of Somewhere
Homer: Bill Bailey
Ham & Sam: I'm Thinking Tonight of My Blue Eyes
Dad: The Martins and the 'Coys
Billie: Somebody Loves You
Trio: My Grandfather's Clock
Minnie: When My Dreamboat Comes Home
Ham: Harbor Lights
Homer: Riding on That New River Train Steel
Guitar: Aloha Oy
Zeb: Frankie & Johnny
Billie & Homer: Billy Boy
Sam: Always
Billie: Look Down That Lonesome Road
Hoedown: Waiting on the *Robert E. Lee*
Closing: Wait For Me at the Close of a Long, Long Day

This was a lot for a one-hour show, and Daniel admitted that it is possible that all the songs listed were not played on the same program, but she told the authors that they packed a lot into the time allowed.

Daniel also remembers that she sang "East Bound Train," "Boy with a Twisted Knee," "We Buried Her Beneath the Willow," "The Old Sunbonnet That She Used to Wear," "A Tisket, a Tasket," and "Basin Street Blues."[100]

"I had a very soft voice, had to get as close to the microphone as possible," Daniel says. "Of course, neither the studio audience nor the musicians could hear me. Dad [McAllister] had to stand with his ear as close to my mouth as possible to hear me and he would direct the band that way."[101]

Daniel's parents would listen intently to the radio shows, according to Daniel's sister, Kingsland Loughlin. "They would tell me to be quiet,

so I would just go outside.... That's why I don't remember a lot about her
time at WBT. But Mother especially listened. If she thought that Billie
was presented in a bad way, or if they did not allot enough time for Billie to sing, Mother was on the telephone with Dad Briarhopper [Johnny
McAllister] and gave it to him."[102]

Charles Crutchfield, Daniel recollects, was doing commercials making fun of the sponsor's products. "One of our sponsors was Kolor Bak, a
hair dye. Mr. Crutchfield said (he really did), 'I'm tellin' you folks, if you
want to get rid of the gray, use Kolor Bak. I guarantee, you might lose
most of your hair, but what you have left won't be gray anymore.[103] The
stage show was about the same, except we dressed up like 'Briarhoppers,'
with overalls and the like."[104]

Loughlin remembers that her parents did not approve of her sister Billie's going to these shows. "Father would just not allow it, but Billie would
pitch a fit to the point where he finally relented. That happened a lot!"[105]

Daniel remembers some "incidents" that occurred during stage shows:

Dad [McAllister] had never done this before and didn't tell anybody he was
going to do it. He bought some of those little balls [firecrackers] that you
throw down and they explode. They really sounded like a shot [from a gun].
Well, this night, before he went on stage, he threw several of these balls
down and ran out on stage, as though someone was shooting at him. Thorpe
Westerfield was back stage waiting to go on, and when he heard these explo-
sions he really did think somebody was shooting, and he beat Dad out on the
stage. He almost had a heart attack, was as white as a sheet. It was so funny!
He never lived that down; we laughed for months.

Another instance was when Dad would call me out, I would just come
walking on stage.... Well, he told me to run out on the stage. I had on new
patent leather Mary Janes [shoes] and the soles were slick as glass. The show
this night was in a brand new club with new hardwood floors. When Dad
called me out, I backed up, took a running start and went flying out on the
stage. First, I knocked Dad and the microphone down, then I knocked Bill
Davis and his bass fiddle down. I couldn't get off the stage, I knocked everybody down and then I fell down. Well, it wasn't funny; I was embarrassed to
tears. Everybody was laughing. I will never forget that.[106]

Daniel also remembered a trip to Columbia, South Carolina:

They were having this huge show in Columbia, SC. Entertainers from all
over the South were to appear (I was 16 at the time, it was the last year I was
on the show). For some reason, I was riding with the Rangers Quartet. Well,
prohibition had ended, but not in North Carolina. As soon as we crossed the
state line, I believe in York, SC, they stopped and went in the package store.
I asked one of them what were they going to buy, and he laughed and said,
"Whiskey." I was horrified! Dad nor Clarence had ever stopped at a whiskey

store. I got very indignant and got out of the car and started walking. They begged me to get back in the car, but I wouldn't. They asked me if I was going to walk all the way to Columbia, and I said no, that I was going to walk until I saw a policeman, and then I was going to have them arrested and maybe they'd take me to Columbia. They kept trying to coax me to get back in the car, and finally they promised me that if I would just get back in the car, they wouldn't drink a drop; they wouldn't even break the seal. So, I got back in the car with them, and we got to Columbia. By this time they were all about to die laughing, and, of course, they couldn't wait to tell everybody. I didn't think it was funny, though. They just never had to contend with a little girl like me.[107]

Loughlin remembered one incident in a WBT Briarhopper stage show: "We were not encouraged to go to the shows by Mother and Father, but we did go one time. Johnny McAllister saw me and made me bring my chair up there next to the stage so that I could see the show better. I was so embarrassed about it all.... I was really shy and they were the Briarhoppers, for goodness' sakes."[108]

Briarhopper Family Popularity

Daniel said that in the 1930s, their popularity was great: "Our following was astronomical. The mail poured in from all over the eastern seaboard. 'From Maine to Miami' was WBT's motto, and the mail proved it."

Daniel says her aunt used to take her and her sister to Montreat, North Carolina, which is in the Black Mountain area of North Carolina:

One year, the milkman came by and found out that I was Billie Briarhopper. He said that he'd give me a quart of milk if I'd sing a song for him. Well, I kept on singing and before he left, I had that whole creek in front of the house filled up with sweet milk, buttermilk, chocolate milk, and butter. The Foremost milkman did not deliver much milk that day.[109]

I have so many, many happy memories of that part of my life. I didn't always like the songs I had to sing, but I had to sing the most requested songs.... Personal appearances were lots of fun, too. I suppose that I have been in every town, in every school ... in the Piedmont and western parts of North and South Carolina and Virginia. We got to one place one night, way back in the mountains, and they didn't have electricity. I couldn't sing, because the PA [public address system] wouldn't work. Sometimes we'd get to a place and they'd have a spread you wouldn't believe. Country ham and fried chicken and homemade pies and cakes and everything was so good.... [110]

Changing Briarhoppers

Billie Burton Daniel shared her memories of when cast members arrived and left the show. She remembers that Jane Bartlett left the second year that Daniel was there. According to Daniel, Bartlett and Claire Shadwell had their own show, called *The Old Shepherd and Jane*. She continues:

> Don White left soon after [Bartlett]. Charlie Davis, another of Bill (Davis') sons joined the show the second year (I was there). Elmer Warren joined the show the third year (I was there). We called him "Hank." Gibb Young came on the show about the same time. Johnny McAllister left the show in 1939 or 1940, and it was never the same. I honestly don't know, but I believe that there was some friction between "Dad" and Mr. Crutchfield. When "Dad" left, Bill Davis took over and by this time Bill Bivens was the announcer. Lee Kirby announced some too, as did J.B. Clark.

Clarence left the fourth year (1940).... [T]he Oklahoma Sweethearts and Floyd and Mildred joined the show.... Mr. Crutchfield was by now the station manager and not announcing the show.... Bill Bivens was the announcer and everything was different.... Bill Davis came back and became the show's manager, and his sons Charlie and Judge came back ... Gibb was still there.... We didn't have a piano player anymore and I didn't fit in.... [T]here may have been a little resentment because of my loyalty to McAllister and Etters.... [T]he reason that I left was because the show went off for the summer and my family moved to Wilmington.... [T]hat was 1941, my sixth year on the show.... I probably should have left with McAllister and Etters because it was never the same.

When asked when she knew that the variety show was changing to a string band/hillbilly music format, Daniel said, "It was when Dad [McAllister] and Clarence [Etters] left. That is, more than likely, why they left. If Dad couldn't do things his way, he wouldn't do them.... [T]here was some friction between Dad and Charles Crutchfield. They just didn't like each other."[111]

Daniel followed this thought in an email to the authors: "Dad and Mr. Crutchfield were more entertaining than Lum and Abner. The banter between them was wonderful!!! I've never understood why they didn't like each other."[112]

New Members

Mildred and Floyd were a singing duo with the Briarhoppers toward the end of the decade. Their participation in the group is documented by several photographs, and they are slightly remembered by Daniel and Carson. Of all the people interviewed, most did not remember the children's full names, or whatever happened to them after their time on WBT.

Billie Burton Daniel had some memories of the duet: "Mildred and Floyd were younger than I, and I grew to be very fond of them, especially Mildred. She loved my clothes, so I gave her some of my prettiest dresses. They were very nice children, but different. They sang songs that I had never heard before, mostly hymns, but not the hymns that I knew. They were from South Carolina, I think. I wish I knew more."[113]

The Oklahoma Sweethearts

There is no information, other than that told by Daniel, of the Oklahoma Sweethearts' time with the Briarhoppers or who they actually were.

Charlotte as a Growing Musical Mecca

At this time Charlotte, North Carolina, was a precursor to Nashville's title of "Music City USA." Advertisers like the Crazy Water Crystals Company and the Patent Medicine Company bought time and sponsored shows on the radio. RCA Victor sent field crews to record the music coming from the area and eventually set up a permanent studio, the last site being a suite of rooms on the tenth floor of the Hotel Charlotte, recording the Golden Gate Quartet, the Monroe Brothers, and Uncle Dave Macon, among others.[114]

Sociologist Liston Pope noted in the 1930s this growing trend in music that WBT was promoting: "'Hillbilly' music is very popular and, indeed is still secretly preferred to opera by most uptown citizens." Charlotte had become a major center for the recording and broadcast of "'hillbilly' music, and the talent assembled in the city could compete with any in the world."[115] More than 500 recordings came out of those recording sessions.[116] The Monroe Brothers recorded their most famous song, "What Would You Give in Exchange for Your Soul?" in Charlotte in 1936.[117]

The Carter Family, already recording stars since their debut albums made in Bristol in 1927, recorded in Charlotte in 1931, producing seven songs for RCA Victor, according to *The Charlotte Country Music Story*. Twenty-two more sessions were recorded in 1938, this time for Decca Records.[118]

But not all of the new recording was glamorous. RCA Victor's rep-

resentative, Eli Oberstein, came to Charlotte to sign talent and to over-
see the recording sessions, according to reporter Lew Powell in his July 18,
1982, article in the *Charlotte Observer* entitled "Charlotte's Recording
Years."

Powell says Oberstein's business practices were "questionable," but
everybody liked him. In the article, Fred Kirby remembers, "[Oberstein]
was auditioning people, and anything that you wrote yourself, he'd take
it.... He didn't want to go through a lot of publishers.... I don't think any
of us realized much out of the recordings. We were mostly new to the
business."[119]

"One of the things that made this music so exciting was the excitement of the city," Tom Hanchett, historian of the Levine Museum of the
New South, said in a 1999 interview. "The cotton factories brought people from the farms to the cities, and that mobilization created an emo-
tionally charged time. The music reflected that. It was full of excitement
and possibility."[120]

This excitement can be felt in the news article proclaiming the arrival
of Oberstein and his intentions of making records, found in the *Charlotte
News* on January 26, 1938:

> Mr. Oberstein and his assistants will be here the rest of the week making
> phonograph records at the Hotel Charlotte. They will make some 300 selec-
> tions from 32 units (bands), including Jimmie Livingston and his band, who
> play here. Most of the others will be hill billies [*sic*].
> "There were 750,000 records sold last year [1937]," V.H. Sills of the record
> department here said. "The five and ten cent stores and the service stations
> dispose of more 35-cent records than you could smash with a steam roller."
> Most of the hill billy records are made in and around Charlotte. For
> instance, today there are more than 30 mountain music bands in the city,
> coming from the Carolinas, Virginia, Tennessee, and West Virginia.[121]

This was a golden musical age for Charlotte. Major gospel, blues, big
band, and country artists were drawn to Charlotte to make records.[122] "I
don't think people are aware of just how strong a musical influence this
area has had," said Lew Herman, a Charlotte librarian who conceived the
idea of putting together a history of Charlotte music in the Mecklenburg
County Public Library. The thing that put Charlotte on the map was hillbilly music and blues music.[123]

String band music "came much closer to the spirit of the dance parties that entertained the Piedmont's residents long before the first professional orchestra set foot in the area. Like the lives of their makers, hillbilly
tunes had changed a great deal since they were played for corn shuckings

and tobacco curings in the years when Charlotte was little more that a crossroads town.... Charlotte had become a major center for the recording and broadcast of 'hillbilly' music, and the talent assembled in the city could compete with any in the world."[124]

Not only were famous musicians coming to Charlotte to record, they were also coming to be on the WBT Briarhopper radio show. Daniel remembers when Gene Austin and Gene Autry were guests on the Briarhopper Show. "Gene Austin was a guest, which thrilled Homer [Drye]. Homer made fun of him because Gene was wearing yellow pants... [A]bout a month later, Gene Autry comes on our show and he was wearing a yellow cowboy suit! I really teased Homer about that."[125]

The authors located a discography for Decca Records showing that in 1937 and 1938 Homer Drye recorded ten songs, including "Bill Bailey," and "I Am Just What I Am," in Charlotte, North Carolina. Some of the Decca notes suggest Johnny McAllister (spelled Johnny Macalester) and Big Bill Davis were background musicians. The notes also suggest other musicians who were unknown. If this is the case, these could be the only non-radio show recordings of the 1930s-era Briarhoppers.

The End of the Briarhopper Variety Show

There is evidence of the actual members of the Briarhoppers at the end of 1939. The authors purchased a calendar from e-Bay showing the Briarhoppers, the Carter Family, and the months of 1940. The Briarhoppers that are shown, and the authors are assuming that a contemporary photograph was used for this promotion, are as follows: the announcer (Charles Crutchfield); Dad (John McAllister); Hank Warren; Zeb Briarhopper (Thorpe Westerfield); Tex Martin (Martin Schopp); Curley (Cecil Campbell); Bill Briarhopper (Bill Davis); Montana Jack (Jack Gillette); Horsethief Harry (Harry Blair); Elmer Briarhopper (Clarence Etters). This calendar was sponsored by Zymole Trokeys, a type of cough drop.

If we go by Daniel's recollections, this photo was made right before Etters, Westerfield, and McAllister left. Daniel left in 1941, and, probably, Campbell, Martin, Gillette, and Blair (The Tennessee Ramblers) were hired before Daniel had moved on. This photo, therefore, is a good representation of the members of the Briarhoppers just prior to 1941.

Needless to say, the Briarhopper Family began to see changes, especially by Charles Crutchfield. With many of the original members leaving, Daniel knew something was up that would not involve Tin Pan Alley songs and Irish lullabies. It would involve a type of music that would be a precursor to bluegrass and *O Brother, Where Art Thou?* Call it "hillbilly" or call it "string music," the change that would take place in the Briarhopper household would be a paradigm shift for WBT radio and for the South.

Timeline—1930s

1931— The Empire State Building opened. Al Capone was convicted on charges of tax evasion. Pearl Buck's *The Good Earth* was published. Japanese troops occupied Manchuria.

1932— WSM grew to 50,000 watts. WLS moved to the Eighth Street Theater. Amelia Earhart became the first woman to fly solo across the Atlantic.

1933— WBT grew to 50,000 watts and Charles Crutchfield was hired. Jimmie Rodgers died of TB in a New York City hotel after recording his last dozen sides for a record company. Adolph Hitler was elected chancellor of Germany and the first concentration camps were built in Germany.

1934— WBT Briarhoppers were formed as a variety show with Johnny McAllister as program director. Adolph Hitler was elected fuehrer of Germany.

1934— Don White and Big Bill Davis joined the WBT Briarhoppers.

1936— Edward VIII became the king of Britain, but abdicated the throne for a divorced woman. Jesse Owens showed up Hitler at the Olympic Games in Berlin.

1938— Roy Acuff made his first *Grand Ole Opry* appearance. Riots against Jews began in Germany. Germany began invading European countries.

1939— Fred Kirby joined the WBT Briarhoppers; Bill Monroe joined the *Grand Ole Opry*. Germany invaded Poland, which started World War II.

America's Musical Taste:

The top record for this decade was Judy Garland's "Somewhere Over The Rainbow."

3

The 1940s: The Golden Age of the WBT Briarhoppers

The decade of the 1940s was the most successful period of time for the WBT Briarhopper family. It was in this decade that the "Classic" WBT Briarhoppers (as defined by this book's authors) came together and formed what would become the longest-lived string band in America.

The "Classic" WBT Briarhoppers and Special Guests

Billie Burton Daniel said in an email to the authors, "In the 1940s, when the others came on board, it evolved into a true country show. By this time, however, the original cast had gone."

In 1941, the "Briarhopper Family" disbanded. However, Daniel had a brief extension on the show, mostly due to trickery. She says:

> Mr. Crutchfield called me into his office and told me that they were taking me off the show because I wasn't a little girl anymore and that they needed someone who could, and would, sing country, that country music was the coming thing. He [Crutchfield] knew that I hated country music. I just didn't understand it, and I couldn't, I wouldn't sing it. Well, that just broke my heart ... and I really did not want to leave the show. I still can't believe that I did this. I persuaded Clarence [Etters] to go along with it.... I disguised my voice and called and made an appointment to have an audition for the [Briarhopper] program. I told him that my name was Sally Ruth Perkins. Clarence and I went into one of the smaller studios on the appointed day. Mr. Crutchfield was in his office (like I knew he would be) listening, so he couldn't see me. I sang "Beautiful Brown Eyes" like it had never been sung before. I mean I just really twanged it up. It was terrible. Nothing ever was uglier than that. Do you know what Mr. Crutchfield did? He loved it. He said that I was exactly what he'd been looking for, and he hired me on the

spot ... (later) I heard Mr. Crutchfield's voice ..." Miss Perkins, we're so glad to have you on the show, but I want you to sing as much like Billie as you can." He had known all along.... [1]

Daniel's extension lasted less than one year, until she turned seventeen: "My last show was in the summer of June 1941. The program usually went off for the summer, sometimes it didn't. That summer it did. It wasn't the same anymore ... we didn't even have a piano player.... My family moved to Wilmington [North Carolina]. I remember that the Johnson Family was on our last show."[2]

According to Billie Ann Newman Carson, when Crutchfield became the head of the Briarhoppers, friction occurred between him and McAllister, who, as Daniel said earlier, "ruled with an iron fist." McAllister and his family left Charlotte for good.[3]

As Daniel said, country music was the coming thing. During this decade within the WBT Briarhopper family, country musicians who were brought in made the show different. The new members of the group would include Whitey & Hogan, Shannon Grayson, Claude Casey, and others who joined Warren and Davis on the show.

Claude Casey

Casey was born in Enoree, South Carolina, on September 13, 1912. His grandfather, father, and mother played fiddle and his aunt played banjo. Claude remembered that "[t]his is how my mother and father first met, playing for a dance."[4]

Casey moved to the Shenandoah Valley of Virginia and then into Danville, Virginia, in his early teens. He was influenced by string-band musicians such as Charlie Poole, fiddler Charlie Laprade, and guitarist Elton Biggers. While in high school, Casey began playing guitar with local string bands the Piedmont Serenaders and the Schoolfield Woodchoppers and took up singing.[5]

In 1929, he made his first radio appearance on WBTM in Danville. He landed a fifteen-minute program on Saturday mornings billed as the Carolina Hobo and soon began broadcasting with friends Jake King, Tex Isley, and Marvin Fowler as the Pine State Playboys.[6]

The Pine State Playboys broke up in the early 1930s, but reformed with different personnel many times. In 1936, Casey hitchhiked to New York in order to work for Art Satherly of the American Record Corporation, recording such numbers as "Memories of Charlie Poole" and "Moonshine in the North Carolina Hills." He won an appearance on Major Bowes'

Amateur Hour in New York and toured with the Bowes organization.[7] In 1938, he brought together the Pine State Playboys and recorded for RCA Victor in Rock Hill, South Carolina. In 1940, Casey worked for Gordon and Erwin Rouse, the writers of "The Orange Blossom Special."[8]

It was during this time that music jobs for Casey were not as lucrative as he thought, and he began considering whether or not he should continue being an entertainer.[9] He told John Rumble in an interview:

Homer Christopher, who I had met, who was a wonderful person, I was in his room talking to him, and told him that I was going to go back [home] and get me a job and get out of the [music] business. He says, "Well, Claude, they're looking

Claude Casey, early 1940s. Courtesy Tom Hanchett.

for someone at WBT, a young fellow, somebody at WBT that can sing," because Homer Briarhopper, Homer A. Briarhopper [Homer Drye], had left with Johnny McAllister and gone to WPTF in Raleigh, North Carolina. So he says, "Why don't you go up there and talk to them, give them an audition?" ... So I went up, and I talked to [Charles] Crutchfield. He asked me how old I was and all, a bunch of stuff. He says, "I'd like to hear you sing a song." So he took me in the studio there, [with] Bill Davis and Gibb Young, Hank [Warren], and Floyd and Mildred, and the whole bunch of them, and I sang a couple of songs, let out two or three of those high yodels, and he says, "Come in here a minute."[10]

Casey walked into the offices of Charles Crutchfield in 1941 and was hired and put on the air that day. John Rumble asked Casey how much money he made at WBT. "Twelve dollars a week," Casey responded.[11]

Casey became a featured singer on the *Dixie Farm Club* and the Briarhopper radio show. "Everyone who worked at WBT was a Briarhopper," Casey said, as he soon joined the Briarhoppers and the Tennessee Ramblers. "Crutch [Charles Crutchfield] ... was the man, though. He's responsible for

Claude Casey. I've given him credit all these years.... He's the one that put me on WBT...."[12]

When Casey was employed at WBT, he was not a member of the musician's union, and it took a while to become a member. "[T]he union was so strong in Charlotte until they wouldn't let me play guitar.... So eventually I stayed six months there singing with my hands behind my back."[13] Casey would eventually join the musician's union.

He made his first movie, *Swing Your Partner*, with the Tennessee Ramblers in 1943 and went on to make ten more films in the next few years.[14] After World War II, Casey formed Claude Casey and the Sage Dusters, a cowboy band.

Dewey Price

The authors came across Dewey Price's name from a 1989 radio recording from the *Hello Henry Show*, one of the programs on WBT radio. When asked, "Who were members of the Briarhoppers when you joined?" Roy "Whitey" Grant said that Price was not a Briarhopper for any amount of time. The authors have not found any more data on this person.

Billie Ann Newman

Billie Ann Newman was a jazz/"torch" singer who was a part of the Briarhopper family show, but was never a member of the WBT Briarhoppers. Daniel recalled Newman:

> I really don't know all that much. We were near the same age, but we were not very much alike. Billie Anne had a really pretty voice, and every time I saw her, she was all dressed up and looked like a show girl (even when we were children). She wore makeup and white boots (I thought that she was beautiful). She was on Holly Smith's amateur show a lot, and she was good. She had some sustaining shows on WBT, and when we started the *Carolina Jamboree*, she was on that. Her older sister, Vivian, was with her a lot and

Opposite: Zymole Trokey Calendar, 1940. Top left to right: Charles Crutchfield (sitting); Johnny McAllister (directing); Hank Warren (fiddle); Thorpe Westerfield (guitar); Tex Martin (sitting in back); Cecil Campbell (at music stand); Bill Davis (bass); Jack Gillette (fiddle); Harry Blair (seated with black hat); Clarence Etters (at piano); Mildred and Floyd (in front of piano). Bottom back row left to right: A.P. Carter; Janette Carter; Brother Bill (last name unknown); Sara Carter; Maybelle Carter. Front row left to right: Helen, Anita, and June Carter. Authors' collection.

she was beautiful as well. I remember one night she was down on the program to sing a song that I wanted to sing, and I got mad, because I didn't like the song that they wanted me to sing. I caused a scene and Mr. Crutchfield really talked to me about that.

I liked Billie's family, especially her father. After we grew up, she sang with some of the local bands around town.[15]

Carson, now retired and living in Charlotte, North Carolina, said to the authors in a telephone interview on December 15, 2005:

I got there [WBT] about 1940. Now people would think that I was Billie Burton because of our same name. I was never a Briarhopper, although a lot of people thought that I was. I sang on the *Dixie Jamboree* that the Briarhoppers and the Johnson Family were on. It was on the Dixie Network that went through CBS for the southeastern region. I would also go on the personal appearances with them....[16] We all had a wonderful closeness about us.... I left in 1948 and got married.

We add Newman into the story of the Briarhoppers because not only was she an entertainer on WBT, but she was also a witness to the 1930s and 1940s versions of the Briarhoppers.

Whitey & Hogan

In 1941, Charles Crutchfield made a gutsy decision that would forever revolutionize the music of the WBT Briarhoppers and the popularity of WBT radio itself. The hiring of Roy "Whitey" Grant and Arval Hogan, a duet with a radio spot on WGNC in Gastonia, North Carolina, would change old-time string band music to a true precursor of the bluegrass rhythm set by Bill Monroe and his Blue Grass Boys with Monroe's hiring of Lester Flatt and Earl Scruggs in 1945.

Working for $7.50 per week, Roy Grant and Arval Hogan met at the Firestone Mill (formerly the infamous Loray Mill, site of a workers' strike in 1929 where a worker and a policeman were killed) in Gastonia, North Carolina. Working during the day, they sang songs in the canteen during lunchtime.[17]

Roy "Whitey" Grant was born on April 7, 1916, in Shelby, North Carolina. At the age of nine, Whitey got the idea to play a guitar. "You see, I liked the guitar, but I didn't have one. I noticed that at parties the guitar player always got the girls. A neighbor of mine, Walter Hollyfield, wrote down all of the chords for me. I learned 'em like that."[18]

His guitar was a Martin D-18 that he bought in 1944 at a Spartanburg furniture store. "I paid $104 for it. Anyway, I did this to impress a

Roy "Whitey" Grant (left) and Arval Hogan (right) in 1941. Courtesy Tom Hanchett.

girl named Polly. It took me three years to convince her to marry me. People said that it wouldn't last, but we will have been married seventy years on July 13, 2005."[19]

Arval Hogan was born on July 24, 1919, at Robbinsville, North Carolina. Hogan, a guitar player, never saw a mandolin until his brother ordered one from Sears and Roebuck for $3.50:[20] "I bought it [the mandolin that he used as a performer] in 1940 for $125 from Jones Furniture Store in Gastonia."[21]

In an interview with Ray Thigpen in the May 1989 edition of *Bluegrass Unlimited* Hogan said, "When I finally got that mandolin, I sat up all night practicing by listening to an old Victrola record by the Scottsdale String Band, and before morning, I had learned to play 'Chinese Breakdown.'"[22]

Whitey and Hogan first got together on a Sunday afternoon in 1935 near the Firestone Mill water tank off Garrison Boulevard in Gastonia, according to Grant. In an October 25, 1985 *Charlotte Observer* story, Grant told the following story to reporter Kathy Haight: "We were neighbors and didn't know it. I was living at 905 West Fifth Street and I was picking the guitar with my brother-in-law, William Rumfelt. We were playing 'Red River Valley.' Hogan walked by us and said, 'Hey, that

1940

WITH EVERY GOOD WISH
FOR HAPPY HOLIDAYS
To my great Uncle
Henry Burton

(over)

Billie Burton

WBT Christmas postcard featuring Billie Burton, 1940. Courtesy Billie Burton Daniel.

sounds pretty good.' He [Hogan] said that he played with his brother but that he worked on a different shift. He said that we ought to get together."[23]

That Monday, the two tried singing old-time gospel songs to the accompaniment of Grant's guitar and Hogan's mandolin, Grant said in that interview:

> We found out that we both liked music and we both liked Jimmie Rodgers, so we would get together at lunch with our instruments and we would eat and play.[24] The first songs that we learned were from a song book by Carl and Hardy. The first that we tried was "No Place to Put Down My Head." Then we started to sing gospel songs. On weekends we started singing at country churches. We went all over the Carolinas and Georgia. My dad started going with us and he was the MC. That was in the middle of the Depression, and if we made a dollar, that was good money.[25] Whitey and Hogan made their radio debut over WSPA in Spartanburg, South Carolina, as the Spindle City Boys.[26]

Grant admits, "I never got to meet Jimmie Rodgers, but my nephew did. Woodrow Grant was hitchhiking from Gastonia to New York. Along came a T-Model [Ford] and it stopped and picked him up. Jimmie Rodgers was driving the T-Model. Jimmie Rodgers was going to New York to do some records and took my nephew all the way to New York. That was my dealings with Jimmie Rodgers."[27]

Many mill hands joined together, like Whitey and Hogan, to play the music that they heard on records and on radios. Grant recalls, "Everybody tried to make old-time music at the cotton mills.... A lot of the boys that we knew, or heard of, they would get together in the cotton mills and the first thing you know they would form bands.... On Saturday and Sunday, when the mill wasn't running, they had a little bandstand up there and [the bands would] draw a big crowd."[28]

While still employed with the mill, Whitey and Hogan moved to WGNC in Gastonia, North Carolina, in 1939 under the sponsorship of Efird's Department Store. Whitey Grant remembers: "We tried out for a spot on the radio station. There were a lot of people there trying out as well. There were *really good musicians* there. For some reason, they chose me and Hogan." The duo got a fifteen-minute slot on the radio at noon. Grant commented that he was still wondering why they got the job. Soon after, Grant went to the boss and knocked on his door. "I asked him, 'Why did you pick us? You had good musicians who could pick and sing songs.' The boss, who was a musician himself, told Grant, 'Out of all the musicians who were there, you two were the only ones who had their instruments in tune and in tune with each other. I told the programmer who was with me that you guys, if given a chance, will go somewhere and let's give 'em a chance.'"[29]

Grant asked the authors of this book, "Do you know who the first guest on our show on WGNC was? Uncle Dave Macon and his son, Dorris. Uncle Dave was one of the finest guys that I ever met. He thought the world of his son. They were good folk."[30]

Later, the duo broadcast from the Main Street window of a sponsoring furniture store.[31] Grant says:

I remember the name of the furniture store, Rustin Furniture, and we used to sing a theme song for the store, which was to the tune of "Happy Days Are Here Again":

> Rustin Furniture's on the air,
> We'll tell you of all the bargains there.
> Just come down we'll show you with care,
> Rustin Furniture's on the air.

In fact it was on that program that we were ever late for a radio show. Me and Hogan went to the five-and-dime store before our show to look at the goldfish. I didn't think that we were that long, but we heard the store's radio

... they probably raised the volume to get us out of there ... anyway, we heard the announcer say, 'This is the Rustin Radio Show with Whitey & Hogan, but we don't know where Whitey & Hogan are!' We heard that and we started runnin' down the street, all the way across town, until we got to Rustin Furniture, because we were playing in the window at the time. We were so tired, we couldn't sing.... All that we could do was to play our instruments while we huffed and puffed."[32]

The duo's popularity grew to a point where they made some recordings with Decca Records in New York City, and where, between the late 1930s and early 1940s, they recorded over thirty songs for Decca and then for Sonora and Deluxe, including An "Old Log Cabin for Sale," "There's Power Greater Than Atomic," and "Turn Your Radio On."[33]

Grant remembers:

We hadn't been on the radio any time at all, and a man from Charlotte, a Mr. Van Seals, came up to us and said that we did a song on the radio and Decca wants to record it. I asked him which one and he said, "An Old Log Cabin for Sale." He told us to get some more songs together and bring them over to the Decca office in Charlotte. They chose sixteen sides to record. Mr. Dave Capp, I'll never forget, came up and said, "Whitey, I understand that 'The Old Log Cabin for Sale' is a pretty hard song to sing." I told him that that was the only song that we were afraid of. Mr. Capp said for us not to worry, that they would make as many takes as we needed. He then told us to run through it one time. Well, we sang the song and we did it perfect. Then we recorded fifteen other songs and me and Hogan were waiting to do the cabin song last. After the fifteenth song, we told Mr. Capp that we were ready to do the cabin song. Mr. Capp told us that he had recorded me and Hogan doing that song when we practiced it and it was already done. He was a smart man.[34]

"Old Log Cabin for Sale" came from Stamps Baxter Music Company, according to Grant. "Yeah, they thanked us for recording that song, and sent us books of songs for us to look through."[35]

According to Whitey Grant, in 1941 he and Hogan joined the WBT Briarhoppers:

Me and Hogan did a show at a high school in Gastonia ... the promoter wanted us because he knew that we would advertise it on the radio. Each act played twice. After our first set was done, the promoter came up and told us that he didn't get as much money from the gate as he thought and wanted to know if we would take half of what he had promised us. Well, we knew that something was up because the place was packed and people were sitting in the windows and on the rafters. After me and Hogan talked it over, we told the promoter that since he was paying us half, we would only do half of what we were supposed to do, so since we had played one set, we wanted our money. That put the promoter in a bind. We got it all straightened out after that. Anyway, after we finished, Bill Bivens came up to us and asked us if we would like to be with WBT. I said, "Bill, that's our highest ambition, to be on the Briarhopper program and be on a 50,000 watt radio station." He said that he would see if he could do anything for us. A few days later, we got the call from Crutchfield to come over and talk to him. Now, Bivens told us not to take anything under twenty-five dollars a week each.[36]

We were popular at that point, but we still needed our jobs in the mill to feed our family. Well, Crutch [Charles Crutchfield, of WBT Radio] wanted us really bad for his radio show. He called us into his office in Charlotte and said, "Boys, he always called us 'his boys,' I'll tell you what, I will pay you both $25.00 per week to have you on the Briarhoppers." Well, we were making $7.50 per week at the mill, so we thought that we were rich. Of course, we agreed to the deal.[37]

At this time, a job was precious. Whitey and Hogan met with their supervisor at the mill, and told the supervisor that they were working their notice. Grant remembers, "We asked the boss if we bombed out on the radio, could we get our jobs back. The boss said that he would have something for us. If you did not leave on good terms, you were put on a list and you would not be hired there again."[38]

According to Grant, the WBT Briarhoppers consisted of Claude Casey, Fiddlin' Hank Warren, Billie Ann Newman, and Big Bill Davis. "Homer Drye was gone," he says. "In fact, Crutch hired us to take Homer's place. You see, Homer was a small boy when he was hired. In 1941, his voice changed. Crutch told Homer that he had to let him go. Crutch said that he wanted to go to a duo-type singing, and that's how we got our job. It was supposed to last only 3 months, but we were on the air for over a decade."[39]

The very first thing that they noticed at WBT was a pile of unopened mail addressed to the WBT Briarhoppers. According to Grant:

When Hogan and I arrived at WBT, the Briarhoppers weren't doing that well, and they were not checking their mail. Me and Hogan thought that the mail should be checked. The Briarhoppers had letters from schools and civic organizations, but they weren't answering them. Hogan volunteered to go through the mail and began answering them. Before long, we had work four and five nights a week, sometimes six nights a week. At that point, our wives were getting sick of that, travelin' so much, but it was our livelihood. We became accustomed to working so much that when we were at home, we thought that we should be working. That's how we started our public appearance outside of WBT in 1941.[40]

WBT Briarhoppers onstage, 1941. Standing left to right: Arval Hogan; Bill Davis; Eleanor Bryan; Hank Warren (fiddle); Lee Kirby (announcer); Claude Casey; Roy Grant. Kneeling is Homer Christopher. Courtesy Jim Scancarelli.

Sam Poplin

The information on Sam Poplin was gathered through *The Charlotte Country Music Story*, published in 1985 by the North Carolina Arts Council.

Poplin, birth date unknown, grew up in Albemarle, North Carolina. His grandfather was an old-time fiddler who passed on the lure of the fiddle to Poplin.

His first professional musical job was with Fisher Hendley's Carolina Tarheels, and, at seventeen years of age, he traveled with the group to New York to be on the radio by day, playing in clubs by night. By the time he returned to North Carolina, again as written in *The Charlotte Country Music Story*, Poplin had recorded square dance tunes for the Brunswick record label.

In the early 1930s, he worked as a musician and as a carpenter for his father in Albemarle. In 1934, Poplin worked with Fred Russell's Hillbillies on the WBT *Crazy Barn Dance*. When that show was canceled, Poplin returned to Albemarle, but soon after rejoined Fisher Hendley with his new group, the Aristocratic Pigs.

In 1938, Hendley moved his operations from Greenville, South Carolina, to WIS in Columbia, South Carolina, causing Poplin to quit and start up his own band, Sam Poplin and his Adluh Musical Millers, named for the band's sponsor, Adluh Flour Mill. They became a popular band on WIS. According the *The Charlotte Country Music Story*, this band became so popular that Royal Crown Cola sponsored the band for a second daily show on WIS as the Royal Crown Rangers. World War II broke up Poplin's band, and he quit music to work in the shipyards. After the war, he came back to Albemarle, bought a farm, and worked as a machinist.

In 1945, Poplin got back into the music business, joining Curly Williams and the Georgia Peach Pickers at the Barn in Venice, California, where the band shared the stage with Bob Wills and His Texas Playboys. In 1946, Poplin came back to Charlotte, North Carolina, and joined WBT as a musician. At this point, he worked with Claude Casey and the Sage Dusters and with the Briarhoppers, where he played throughout the rest of the decade.[41]

Homer Christopher

Not much is known about Christopher. The authors do know that he played with the Briarhoppers Unit Number 2, where he played the accordion. Grant did say that Christopher made cabinets for him and that Christopher retired to Daytona Beach, Florida. Grant remembers Christopher's dying, but could not remember the year.

Grant says that Christopher was a great artist in making cabinets: "He was a woodworker by occupation and played a good accordion. I believe he was from SC. He was with Briarhoppers and Tennessee Ramblers.... We all worked together like that, you know."[42]

Billie Ann Newman Carson remembered Christopher: "Homer Christopher ... I think that he died. His wife was a seamstress and I took all of my clothes to her. Homer was a very quiet, dry, black-haired guy."[43]

"Homer Christopher sang and played the accordion," Eleanor Bryan Fields said in a telephone interview on December 26, 2005. "I roomed with his family in Charlotte. He had two daughters."

The authors could not find any more information on Homer Christopher.

Nat Richardson

Information on Nat Richardson came from the *WBT's Briarhopper Family Album*, circa 1949, printed by WBT, and paraphrased below:

Born in Newberry, South Carolina, circa 1929, Richardson began playing music on a "dollar fiddle." At the age of sixteen, Richardson convinced his father to purchase a steel guitar, which was a second-hand model with no instructions as to how to play it.

Apparently, Richardson learned how to play the steel guitar, because he got a job as the featured steel guitar player for WAGA in Atlanta, Georgia.

Richardson enjoyed the Briarhoppers' radio show, and when he and his wife visited relatives in Charlotte, Richardson went to audition at WBT, where he received a position on the Briarhoppers on May 23, 1949.

Richardson also performed on WBT's *Carolina Calling*, which was heard coast-to-coast on CBS Radio.

Shannon Grayson

The second paradigm shift occurred when Shannon Grayson joined the Briarhoppers in 1941, "on the good wishes from Whitey and Hogan," Grant remembers in his April 15, 2005, interview.

Prior to Grayson's hiring, there were few string bands that had a finger-picking banjo player, Wade Mainer and Snuffy Jenkins being two of the few pickers in the music industry. Grayson added his version of both two-finger and three-finger picking to the changing WBT Briarhopper musical format that brought the band closer to the bluegrass sound. With Bill Monroe at WBT and in the vicinity, one can assume that he heard the WBT Briarhoppers, Mainers Mountaineers, and Byron Parker's band with Snuffy Jenkins, combining those sounds with the Scottish lilts and old-time fiddle playing of his Uncle Pen, to form what is now called "bluegrass."

Grayson, born on September 30, 1916, in Sunshine, North Carolina, was the guitar and banjo player who was influenced by DeWitt "Snuffy" Jenkins. Jenkins, also a North Carolina native, is credited with being the first banjo player to play three-finger bluegrass style on the radio, and has been mentioned by Earl Scruggs and Don Reno as being a main influence in their respective banjo playing.

Grayson played both a two-finger style of banjo that had a bluegrass tempo, unlike mountain-style two-finger styles that replicated the clawhammer style cadence, and a three-finger roll style. His style was between Wade

Peruna Calendar, 1941. Back row left to right: Charlie Davis; Gibb Young (near microphone); Roger Davis; Claude Casey. Front row left to right: Bill Bivens (sitting); Hank Warren; Billie Burton; Mildred and Floyd; Bill Davis. Courtesy Jim Scancarelli.

The Carlisle Brothers with Shannon Grayson — early 1940. Left to right: Bill Carlisle; Shannon Grayson; Little Tommy Carlisle; Cliff Carlisle. Courtesy Tom Hanchett.

Mainer's, another North Carolinian who developed a unique two-finger style before bluegrass, and Jenkins': choppy, rugged, and not up to what is now called bluegrass style picking. But Grayson's sound was a precursor to bluegrass: syncopated and unique. His playing is what separates the Briarhoppers from other string bands of the early 1940s. To give you an example of the degree of separation, Bill Monroe's Bluegrass Boys had Dave "Stringbean" Akeman playing clawhammer banjo. It is probable that Shannon Grayson's addition gave the Briarhoppers the bluegrass drive in 1941 before Bill Monroe added Earl Scruggs in 1945.

Wade Mainer, commenting on the origins of bluegrass banjo, said in an interview with the authors on April 27, 2000:

> In my opinion, the way I see it, and I heard it all back then, there was bluegrass before Bill Monroe ever got into bluegrass. There are several tunes we recorded where the banjo sounds like bluegrass. The Morris Brothers also were playin' like that. Bill Monroe wasn't doin' any good, let me tell you, until he added a banjo into his group. Then his name was "Blue Grass Boys" and the name stuck for his music. I give credit to Bill. He probably was the man who made the music faster. But some people say he started it and some say we started it.[44]

Grayson's musical experience began as a young child, playing the pump organ at the age of six, and later he mastered the banjo and guitar. Grayson almost quit the banjo until he heard Snuffy Jenkins play, and Grayson considered Jenkins his biggest influence on the banjo.[45]

Grayson grew up in the North Carolina region known as "banjo country," an area that this author considers being from Asheville to the west to Lincoln County to the east, Catawba County to the north, and Cleveland County to the south. Snuffy Jenkins, Wade Mainer, Smith Hammett and Rex Brooks (cited by both Jenkins and Scruggs as major banjo influences in their lives), and Hoke Jenkins (Snuffy's nephew), grew up in this region and defined their banjo picking here. The authors want to note that we are not "snubbing" the Round Peak and Galax area of Virginia and the North Carolina counties near the Virginia state line. This area is more known for clawhammer or mountain style banjo playing than a two-or three-finger picking style of banjo playing.

To know Shannon Grayson, one needs to know a little about Snuffy Jenkins.

Polly Grant, Whitey's wife, remembered Snuffy Jenkins as a young man. "Before he got famous with Pappy Sherrill and the Hired Hands, Snuffy used to play banjo at my dad's corn shuckin's."[46] Whitey was there at those corn shuckings, but admits that he did not pay much attention to the three-finger style that Jenkins made famous. "I'm ashamed of myself for that.... I was only interested in Polly and the guitar ... I did not pay much attention to the banjo."

The authors added this information on Snuffy Jenkins to show where Grayson was in the "timeline of banjo picking." From our research, Snuffy learned from Brooks and Hammett and from classical banjo records. Grayson probably heard Jenkins before Scruggs and Reno since Grayson lived closer to Jenkins. From a pure distillation of the research, the alpha timeline for bluegrass picking is: Brooks and Hammett; Jenkins; GRAYSON; Scruggs, Reno, and Ralph Stanley, all of whom learned from or heard Jenkins at about the same time. Branching off from this line would be pickers like Johnny Whisnant, who learned, independently of Jenkins, a rolling three-finger style.

Banjoist David Holt knew Grayson after Holt moved to the North Carolina mountains in the 1970s. Holt told the authors that Grayson's banjo style was an early transitional bluegrass style heavily influenced by old-time string band music. Grayson's playing was not as driving as Earl Scruggs' playing, Holt remembered, but "it fit perfectly with the band."[47]

According to Grayson's daughter, Gina Grayson Robinson, her father showed musical talent at a young age. He began playing with the family's old foot organ. "He was so small that he had to pedal with one foot in order to reach above his head to the keys in order to play," she said. Soon after, a friend came by to see his parents, and the friend had a mandolin. "He cried and pitched such a fit that his Dad bought it." After mastering the mandolin, Grayson purchased a banjo.[48]

Grayson's first professional job was with Art Mix, brother of cowboy movie star Tom Mix. Then, Grayson made his radio debut on WSOC in Charlotte, North Carolina, with "Jumpin'" Bill Carlisle, a future *Grand Ole Opry* star.[49] Next Grayson joined Carlisle and his brother, Cliff, in Knoxville, performing as the Carlisle Brothers.[50] Cliff had worked, traveled, and recorded with the legendary performer Jimmie Rodgers."[51]

Gina Robinson says that her father talked a lot about his time with the Carlisle Brothers. "Playing with them must have been one of the happiest times for Dad. He spoke so fondly of them and Bill [Carlisle] was a card anyway. Dad seemed the happiest and would laugh the hardest when he was around Bill. They would both say of each other, 'I love him like a brother,' and I'm sure Dad meant it."[52]

Bill Carlisle was traveling through the area and heard the Briarhoppers radio show. According to Grant, Shannon Grayson was with Carlisle in the car. "I was told that Bill Carlisle heard us on the radio; he turned to Shannon and said, 'At least WBT got somebody who can sing!'"[53]

Grayson caught the ear of Whitey Grant. "Me and Hogan played with Shannon before we got to WBT. It was up in Rutherfordton, North Carolina, and I thought he was outstanding. He could play the guitar, mandolin, and banjo," Grant said. "We saw him with Bill Carlisle and we thought that he would be a great addition to the group. Then, the Carlisles went to Nashville and left old Shannon out in the cold. We went to Crutch [Charles Crutchfield] to tell him about this banjo player and that he would be a good fit."[54]

Polly Grant remembered that, just after Grayson was hired, she and her husband moved into a house that Grayson owned. "When Shannon got married, his wife's dad built them a home for a wedding gift. When they had a couple of kids, the house was too small so Shannon built a nice brick home next door. Shannon let us live in the small house until we could buy our own home."[55]

In a May 2005 telephone interview, Wade Mainer especially remembers Grayson: "He was a fine feller and a great musician. He really helped me a lot on the *Mid-Day Merry-Go-Round* radio show in Knoxville. I'd be short a musician and Shannon would come over and fill-in.... He could play a lot of instruments."[56]

In 1944, Grayson brought his unique style of banjo picking to the WBT Briarhoppers, where he would stay until the program's close in 1951. However, Grayson didn't make the "first team" at the beginning. "Actually, the Briarhoppers got so popular, we had to have a second band so that we could meet all of our commitments," says Grant.[57]

Crutchfield assembled "The Briarhoppers, Unit Number 2," which consisted of Grayson, Homer Christopher, Claude Casey, and Sam Poplin.[58]

According to the Website http://www.music.com, Eugene Chadbourne writes, "Sometimes the demand [for the WBT Briarhoppers] was so great for this group, that the group members spread themselves out between two satellite versions of the bands, each filled with hired-gun pickers. 'You almost couldn't tell one from the other,' [Shannon] Grayson claimed in an interview."[59]

"Shannon always loved to tell a story about being born in Sunshine, North Carolina," Grant said in a 1993 interview. "He'd say 'I was born in Sunshine, which is close to Golden Valley, which is close to Bostic.' He'd tell folks that there was a 4-inch post in the middle of town; on one side the sign said Golden Valley, on another side it said Golden Valley, and if you missed the post, you missed the town."[60]

Grayson also was a member of the hillbilly comic group, the Hot Shot Elmer's Family. This group played on Knoxville's (Tennessee) radio station, WNOX.[61]

Grayson was a very popular musician in the Carolinas and the South, especially with his banjo picking style. "I was told by the director of the Levine Museum of the South (in Charlotte, North Carolina), that he had one of Dad's records on his desk.... He offered to give it to me, the record, but I told him no, I liked it right where he had it."[62]

Fred Kirby and "Atomic Power"

Fred Kirby recorded a national hit in 1946, "Atomic Power." According to Charles K. Wolfe, coeditor of *Country Music Goes to War*, and writer of the essay "Jesus Hits Like an Atomic Bomb," this was the first song that dealt with the atomic bomb.

According to Wolfe, Kirby wrote the song the day after the United States dropped an atomic bomb on Hiroshima, Japan. Kirby began singing the song on his local radio shows. Wolfe wrote that Kirby thought that someone from the publishing firm of Leeds Music Corporation in New York heard Kirby on the radio. Leeds flew a representative down to Charlotte to obtain publication rights to the song. Leeds also contacted RCA Victor, who asked Kirby to record only that song and one other song. "I didn't think it was worthwhile to go all the way to New York to tape two sides," Kirby said in Wolfe's article, "... Sonora Record Company came down here to Charlotte and offered me a $2,000 bonus if I would record with them, and they would give me eight sides."[63]

Of course, Sonora was not RCA Victor, and Sonora did not have the vast distribution program that RCA Victor had. The Buchanan Brothers recorded the song with RCA Victor. *Billboard Magazine* named the release of both versions of the song on May 1, 1946. *Billboard's* May 25, 1946, issue stated, "The whole world is talking about 'Atomic Power,' the greatest folk song in twenty years."[64] The Buchanan Brothers' version of the song climbed onto a list of the "Most Played Juke Box Folk Records," on June 29, 1946. Kirby received most of his composer royalties from this version of the song.[65]

Kirby became so identified with the song that it threatened to surpass everything that he had accomplished to date, according to Wolfe. The most memorable aspect of this was when Kirby was asked to ride in the January 1949 inauguration parade of President Harry S Truman. "I was passing by the reviewing stand, the stand with Truman and [Vice President Alben] Barkley, and our chief of police from Charlotte was just beyond that place and he could not resist — well, he did it before he even thought of it — [the police chief] yelled 'Atomic Power' just as I had bowed to the President and Barkley and the people in the stands. It scared me to death!"

Kirby remembered when returning soldiers would come up to him and tell him that they had heard "Atomic Power" translated into Japanese and German.[66] Kirby also helped the war effort by selling war bonds in St. Louis. "I was the Victory Cowboy who sold over a couple million dollars worth of war bonds. Don White and I also continued our duet as The Carolina Boys, Fred and Don."

On the heels of Kirby's success with "Atomic Power," Whitey and Hogan thought of a song in a similar vein, which would be titled, "There's a Power Greater Than Atomic." Hogan says in Wolfe's article that he and Whitey read about peacetime atomic weapons tests in July 1946. The U.S. government placed ninety ships off Bikini Atoll in the Pacific. Atomic bombs were detonated over the ships. From the ninety ships in the ocean, only five sank. A second test had similar results. "We got to thinking about

A rare early 1950s picture showing WBT Briarhopper Fred Kirby and his horse, Calico, onstage for the Union Christmas Party, at Cooleemee School, Cooleemee, North Carolina. Note the segregated audience. Photo taken by Harold Foster. Courtesy the Textile Heritage Center, Cooleemee Historical Society.

when they had that big test in the Pacific; those ships still standing after the blast, that's what gave us the idea (about the song)," Grant added, then continued:

Hogan and myself, both being children of devout Christians, the idea came to us one night going to a personal appearance. And I said, "Well, gee whiz, somewhere in the world there ought to be a power greater than atomic," and we put two and two together and starting writing words that night and in a short while the song was completed. We didn't do anything with it until Fred (Kirby's) song started dying down. Then we turned ours over to our publisher, Hill and Range, and we recorded it. We recorded our version in the WBT studios in Charlotte, for the DeLuxe label. The Buchanan Brothers in New York also recorded it on the RCA Victor label, and since Victor had better coverage and better distribution, it did pretty good for us.[67]

In John Rumble's interviews with Whitey and Hogan, Grant remembers discussing the song with Kirby: "We were riding one night on a personal appearance, and we were still working on the song in the backseat of the car. We were writing it, and Fred, Fred Kirby, good friend of ours

... said, 'Whitey, please don't do anything with the song until mine has its play.' We had an oral agreement that we wouldn't do anything with the song until his started to decline....[68]

Eleanor Bryan Fields

Eleanor Bryan became a Briarhopper sometime in 1939 or 1940. The authors have picture evidence of Bryan's being a part of the group in 1939 for a 1940 calendar shot. According to Roy Grant, Eleanor was a yodeler and singer. He said, "Claude Casey got her the job 'cause she sure could yodel.... She could out-yodel Patsy Montana, she was that good."[69]

The authors found Fields in her hometown of Goldsboro, North Carolina, and she related how she became a Briarhopper, in a December 26, 2005, telephone interview: "A friend of mine got a guitar for a present, and I really liked it. So much that I got me one, a Gibson Jumbo guitar.

THE BRIARHOPPERS, WBT—Standing left to right: Whitey & Hogan, Bill Briarhopper, Gi Young, and Claude Casey. Seated at table, Charlie Crutchfield and Grady Cole. In front o table, Eleanor Bryan, Homer Christopher and Hank Briarhopper.

Peruna advertisement with Grady Cole. Grady Cole in separate photo. Standing left to right: Roy Grant; Arval Hogan; Bill Davis; Gibb Young; Claude Casey. Seated left to right: Charles Crutchfield; Grady Cole. Kneeling: Eleanor Bryan; Homer Christopher; Hank Warren. Courtesy of Jim Scancarelli.

I learned to play and soon began playing on WGVR in Goldsboro. They had a Saturday night radio show where they would let people come in and play and sing. It was either here or at another jamboree where I met Claude Casey. He wanted to write my name down and go back and talk to Charles Crutchfield to see if I could get on the Briarhopper program."

Fields remembers that the members of the WBT Briarhoppers when she joined in 1942 were Claude Casey, Whitey & Hogan, Homer Christopher, Hank Warren, and Bill Davis. She also fondly remembers Charles Crutchfield: "He was very nice to me. I had no personal dealings with him, only at the radio station. He would try to mess me up when we were on the radio. Whitey and Hogan would sing the theme song and I would come in singing behind them. Crutchfield would light a match and stick it in my shoe. That's pretty crazy, wasn't it?"[70] Claude Casey thought that Fields would be a good choice because of her yodeling. She said, "I learned from Patsy Montana ... never met her, but listened to her on the radio. Me and Claude would do a few songs and both of us would yodel. It went over pretty well."[71]

Fields boarded with Homer Christopher's family while she was in Charlotte. "Homer was a quiet man who could sing and play the accordion. I remember that he had two daughters. I don't remember too much else. I also stayed with Hogan and his wife, Evelyn, when they lived in Gastonia. They were so sweet to me."[72]

Fields was only a Briarhopper for a short time. "I was a Briarhopper one season and I went back home to go back to high school in Goldsboro. This was the first time when I was away from home, and I missed my family."

Fields started a trio with her sister and a cousin, and they performed in the Goldsboro area during the mid 1940s. Soon, they set their sights for Nashville. Fields said, "Me and my sister and my cousin formed a trio that sang locally at the radio stations in the 1950s. And we went to Nashville. We stayed at the hotel near WSM, the Clarkston Hotel, next door to the radio station. We stayed there. And Lew Childre was staying there, too. That's how we met."[73]

Lew Childre was a musician who would become a member of the Grand Ole Opry. Young Eleanor Bryan married Childre in Nashville "just long enough to have two children with him.... We might have been married a few years ... I can't remember. My family wanted me back home so that I could be a little girl again, so we divorced and I came back to Goldsboro."[74] After having her children, Fields basically quit the music business.

Don White and Cecil Campbell with Roy Rogers, September 1943. Left to right: Don White; unknown; Roy Rogers; unknown; Cecil Campbell. Courtesy Dwight Moody.

Don White & Claude Casey

Don White continued to spread his wings. He and Claude Casey did a movie, as mentioned earlier. Don also was in the movie *My Darling Clementine* starring Roy Acuff and his Smokey Mountain Boys.

Arthur Smith

Arthur "Guitar Boogie" Smith was another major artist to play a part with the WBT Briarhoppers. Many cite Smith as being a member of the band, but according to Grant, Smith was a solo member starring on the Briarhoppers' radio show:

"Arthur never was a Briarhopper, and didn't need to be. He had his own thing going, built a good musical group into the Crackerjacks, and hosted *Carolina Calling* on WBT. He had his brothers with him, Sonny and Ralph. We were all separate but we were all together. It was funny that way."[75]

Grand Ole Opry member George Hamilton IV, a musical partner with Smith for many years, told the authors Smith never mentioned that he was ever a member of the WBT Briarhoppers. "Arthur always spoke of the Briarhoppers with the greatest respect," Hamilton IV said in a telephone interview with the authors on January 23, 2006.

The WBT Briarhopper Radio Show

The WBT Briarhoppers' half-hour radio show came on six days a week on WBT at 4:00 P.M. From the VHS tape entitled "Charlotte Country Music Story," produced by WTVI, Charlotte's PBS television station, in 1985, the WBT Briarhopper show started like this:

You're listening to WBT, Charlotte, North Carolina, 4 P.M.,

B-U-L-O-V-A, Bulova Watch Time, courtesy Bulova Watch Company, Fifth Avenue, New York.

(The announcer says), *"Do y'all know what hit is?"*

(The band would respond), *"No!"*

(The announcer's answer would be), *"Hit's Briarhopper Time!"*

The band would then play their signature song, "Wait Till the Sun Shines, Nellie."

"I don't know how that song became our theme song," Whitey said in 2005. "They were singin' it when me and Hogan got there [to WBT] in 1941. I never did ask, and I hate that."[76]

Billie Burton Daniel knew why that was the theme song for the Briarhoppers: "That song was Johnny McAllister's favorite song. He picked it and that's what we sang to open the show."[77]

The song "Wait Till the Sun Shines, Nellie," was written in 1907 by Harry Von Tilzer, the man who also wrote "Bird in a Gilded Cage." Von Tilzer was born in Detroit, Michigan under the name Harry Gummbinsky in 1872. Harry joined a traveling circus at age 14, where he took the new name of Harry Von Tilzer and soon became successful playing the piano and writing compositions.

Tilzer started a publishing company with his brother, Albert, in 1902. Among the songs that Von Tilzer wrote were "Only a Bird in a Gilded Cage," "I Want a Girl Just Like the Girl Who Married Dear Old Dad," and "Wait Till the Sun Shines, Nellie." Von Tilzer cowrote "Take Me Out to the Ball Game."[78]

The chorus of "Do y'all know what hit is?" is also explainable. Daniel says, "Crutchfield I guess got a little bored one day as we were getting ready for the radio show. We were ready to go on and all of a sudden, Crutch

yells out 'Do you know what hit is?' We didn't know what he was talking
about and we answered back, 'No, what is it?' and Crutch said that 'Hit's
Briarhopper Time.' The audience loved it. It became as much of our show
as we were."

However, there seems to be precedence for this opening line. Billie
Burton Daniel said in an email to the authors that a similar introduction
was used on the Briarhopper family show of the 1930s. "How wonderful
it would be if I could go back to then, to just one more time, hear Mr.
Crutchfield say, 'Hey, Pappy, what time is it?' and to hear Dad [McAllis-
ter] answer, 'Why, Crutch, hit's Briarhopper time!'"[79]

After the theme song, Crutchfield would say something like, "Howdy
neighbors, it's the Briarhoppers again.... Fiddlin' Hank and Don White,
Claude Casey, Fred Kirby, Whitey & Hogan, Shannon Grayson, Curly
Campbell, and our special guests, the Johnson Family, featuring little 14-
year-old Betty Johnson ... all sponsored by Kolor-Bak, Peruna, Zymole
Trokeys, and Radio Girl Perfume. Now, here's Fiddlin' Hank and the Fiddlin' Briarhoppers!"

The WBT Briarhoppers would launch into some kind of hoedown,
usually led by Fiddlin' Hank Warren. After the song, Crutchfield would
then introduce the individual band members who would then sing a song
or pick a tune. Then Crutchfield would go into some off-the-cuff commercials for the show's sponsors, some very derogatory about the product.... The audience loved it.[80]

At the end of the show, Crutchfield would sign off, saying something
similar to "Well, neighbors, I reckon that's it. The Lone Ranger and his
horse Silver and their buddy, Tonto, are in the next studio rarin' to put on
a good program on the air here at WBT, so all of the Briarhoppers and
the Johnson Family and the rest of us will be gittin' 'til tomorrow — same
time, same station, and probably the same songs and the same commercials. So long, neighbors."[81]

Roy Grant went into detail with John Rumble about how the radio
program was planned prior to broadcast:

[O]n radio, that was one of my jobs, to build the format of the program. What
I would do is, look over all of the mail that had come in for this particular day.
We received scads of mail each day. Any mail that wasn't personal [and] it was
just for requests, the guys would flip it to me. I made up the program according
to that, other than sometimes we had special numbers, like one of our own
family members was having a birthday or an anniversary or something like that.
We'd do something special for them, something that they had wanted us to do.
But most of the time, it was made up strictly of requests for that particular time.

We would open our radio program with a breakdown, of course, and then we would have a solo, then maybe a trio, then Hogan and myself would sing a duet, and maybe we would have a comical number too in there or an instrumentation number that was a little out of the ordinary. Then we would repeat again as far as we could, because when Mr. Crutchfield started talking about his products, there was no end to that. He could go on. He made fun of the products, and that's what sold the product. He never did a commercial straight, I don't think, in his life.

Hogan added during the same interview, "Well, on the radio program, we would stick mostly to the program that was outlined there unless we got a special call. For instance, one day, the girl operator came running in there [the studio] with a request written down and handed to Mr. Crutchfield. It was from the president and the owner of Cannon Cotton Mill, Mr. Cannon, requesting that Hank [Warren] play 'Cackling Hen' for him on the fiddle. So we replaced one of the numbers then with 'Cackling Hen,' because that was a special request, you see."[82]

Charles Crutchfield reflected in an interview in 1982: "We had no rehearsals. The Briarhopper program was on for years and years and I don't think that we ever had a rehearsal. Didn't even read new scripts. Once a sponsor called and said that they had sold out [of a product that was being advertised on the radio show] two months ago and didn't we even read scripts? They [the scripts] were in the drawer."[83]

The Community Response to the "New" Briarhoppers

The 1940s were the heyday for the WBT Briarhoppers. At this time within the United States, Americans were very accepting of old time string band music, either on the radio or in person. "That was the only entertainment we had," Bill Warlick said. Warlick, a former biology teacher and full-time farmer, remembers the time in the 1940s when all of the farmwork was done before school and after school. "We had to hustle to get the work done so we could get to the radio and tune in the *Lone Ranger* and the Briarhoppers."

Warlick told his son, "We used to run home from school, get some cold sausage and a piece of bread, fill the wood box full of wood, and turn on the radio to hear the *Lone Ranger* and after that show, we would hear 'Wait Till the Sun Shines, Nellie.' We knew that the Briarhoppers were ready to play."[84]

Jack Lawrence, a famous guitar player and long-time musical partner with Doc Watson, wrote in an editorial, "A young Arthel (Doc) Watson's

The WBT Briarhoppers with Arthur Smith, early 1940s. Back row left to right: Don White; Bill Davis; Fred Kirby; Harry Blair; Claude Casey; Arthur Smith. Front row left to right: Roy Grant; Cecil Campbell; Arval Hogan; Hank Warren. Courtesy Tom Hanchett.

only respites from severe loneliness were the sounds of Whitey and Hogan (and the Briarhoppers) and the big Malley steam locomotives that ran behind his dorm at the N.C. School for the Blind in Raleigh (North Carolina)."[85]

John Carpenter, a retired agri-chemical executive living in Laurinburg, North Carolina, grew up in Cherryville, North Carolina, and lived on his family's farm. He said, "Dad told us that we had to get the hogs fed and all of the work done before 4:30 P.M. rolled around. We raced to get in the house to hear the Briarhoppers. They were a part of our family. 'Briarhopper Time' took us away from the hard work, the war, the memories of the Depression, all of that."[86]

North Carolina Representative Joe Kiser remembered hearing the WBT Briarhoppers from his childhood home in Henry, North Carolina. "I remember rushing home to get the chores done so that we could turn on the radio at 4:30 P.M. for the Briarhoppers Show," Kiser said in a telephone interview with the authors. "I remember seeing the Briarhoppers perform at the school. The WBT Briarhoppers brought joy to all who heard them and their music is what formed the basis of what I know as country music. They are indeed a state and a national treasure."[87]

In the January 2003 edition of *Our State*, an article on the Briarhoppers states, "Rumor has it that Billy Graham says that the cows on his childhood farm milked better during 'Briarhopper Time.'"[88]

A bluegrass legend, an International Bluegrass Music Association Hall of Fame inductee, and a member of Charlie Monroe's band and of Flatt and Scruggs and the Foggy Mountain Boys, Curly Seckler remembered listening to the WBT Briarhoppers as a teenager in China Grove, North Carolina. "We all listened to the Briarhoppers. I had five brothers and we would enjoy the radio show. It made us get the idea to form a band, and we started playing music when I was fifteen years old."[89]

"The Briarhoppers were the Juilliard String Quartet of country music and theirs was the music of my youth and upbringing in North Carolina," former WBT announcer and famous CBS broadcast journalist Charles Kuralt wrote in the book that he coauthored with Loonis McGlohan, *North Carolina Is My Home*. "I thought that all music was played by guitar, banjo, fiddle, and bass, for that is pretty much all we ever heard on WBT radio."[90]

World War II

World War II meant that many men were shipped off to battle the Axis forces. Kirby left the group and went with White to Cincinnati. During this time, Kirby met some of the most famous people of the time, including Doris Day. As mentioned earlier, U.S. Treasury Secretary Henry Morganthau, Jr., proclaimed Kirby "The Victory Cowboy," for helping sell millions of dollars in war bonds and raising money for charities.[91]

The armed forces listened to the WBT Briarhoppers on the radio, either locally on WBT or on Armed Forces Radio. They became so popular that their presence was requested by a general. According to Grant:

> Crutchfield called us into his office one day and said, "Boys," he always called us his boys, "the general at Maxton Air Force Based is on the telephone and wants to know what it would cost him to have the Briarhoppers play for his troops on a Saturday night." Fiddlin' Hank popped up and said, "Tell him if he brings a plane over to pick us up, we will play for nothin.'" Crutch relayed the message to the general and came back to tell us that a plane would be at the airport to pick us up next Saturday. So we got on the plane with the Johnson Family and we flew to the base to play for the troops. Well, we played for 'em. That night, I told the general that I would sure love to see one of his planes swoop down and grab one of those gliders. He said for me to be outside at 7:00 A.M. and that he would show me how it was done. That morning he woke up two crews and had them get in their planes and snatch

two gliders ... all of that because I had asked. I know that the troops wanted to kill me for getting them up early on a Sunday morning.[92]

Grant told John Rumble:

During the war [World War II], the army transported us in the old DC-7s or 8s or 9s. Anyway, you rode in them and you could look out at the wingtips, and they were flapping like a bird wing. But to go to an army base not knowing how you were going to be received or how you were going to be welcomed, that was sort of tough. But after the first one, we learned that that they were just boys away from home, a-longing for a little bit of entertainment. Through the Briarhoppers ... we were able to give them some entertainment and make them forget their problems for a little while. We were hesitant about going to these army bases, because we didn't know we were going to be received or anything like that, but after we found out, then it was one of the greatest thrills we've ever had, entertaining soldiers during the war.[93]

Grant remembers the night that the United States invaded Normandy:

The WBT Briarhoppers, 1942. Back row left to right: Hank Warren; Fred Kirby; Shannon Grayson. Front row left to right: Roy "Whitey" Grant and Arval Hogan. Courtesy Tom Hanchett.

We were playing in Norfolk, Virginia, with Ernest Tubb and the Texas Troubadours, Pee Wee King and the Golden West Boys, and the Duke from Paducah, having a lot of fun. We were backstage shooting the bull when I came up to Tubb and said, "We blew a tire coming up here and we don't have a spare." Tubb said that just so happened that he bought two recapped tires coming up here for $20 apiece and that he would sell me one. We paid him the money and Fred Kirby took the tire and put it in the trunk of our car. Well, we went on our way. While we were on the Shenandoah Parkway, we turned on the radio and heard about the invasion. At that time, we heard a big pop. We stopped the car and all of our tires were good. We were about to get back in the car and I saw dust blowing out from the trunk lid. Fred opened the trunk and the spare had blown all to pieces. The next morning, I got up and wrote Tubb a letter, telling him that the tire blew up in the trunk before it ever touched the ground. I asked him how much he was going to remunerate us for the tire. I got a letter back from Tubb and all it said was "HA! HA! HA!" signed Ernest Tubb.[94]

The WBT Briarhoppers could be heard in Europe over Armed Forces Radio through a CBS transcription of the *Dixie Jamboree* on WBT. Soldiers would listen to Whitey & Hogan and the Briarhoppers and send them cards. "The troops would address the cards and letters to Whitey & Hogan, USA.... That was all that they wrote ... and they would arrive at WBT."

Grant's wife, Polly, added that "WBT was the only station that had the power to be transcribed by CBS and beamed overseas."[95]

"I had the privilege to MC [the show *Carolina Calling*]," Grant recalled in an interview with John Rumble:

It covered the entire CBS [radio] network. And we do know that it covered the entire CBS network. They would transcribe our program in Los Angeles, California. There was no such thing as taping then; it was all big [sixteen-inch] transcriptions. They would transcribe our show in Los Angeles and beam it to the boys fighting in the South Pacific.

I received, and Hogan received, mail from guys that we were in elementary school with that was fighting on Guadalcanal on the battleship *North Carolina* and *Tennessee*. They said it was "like thirty minutes being at home. Keep up the good work." That was one of the highlights of our career, entertaining guys we went to school with [who were] fighting in the South Pacific during the world war.[96]

The statement above is obvious when you enter the Grants' current home in Charlotte. Above one of the doorways hangs an Italian mandolin (affectionately called a "doodlebug" by mandolin players because of its rounded back) that was given to Grant by a soldier coming back from Germany after World War II. "I was given this mandolin.... The guy who gave it to me said that he took it from a German who he had to shoot.

The soldier thought that the German held the mandolin in high esteem since he carried it with him on the battlefield, so he took it and brought it to me knowing that I would give it a good home."[97]

The war also had an effect on the WBT Briarhoppers and the rest of the musicians at WBT. Many of them, including Clarence Etters, Thorpe Westerfield, Gibb Young, and others were either drafted or had volunteered. According to Grant, when a WBT musician got the call to serve his country, there was a ritual that the musicians would do for that person:

> When we were working at WBT during the war, if any particular artist was drafted or called into service, we would all play him a free job [concert], and not charge him a cent.
>
> I was slated to go ... and I missed it [by] four days. I didn't get to go. But the jamboree that the guys all agreed to play with me, I went over to Kings Mountain (North Carolina) and booked a high school auditorium there.... I talked to the principal, and asked him did he have seats in the balcony. He says, "Yes, but they haven't been cleaned up in years.... Dust is, I guess, is a half an inch thick on them."
>
> I said, "Well, can you clean those seats up?'" And he said, "Whitey, you must be crazy, but we'll do it."
>
> I said, "Now, other than that, do you have some chairs that you could put in the back of the auditorium over there, and one row up each aisle in the school [auditorium]?" He says, "Now I know you're crazy, but we'll do it."
>
> So, we booked the school up, and I got all the guys and gals at WBT to go with me — the Rangers Quartet, Grady Cole, the Johnson Family, the Tennessee Ramblers, Billie Ann Newman, and Hogan and myself and my dad did all of the advertising.
>
> So the night of the show, every seat was packed to capacity, and the firemen made Hogan and Hank quit selling tickets because the building was overflowing. I guess more people went home than saw the show that night.[98]

This was one example of how popular the WBT Briarhoppers were during this turbulent time.

The Rise of Radio Advertising

As mentioned earlier, the WBT Briarhopper show was also renowned for their impromptu commercials for the companies that sponsored their show, which included Crazy Water Crystals, Peruna, and Kolor-Bak, owned by the Drug Trade Company.

Crutchfield said, "The Drug Trade Company was looking for a viable hillbilly music market.... The medicine man concept would appeal to more and more people who appreciated hillbilly music more than city folks, I'm guessing."[99]

Charles Crutchfield did most of the commercials on the show when he was the announcer in the 1940s. A *Charlotte Observer* dated December 19, 1977, mentions that Crutchfield hawked "Radio Girl perfume, (K)olor Bak hair dye and patent remedies like Peruna (pronounced Pee-roo-ney) and Crazy Water Crystals. Bill Warlick, father of one of the authors, remembered how a Kolor-Bak commercial went:

"K-O-L-O-R- B-A-K, Kolor-Bak. Sprinkle a few drops on your comb and comb it through your hair, that's all you need. K-O-L-O-R-B-A-K, Kolor Bak."[100]

Rumble's interview with Crutchfield discussed the advertising on the WBT Briarhopper show. Crutchfield played a tape to Rumble regarding a special commercial. The lines in **bold type** are the lines that Crutchfield allegedly said in a 1940s Briarhopper show that the authors read from a

The WBT Briarhoppers, Unit 2. **Left to right: Homer Christopher; Shannon Grayson; Claude Casey; Sam Poplin, circa 1943. Courtesy Tom Hanchett.**

script found in Crutchfield's papers, which are different from the Rumble interview:

Whitey, you and Hogan may look kinda ratty and moth-eaten, but you do sing purdy. By the way, neighbors, if y'all would like to have a picture of Whitey and Hogan and Hank and all the rest of the Briarhoppers, goodness knows why you would, but if you want one, the same picture that about eighteen thousand folks are asking for every week, all you have to do to get one is tear off the top of the box of the stuff we advertise on this Peruny and Kolor-Bak program and mail it to us Briarhoppers, and we will send you one.

Oh, yeah, this junk — I mean, these fine products sure are good, it says here. So remember, neighbors, don't go around losing your job just because you got gray hair. Douse on some of this Kolor-Bak concoction, and that gray hair will be gone **before you can say Homer Briarhopper. It don't say on the paper how it's gonna get gone,** but I don't imagine so many folks would be using Kolor-Bak if it made your gray hair go away, roots and all. Folks, **Aunt Tootie** tells me it turns it sort of black-looking, so I reckon it must be all right. So go out and get yourself a bottle and send in for the picture before we run out of them, it says here. The supply is limited, the man says. Truth, though, is we're up to our ears in these pictures. So if you like the Briarhoppers, for goodness' sake, buy a bottle of this stuff and help us get rid of these ugly pictures. Now this is WBT, just across the street from WAYS [another radio station]. See you tomorrow at four-thirty."[101]

Crutchfield said in the same interview that the show was sponsored by Drug Trade Products Company out of Chicago, Illinois. "They'd buy up companies when they'd go broke ... Kolor-Bak, Radio Girl perfume, and Peruna. I called it 'Pee-roo-ney' on the air ... made fun of the products and the sponsor loved it."

Crutchfield commented on the success of WBT's advertising: "We used to get ten thousand box tops a week from Peruna [boxes] for a [Briarhopper] picture. That's all we gave away. We got ten thousand box tops. They sold for a dollar and a quarter per bottle, and Harry O'Neal, who was [the representative] for Drug Trade Products, told me that to put that bottle on the dealer's shelves, including the carton, all the printing, shipping, everything, including the contents of the bottle, cost eight cents, and they sold it for a dollar and a quarter. And we got ten thousand [box tops] a week!"[102]

"I kidded the commercials and I kidded the talent," Crutchfield said in an interview with John Rumble, "but as far as being a hillbilly or a country guy, I really didn't do that. My stuffy nature, when I was younger, always put a tie on me and dressed me like I shouldn't have dressed as a young fellow."[103]

In a 1986 interview with Lynn Haessly of the Southern Oral History Program at the University of North Carolina, Chapel Hill, Crutchfield commented further about his commercials:

> [T]hey [the sponsors] had the idea that if they had a proper vehicle like radio they could advertise these various products effectively. PE-RU-NA was one; Kolor-Bak hair dye was another; Radio Girl Perfume was another; Zymole Trokeys cough drops was another. They thought radio might sell their products. So they tried radio and they thought that this hillbilly type of music might be best. And they knew that this was a textile center, as Charlotte was at the time. We [WBT] were in the heart of it and we covered an enormous area.... [T]hey [the sponsors] knew that it [the commercials] would reach farmers and the mill workers and the so-called blue-collar people.

Talking about why he did commercials like he did, Crutchfield said:

> Our approach was sort of the [Arthur] Godfrey approach, and that's what the public went for back in those days.

Top: Peruna box and bottle. *Bottom:* Kolor-Bak bottle and box. Both photographs courtesy Tom and Lucy Warlick.

When I was announcing ... I would talk to an individual (instead of everyone who was listening) — WBT had a massive audience in those days because they had very little competition. A very few stations were on the air. Rather than talking to thousands of people, why, in my mind, I would talk to one person or two sitting home in a living room, not a mass of people.[104]

[Godfrey] was on WTOP in Washington [D.C.]. But he had a furrier called Slossnick [phonetic], a furrier there in Washington. He used to make more fun of that store and more fun of the furs and Mr. Slossnick personally. He had a great time with that name. But he would — every day, every morning, he had a great commercial on for Slossnik. That was their biggest advertisement. People from all over Virginia and Maryland would come to Washington just to see the store and go in the store to meet Mr. Slossnick. It was one of the most successful things that had ever been on.[105]

When asked whether or not the sponsors were offended by the commercials, Crutchfield said, in the same interview, that they were:

Mr. O'Neal [of the Drug Trade Company] was down here one day on his way to Myrtle Beach and he picked up on the program. He hadn't heard it for two or three years. They were getting lots of mail and a lot of box tops so they didn't pay too much attention. But he heard it and stopped at a filling station and called after the program was over and asked what in the world was going on. I said, "Well, Mr. O'Neal, this is the way we've been selling your products all along. Do you want us to change it?" He said, "No, I just wondered. I'd never heard anything like that on the radio." I said, "I'll change it if you want to." He said, "No, no, no, keep it like it is!"

Arval Hogan recollected how the advertiser would seasonally change the products around: "See, Peruna was supposed to be a cold medicine, but during the summer you're not supposed to have colds, you know. So, they would replace Peruna with Radio Girl Perfume ... and Kolorback [sic] and the [Zymole] Trokeys. So that was the summer sponsor, you see."[106]

Radio Girl Perfume in two sizes. Courtesy Tom and Lucy Warlick.

Roy Grant remembers, "We used to have a lot of fun. Crutchfield would say, 'We don't care what you do with it. Put it in the radiator of your car; it'll clean it out,' and stuff like that."[107]

Grant remembers a story that involved his daughter: "Yvonne, our oldest daughter, used to work at a bank in Charlotte, and the bank pres-

Now on tour — **TWO OF THE NATION'S TOP ENTERTAINERS**

CLAUDE CASEY *and* FRED KIRBY

Direct From

WBT **CAROLINA HAYRIDE** • CBS **CAROLINA CALLING**

Presenting

The BRIARHOPPERS
AN OUTSTANDING 30 MINUTE STAGE SHOW

• • •

RCA VICTOR — SONORA AND SUPER DISC RECORDING ARTISTS

CLAUDE CASEY'S

RCA VICTOR RECORDS
"Look in the Looking Glass"
"Days Are Long, Nights Are Lonely"
"Journey's End"
"I Wish I Had Kissed You Goodbye"
"Two Little Girls With Golden Curls"
"My Little Tootsie"
"I Wish I'd Never Met You"
"Family Reunion In Heaven"

SUPER DISC RECORDS
"Juke Box Gal"
"Carolina Waltz"
"It's Hard To Lose These Lonesome Blues"
"Living In Dreams"
Appeared in Republic Picture
"Swing Your Partner"

FRED KIRBY'S

SONORA RECORDS
"Atomic Power"
"Honey Be My Honey Bee"
"I've Been A Fool Too Often"
"My War Torn Heart"
"The Wreck of The Old 97"
"Deep In The Bottom of The Sea"
"Boogie Woogie Farmer"
"My Little Boy Blue"
"Casey Jones"
"It's The Beginning of The End"

"That's How Much I Love You"
"After All These Years"
"Downright Lonely, Downright Blue"
"I Can't Tell That Lie to My Heart"

SUPER DISC RECORDS
"God Made This Country"
"The Almighty Dollar"
"I Thank My Lucky Star"
"A Greater Power"

Tour advertisement for Claude Casey and Fred Kirby and the WBT Briarhoppers, mid 1940s. Courtesy Jim Scancarelli.

ident came in one day and said to her that he had something for her that she might like. She had no idea what he could have. He went back to his office and walked back to where Yvonne was standing. He had his hands behind his back. Yvonne was a little nervous until he brought his hands from behind his back and it was a bottle of Peruna, complete with the box. I think she still has it today."[108]

Crutchfield's Aunt Tootie and Peruna

On the radio show, Crutchfield would sometimes refer to letters that he received from his "Aunt Tootie," who lived in Pelzer, South Carolina. Aunt Tootie would become a figure who could sell patent medicine at a greater volume than the actual sales personnel of the patent medicine companies could do.

Robert Inman, in a column in the *Charlotte Observer*, recalled a conversation that he had with then-85-year-old Crutchfield in the 1980s, about a famous commercial that Crutchfield did for Peruna. Crutchfield had told this story on a 1940s WBT Briarhopper show, which was re-created in the 1985 production *The Charlotte Country Music Story*, in which Crutchfield reads a letter from his aunt. In the Inman column, Aunt Tootie called Crutchfield on the telephone, but the commercial went like this:

> Aunt Tootie (called/wrote me a letter) ... raving about this new Peruna product. It had changed her life, she said.
> "How much of it are you taking?"
> "A bottle a day," she answered. "I'm sleeping better than ever, my appetite is excellent, I feel wonderful."

What Aunt Tootie didn't know ... was that Peruna was about 40 percent alcohol (in *The Charlotte Country Music Story*, Crutchfield says it is 40 proof, or 80 percent alcohol). Dear Aunt Tootie, a teetotaling, churchgoing lady, had a constant buzz on.[109]

Crutchfield also had a basic commercial for Peruna, which was conveyed in *The Charlotte Country Music Story*. This text was taken from a script found in Crutchfield's files:

> Neighbors ... do some of you all get up in the morning feeling run down, drug out? Do some of you ladies feel like you just can't possibly get the kids dressed, feed 'em, and then go around the neighborhood picking up all those other screaming young'uns in time for school? Then when you finally try to start the car, you discover it's out of gas or the battery is dead ... so you run in the house and scream to your husband — makin' him sorry he woke up at all?
> Well, there's no reason for all of this haggard feelin' and confusion. The

answer is Peruna (not the dog food — the tonic) ... spelled P-E-R-U-N-A. Now Peruna won't recharge your car battery, but it sure will recharge yours. Folks who take Peruna every day tell me that they wake up in the morning feelin' like a million. And even at night ... they say it's a pleasure cookin' supper, helpin' with the homework and scrubbin' the kids for bed. Peruna is not a cure-all, but it will get rid of that run-down, dragged-out feelin' ... and listen to this: When you buy a bottle of Peruna (all the better drug stores have it), just tear off the top of the carton it comes in, write your name and address on the back of the box-top and send it to the Briarhoppers here at WBT. As soon as we get it, we'll mail you one of those pictures of the Briarhoppers we have been talking about — Whitey & Hogan, Hank, Fred Kirby, Claude Casey, Don White ... the same bunch that makes all this noise on the radio every afternoon at four o'clock. As a matter of fact, if you'll tear off the top of your radio, we'll send you the Briarhoppers!

According to the Crutchfield children, Aunt Tootie was really Charles Crutchfield's mother, who wrote her son about Peruna and experienced the mix-up in how much to take per day.

Crutchfield's antics would affect those not on the Briarhopper Show. Grant remembered:

My dad, bless his heart, Crutchfield used to kid my dad. Every day he would kid him about going over to the widder's [widow's] house. My mother died when I was very young. And Crutchfield used to kid my dad about going over to the widder's house to put a post in their garden and so forth, helping them clean their attics.

Crutchfield caused my daddy to become so popular on the radio program. And he never said a word on it, never played an instrument, but Crutchfield caused my daddy to become so popular by just kidding him in a roundabout way on the program, that when we would go to these country schoolhouses back in those days to play a program, they would say, "Whitey, where's your dad?" "Hogan, where's Whitey's dad? Is he along with you tonight?" He just had a way that he could build somebody up to the limit. He just had a knack of doing that.[110]

Grant said in the same interview how Crutchfield would describe the members of the Briarhoppers to the radio audience:

He [Crutchfield] would go on for hours about us [Whitey and Hogan] being barefooted and dirty-faced and so forth and so on, and the people loved it. Claude Casey was "the lady-killer." He'd build Claude up as "The Ladies Home Companion" or "the Boy with the Golden Voice." And the young girls just ate that up. Fred Kirby ... [Crutchfield] caused the children to fall in love with Fred Kirby, and they still do ... talking about Fred's horse Calico ... and Fred didn't have a horse. And it got to the point here he had to get one because Crutch had built him so high that he had to get a horse and start taking it [with him].[111]

The WBT Briarhoppers' Stage Show

Doing a radio show was only part of the work performed by the WBT Briarhoppers. Most of their income came from stage shows that they took on the road. It was there that they could sell pictures, songbooks, and other Briarhopper paraphernalia.

Much planning had to be done in order to get the right music mix for that particular audience. Sometimes, decisions had to be made at the spur of the moment. Grant commented that there was one group of Briarhoppers that did more work in this area and was more successful than any other combination, and that group was comprised of Kirby, Casey, Warren, Davis, and Whitey and Hogan: "Fred had the kids; me and Hogan had the old folks with the country hymns, Claude Casey had a lock on the teenagers, Hank and Bill would finish up the shows. That was a terrific combination and the crowds ate it up. We never had a better format for the audience than that version of the Briarhoppers."[112]

Arval Hogan remembered how the stage show started, which was similar to the radio show: "I would say, 'Now do y'all know what hit is?' They [the Briarhoppers] would say, 'No, what is it, Hogan?' I'd say, 'Hit's Briarhopper time,' then we would do our theme song ('Wait Till the Sun Shines, Nellie') and then we would do our regular routine of songs for, say, thirty minutes. Then we would do a little skit. We called one of them we did, a little show we put on, we called it *Little Nellie*. It was a comedy we did. Then another one we had was *Plunk and Unplunk*, which would run fifteen to twenty minutes, you know."[113]

Hogan described the various skits that the WBT Briarhoppers did during their stage shows

> Claude Casey learned the *Little Nellie* somewhere during his traveling around, and he came up with the idea (of us) doing *Little Nellie*. He taught us all our parts and showed us how it went, and we went from there. Then we got *Plunk and Unplunk* from Homer Sherrill in Columbia [South Carolina]. He gave us the routine on it.
>
> During the show, Hank [Warren] would cut in between songs occasionally, and pull some of his gags, you know, with the straight man, ever who it was, Whitey or Claude [Casey] or Fred [Kirby]. We had three MCs, so ever which one was MC'ing, why, they would do some gags with Hank occasionally along....

Hogan also described how the group developed skits: "Every once in a while, we'd find an old medicine man, and he would give us a little idea of some of the skits. We would all get together and put them together and

WBT Radio Stars comprised of the WBT Briarhoppers, Arthur Smith and the Crackerjacks, and the Johnson Family, mid 1940s. Back row left to right: Bill Davis; Sam Poplin; Homer Christopher; Fred Kirby; Arthur Smith, Ralph Smith. Second row left to right: Arval Hogan; Hank Warren; Claude Casey; Dewey Price; Sonny Smith; Roy Grant; Roy Lear. Front row left to right: Jim Johnson; Betty Johnson; Bob Johnson; Grady Cole (standing); Kenneth Johnson; Lydia Johnson; Jesse Johnson. Courtesy Jim Scancarelli.

then start doing them on stage. The people loved them, and we loved to do them. We would dress up in character."[114]

The audience would play a big role in the WBT Briarhopper stage show. Hogan further reflects: "[T]hey [the audience] would pass notes up, requesting songs. We took a little intermission in the middle of our show, and sold pictures.... [W]e used to take [Charles] Crutchfield's picture with us and sell them.... We all had pictures to sell to the audience, so we would take an intermission and mingle with the audience and pick up requests and talk with them, whatever they wanted to talk about, and just enjoy a few minutes with the audience."[115]

Grant explained why the WBT Briarhoppers sold pictures of Charles Crutchfield "[Crutchfield] was so popular, and people would request [photographs of Crutchfield]. That's how we started selling his picture, by people wanting to know what Crutchfield looked like, asking us questions about Mr. Crutchfield, and said they would just like to know what he looked like and all. So we just got the idea, well, if he'd let us, why, we'll let him have some pictures made and we'll take them out and sell them and give him the proceeds from it, so we did. Then people appreciated it a lot."

Hogan added, "It's hard to realize, now that we're so used to television, that in those days, people just had to listen to you on the radio and sort of picture in their own minds what you look like. So when we would offer these pictures for sale, boy, they wanted pictures of each individual person. On our program ... if we had sold one picture with the entire group, that would have hurt our profits. So each act — Whitey & Hogan, Fred Kirby, Claude Casey, Fiddling Hank, and Big Bill Davis — each one of us had our own picture and we sold it."[116]

Grant remembered in the Rumble interview an incident where, whether on purpose or not, a fan did not pay the right price for a picture. Grant says: "We would sell a picture for ten cent[s] for an eight-by-ten. During the war, we were playing a theater in Spartanburg, South Carolina, and we were hawking our pictures during intermission. Some fellow motioned for Hogan that he wanted one of the pictures. Hogan said, 'OK, I'll pass it down, and you start the dime on the other end, and I'll start the picture on this end.' So when the dime got to Hogan, it wasn't a dime, it was one of those silver-looking pennies that they made during the war. Hogan kidded the man, he said, 'Fellow, I got your dime, but it isn't a dime, it was a penny. Don't worry, I still made a profit.'"

Grant explained how a profit was made. "We would send one eight-by-ten glossy to a company in Chicago, I believe it was, and they would run us off a thousand multi-prints that they called it. It was very thin paper, not the regular paper that eight-by-ten glossies are on now. It was sort of like a sheet of tablet paper, actually. It was that thin. But we could get them for about three-quarters of a cent each. Well, we made a profit if we sold them for a penny, but we'd sell them for a dime."[117]

The WBT Briarhoppers had a broad fan base during their heyday, which was a time of segregation, and the Briarhoppers were not excluded from segregation's effects on their fans. "A lot of times, we played where there was blacks and whites," recalled Grant, "and a lot of places we played where blacks have told us they would have loved to have come out and seen our show, but they couldn't. That made us feel real bad, because the blacks wanted to see us in the early days of radio and had no way to come out. As soon as [integration] started, then the blacks were thrilled that they could come out and see the Briarhoppers. Even today we play these senior citizen places, and the black people just love to talk with us because they did not get the privilege in the early days."[118]

Grant especially remembered an instance in the 1940s regarding a segregated crowd. He says, "I'll never forget down in Pembroke, North Carolina, one night, before integration," Grant told Rumble in their interview:

> We played a theater down there that had two or three partitions. We had three races of people at one show. We had black, we had Indian, we had white. Now that was early days of radio. But we thoroughly enjoyed it.
>
> Hank would walk down the divider. It was a wide divider, right down the main auditorium. Blacks sat on one side, and whites sat on the other side, and the Indians sat in the balcony. Hank would walk down the divider and play his fiddle like an acrobat to both sides and all the way to the balcony and look up and play it for the Indians up in the balcony.[119]

WBT Briarhopper Announcers

During this decade, Charles Crutchfield began to take on more management responsibilities at WBT. It was during this time when numerous WBT employees had the coveted role as the Briarhopper announcer.

Roy Grant, in an interview with the authors, remembers that "Crutch [Crutchfield], Curt Webster, Lee Kirby, Bill Bivens, Grady Cole (on live shows), Lonzo Squires, Fletcher Austin, and various Briarhopper musicians would do the announcin' on the show."[120]

"Grady Cole was a card," Bluegrass legend Curly Seckler remembers. Curly was a member of Charlie Monroe's band after Charlie split with his brother, Bill. "We would be playing on the radio, in front of the mike, early in the morning. Grady Cole would come in the studio while we were on the air and drop his pants ... down to his ankles.... He said he did that to wake us up."[121]

Briarhopper Stories

Grant remembered many stories about doing shows outside of the radio show. "We had a lot of people who wanted the Briarhoppers to come over and play, but they didn't want their neighbors to know that they liked country music. Well, they would ask us to come in the back door, and we would say 'no, no.' Crutchfield already warned us about this and told us if we were asked to go in the back door to raise our price because 'they're willin' to pay it and they got it to spend.' So, when we were asked to come

The WBT Briarhoppers in the mid 1940s. Back row left to right: Roy Grant; Shannon Grayson; Arval Hogan. Front row left to right: Fred Kirby and Hank Warren. Courtesy Jim Scancarelli.

in the back door, we would first say 'no.' Then they would ask us how much they would have to pay to get us to come and play, and we would give them an outlandish fee, and seven times out of ten, they would go for it."[122]

Whitey and Hogan told Rumble that the WBT Briarhoppers would go and play private concerts for one of Charlotte's premier industrialists, and of being asked to arrive under cover of darkness, so that his musical tastes would remain a secret.[123]

Throughout the 1940s, the WBT Briarhoppers dominated the radio airwaves and maintained a strong popularity up and down the East Coast. At their height, the group was receiving over 10,000 pieces of mail per week.[124] Most of the most memorable Briarhopper stories were from this decade.

Grant remembers:

We had a lot of fun with patrolmen. They knew us all up and down the eastern seaboard, of course, and they knew our car. They would stop us as we would come into town and they would want to talk and all, which would almost cause us to be late for our performance. Crutch would call out the patrolmen's names on the air, "My boys will be coming through your area in a little while. If they are in a hurry, please don't stop them on the way in; stop them on the way out." They would! We had a lot of fun.

We were playing in Waxhaw, NC, one day. We had to play the first show, get back to Charlotte to do the radio show, and then get back to Waxhaw to play the second show. We were pretty well timed-out. We had a real good friend, C.J. Rogers, who was a patrolman and he had a trainee that night. He knew that we would be traveling between Waxhaw and Charlotte sometime during that day, and that we would be in a hurry. So to save time, Hank kept on his comedy outfit, the big britches, fake red freckles, blacked-out teeth, and red wig, while we traveled back and forth. Well, I saw the patrol car up the road. The trainee, who knew nothing about the Briarhoppers, chased us down and pulled us over. The trainee saw Hank in his get-up, and Hank started to make faces at the patrolman. The new man asked us why we were in such a hurry. Hank told him, "Hey, we're in no hurry, but you must be, and we should perform a Citizen's Arrest on you for speeding." The young cop said, "No sir, you were speeding!" Hank said, "No, you had to have been speeding in order to catch up with us." So the trainee gave up and went back to the patrol car where C.J. Rogers was sitting. Rogers came out of the car, came up to us, and said, "You boys played your parts well, now do your broadcast!"[125]

Grant recalls one night when the band got lost on the way to a show. "One night we were on the road in Virginia and Claude Casey says, 'We might be lost but we're on a good road.'"[126]

Grant also remembers being with Curt Webster, an announcer at WBT. Webster was credited with reviving the career of Ted Weems on a national level by playing Weem's song, "Heartaches," which was estimated to sell several million copies after being almost forgotten. "Curt and Ted and I were sitting on a bench at WBT after Curt had brought back the tune. Ted told Curt that if he needed anything, just ask. Curt said that he would appreciate $1,000 for a down payment on a T-Model. Everybody laughed because Curt was jokin' with Ted. Three weeks later, Curt and I were sittin' in the same place, reading our mail at WBT, and Curt said that he had a letter from Ted.... It had $1,000 inside."[127]

During the 1940s, the song "Chattanooga Choo Choo" was a hit. The WBT Briarhoppers did not have that song in their program. Grant remembers in 2005:

Lee Kirby was an announcer one day when Crutchfield was on vacation, and he asked us if we would sing it. I told him that I didn't think that we could do it justice. He kept on pesterin' us about it on the radio show until I said on the air that the Briarhoppers would do it on an upcoming show. Well,

Lee Kirby advertised this for a full week on WBT. We had to move down-stairs into the largest studio that WBT had and still people were jammed in there. They packed Third Street in Charlotte to the point a car could not get through. The police told the station that they had to do something about the blocked street. WBT told the police that the street was their problem and that everyone wanted to hear the Briarhoppers sing "Chattanooga Choo Choo." The police gave up and blocked off the entire street until our show was over.[128]

When Warren's wife was pregnant with their fourth child, there was a contest held over the airwaves to name the baby. According to son Larry Warren, "Some lady wrote in the name 'Larry' and won ten dollars or something like that. I believe that she lived in Newton, North Carolina. Some wild names came in, like 'Horatio Alger,' stuff like that."[129]

William Smith of Lenoir, North Carolina, shared some information about a Briarhopper radio offer made in the 1940s. In a May 30, 2005, email to the authors of this book, Smith remembers that an announce-ment was made that the Briarhoppers would give guitar lessons at $5 per session if a certain telephone number was dialed:

By the time the decision (i.e., Mother's approval) was made, the phone call was too late to reach the cast member who made the offer. But, Shannon Grayson took the call and volunteered to supply the instruction to my older brother. At the time, Shannon must have been in his mid-twenties; he arrived with his instrument protruding from the rumble seat of his coupe. During the introduction, he discovered my older brother was a twin. He vol-unteered to teach one the guitar and the other the banjo. I was feeling left out of the fun, but money was in short supply so I was told that I was too young. However, Shannon had the perfect answer, when he said that he could teach me to play the mandolin. He did, but after a year, he found employment elsewhere, so the lessons had to cease.

The three young brothers played sufficiently to entertain occasionally at square dances, at their school assembly, and for some church-related pro-grams. On one occasion, we were asked to entertain the local Women's Christian Temperance Union. Calling upon our "vast" repertoire of tunes which Shannon had taught us, we selected several that we thought would be among our best efforts. [T]he first number was "Little Brown Jug," which generated snickering among some ladies, and indignation among others. This was followed by "Good Old Mountain Dew." Due to the laughter of the audience, we concluded that our appearance had been a rousing success.

The Briarhoppers were sometimes forgetful, especially in regards to each other. Grant remembered:

One time, the Briarhoppers played way out in the country, under a small shed. We played for the crowd. Then we packed up and we left. I was in the car that Fred Kirby was driving. After about a half-hour, I looked around and asked Fred, "Where's Hank?" The other car with the rest of the band passed us and Hank wasn't in it. So, me and Fred turned around, and drove back to where we'd played. A big storm came up and it was rainin' cats and dogs. We got back to where we played and there was Hank, standing under the little shed, just smilin'. Me and Fred apologized. Hank said, "I knew you'd finally come and get me.... I have the gate money in my pocket!"[130]

Grant relayed some other Briarhopper stories to John Rumble about performing shows that were way off the beaten path:

And this particular school that we arrived at this time, it was way back in the country. Bless the folks, they were just as good as they could be. But the thing about it is, there was only four or five people showed up for the program that night. So we put our heads together right quick and said, "Look, we're going to give you your money back. There's just not enough people to put the show on. We're going to give you your money back, and we're going to put our instruments in the car and we're going back home."

One lady came up .... She said, "Whitey, if there's any way in the world you can put on this show.... I wish you would.... I have walked three or four miles. I carried this baby" — she had a baby in her arms — "and I led three others."

And I said, "Lady, wait a minute. Don't you leave.... You have your seat. We're going to do the complete show for free, you and all of your friends that have come out to hear us."

So we sat them down, and we did a complete show. But that's just one instance that we had in our early days of radio. But it just goes to show you how faithful a few people were to you. They would walk for miles and carry a baby, like this lady did. Now, I won't ever forget that.[131]

"We were in Patrick, South Carolina, one night," Grant said as he reflected on another show that was held in a rural place:

It was in the summertime. The show was supposed to start at eight o'clock. At fifteen minutes till eight, there was nobody there except us and the janitor.... And I said, "Come on, boys, let's put these instruments in the car and go back home." The janitor says, "No.... Don't leave.... The building will be full." And I said, "Full at eight o'clock, and nobody here but us and you?" He said, "Yes sir. Don't worry; it will be full."

And just about that time he said that, I started seeing wagons and lanterns and lights coming through the woods from different locations, and believe it or not, at eight o'clock — of course, Hank [Warren] and Hogan were selling tickets like fighting fire — that building was full, and there were people sitting in the windows. We put on the show and went home.[132]

Grant also remembers a story that was told by Shannon Grayson:

I know our banjo player tells about that we played a place one time, and during the middle of the show, this elderly couple got up in the back of the building and came down. They [the building] had two lights, two big lights, floodlights, on either side of the stage, and that's all the lighting there was. About half way during the show, this elderly couple got up and came down and was standing there looking at this light over there. And our banjo player asked him, "Fellow, are you having some kind of problem? Can we help you?" And he [the elderly gentleman] said, "No. Me and maw ain't never seen this much light in one wad, and we wanted to see it."[133]

Grant remembered the kindness of the fans when the group traveled: "They [the fans] would send us gifts. And if we were going to be playing in a little place called, maybe Enoree, South Carolina, invariably someone from Enoree would write to us and want to have supper. We've always called it supper; that's the meal you eat before you go to bed. Well, someone from Enoree would call and ask us if we would have supper with them. And sure, we'd write back and say, 'Yes, we'll have supper with you,' because most of the time, they would have country ham, chicken, and, oh boy, it was a turnout, and we really enjoyed going into the homes and meeting the people."[134]

Sometimes, the fans would act a little weird. Even in the 1940s, there appeared to be groupies, even stalkers. Grant was the recipient of the affections of an unknown fan.

Grant told Rumble:

We had one listener. She lived in North Wilkesboro, North Carolina, and when we would play anywhere near North Wilkesboro, two days later, I would get a letter from this girl telling me where we ate. She would tell me what I ordered. She would tell me if I ate all of it or not. She would tell me how many cups of coffee that the waitress served me.... She wrote to me every time that we played anywhere, and she would tell me where she sat, after she had sat there, because I never did know who she was.

She wrote to me one time and asked if there was anything that I needed in the way of fishing equipment or golfing equipment, anything for my car. Well, one morning I decided to put her to a test and see. And Grady Cole was — we were doing a very, very, very early morning program. Fact is, it was on at 5:00 A.M. He was our announcer. I said, "Grady, sometime during the program this morning, ask me what time it is. Tell me that the clock is over your shoulder and you can't see it."

So during the program Grady said, "Whitey, what time is it by that clock? I'd have to turn around and look at it. It's just hard for me to do it. What time is it?" I said, "Grady, the clock up there is stopped, and my watch, I lost it. I don't know what time it is. The clock up there, it stops. You'll have to ask an engineer what time it is."

[Grady] said, "You lost your watch, Whitey?" And I said, "Yes, the strap broke, and I don't have a watch anymore."

Two days later, I received a nice Elgin wristwatch from this person.

A couple of weeks later I asked Mr. Crutchfield, I said, "Crutch, sometime during the program today, ask me how my fishing is going," and he asked me. I said, "Crutch, my fishing is going to pot. My reel has gone bad. It just won't work at all. Old Hogan is just beating me to death in fishing, because my reel has quit. I just can't fish." Two days later, I received not one, but two reels from this girl, plus every kind of hook that you can imagine, every kind of artificial bait that she could think of; she sent to me. I just — I just never understood it. I never did know who she was. She never did let herself be known. But she just loved to do things like that.[135]

Due to Whitey and Hogan's high singing voices, some fans thought that they were children. Grant remembered one instance of being mistaken for children. "We had one woman down in Blenheim, South Carolina, that was crocheting a little baby bedspread for Hogan and I, because the announcer at the time — and I guess we were young; we sang with a high-pitched voice — he would say, 'Now here's little Whitey and Hogan to sing us a song.' And she wrote us one day that she was crocheting or embroidering or knitting, whatever you do, to make us a spread for our little baby bed. When she found out we were both married and had children of our own, we never did hear from her anymore."[136]

In the era when the United States War Department was translating secret messages from Adolph Hitler while at the same time sending messages to the Allied forces in the Navajo language, and when Captain Midnight secret decoder rings were used by young listeners to decipher mysterious messages from their radio hero, similar espionage went on during the Briarhopper radio broadcasts on WBT.

As Polly Grant told the authors in April 2005, "Whitey would send me secret messages over the radio!"

"We had signals that we would send to our wives over the radio program," Grant said in an April 15, 2005, interview:

When traffic was light, and we knew that we had some time to kill, and we wanted a cup of coffee before we started traveling from the radio station to wherever we were going to play that night, we would get Hank to play, "Polly Put the Kettle On." By that signal, my wife, Polly, knew that we would be coming by for some coffee. If I dedicated to my daddy, bless his heart, a song during the program, the very minute the show was off, that was my signal for him to call me. If I dedicated a song to my brother in Avondale (North Carolina), during the first part of the program, he would know that I would be there the next morning to go squirrel hunting. If I dedicated him a song during the last part of the show, he would know that Hogan would be with me. It got so bad that the people who lived in Avondale who were listening to the show would call my brother and tell him that I was coming to go squirrel hunting.

The WBT Briarhoppers also did volunteer work, playing for hospitals. Grant remembered a special time that they entertained sick patients:

During the 1940s, there was this polio epidemic going on. And we wanted to play for the children in the hospitals, but we were told *no* all of the time because the doctors were afraid that we would catch polio and give it to our families and spread it around. We had to play in the parking lot because the people who wanted to hear us were in the polio ward. The children would wave out of the windows and we would wave back. We got tired of playing in the parking lot and told the nurses to leave the doors open because we were coming in. They did and we did. We did that many times, and nary a one of us got sick or got polio or anything. I guess that was God telling us not to worry about catchin' something ... our entertaining was more important than catchin' polio.[137]

Hogan, also, remembered playing for the children with polio:

[T]he entertaining that we thought we were doing the most good, and we enjoyed doing it the most, was entertaining the polio wards during the polio siege (during the 1940s). They was a polio hospital in Monroe, North Carolina, where the old army camps had been. They converted that into a polio hospital. Then there was one in Hickory [North Carolina]. We'd go up there and entertain them. But we would set aside one Wednesday out of the month just for that purpose, to go and entertain those kids. It was amazing to see those kids; [they] seemed to be having a good time, and them in the condition they were in. It just really done your soul good. But it sure did hurt you to see them in that shape.[138]

When Dewey Price was with the group, he sang with Whitey and Hogan as a special trio. "We got bored one day and we heard that the radio station in Knoxville, Tennessee, was having auditions for groups to perform on the air," Grant said in an interview. "The three of us drove to Knoxville and we made up a name for our group, and I don't remember what that name was. Anyway, we did one song and we were offered a job on the spot. We thought better about it and came back home."[139] Apparently, the trio did the same thing at a radio station in Alabama, according to Grant. Hogan mentioned an instance to John Rumble about another "dream string band" that was contemplated: "Wade Mainer came by there one day to get us [Whitey and Hogan] to go to WIS [in Columbia, South Carolina] to start a program with him, but there wasn't any salary promise, see, so we turned it down."[140]

J.E. Mainer, the elder of the Mainer brothers, wanted Whitey and Hogan for his band. Grant recalled that:

WBT's
BRIARHOPPER
FAMILY ALBUM

With

PICTURES AND SONGS

Sincerely Yours

Fifteen Years On The Air **WBT** Monday Through Saturday

The WBT Briarhopper Family Album in the mid to late 1940s. Left to right: Roy Grant; Nat Richardson; Claude Casey; Arval Hogan. Kneeling is Hank Warren. Courtesy Tim Drye.

J.E. came to our house one night ... well, fact is, that was before Pap [Pappy Sherrill] went down there [with J.E. Mainer's band]. J.E. Mainer and the Crazy Mountaineers, now Snuffy [Jenkins] was working for J.E. then. They came to our house and was playing over at Dallas [North Carolina] and Hogan and myself was gonna work that night with 'em as a guest appearance. We just had a ball that night and after the show was over J.E. wanted to take

Wade Mainer, his brother Wade, and me and Hogan and go on the road, the four of us. And I said, we had too good a setup here and I didn't think we wanted to leave. He wanted Wade, me and Hogan, and J.E. to form a band.[141]

When Bill Monroe formed the Blue Grass Boys, Monroe hired Whitey and Hogan to open for him in Greenville, SC: "Me and Hogan and Grady Cole went down there. When we got there, I didn't see Hogan's mandolin. I asked Grady if he brought it and he said 'no,' and that he thought that I had it. I asked Hogan if he had his mandolin and he said that he thought that we got it. Well, we went to Bill Monroe and told him that we had a problem. He wanted to know what it was and we told him that we didn't have a mandolin because we forgot it. Bill said, 'That's not a problem. Hogan can use mine.' That's what we did."

When asked if Hogan enjoyed playing Monroe's now legendary Gibson mandolin, Grant replied, "Well, he enjoyed it in that he had a mandolin to play, but Hogan said that his personal Gibson mandolin was a whole lot better!"[142]

When the WBT Briarhoppers played in theaters, they had a plan to find out how they were being received by the audience and what they liked and didn't like. "You see, Fiddlin' Hank always wore a costume like a clown. Well, at intermission, Hank would put on his regular clothes and mingle out in the audience, asking them what they like and how they liked Hogan singin' high, stuff like that, and then he would report back to us. Also, Hank's wife, Inez, helped us. She could read lips and she would figure out what everyone was saying about us. She was a great deal of help, and learned a lot of gossip at the same time!"[143]

Even though the WBT Briarhoppers were playing "opry" music, they also got to play with "opera" musicians a few times in Charlotte. Grant remembered an instance where the Charlotte Symphony Orchestra wanted the WBT Briarhoppers on stage with them:

The largest crowd that the Charlotte Symphony Orchestra ever got together in the city of Charlotte, North Carolina, was one that the Charlotte Symphony Orchestra did in conjunction with the Briarhoppers. Hogan and myself, with our fiddle player and banjo player, went down. Mr. Lamàr Stringfield had written a tune about the old traditional "John Henry," and it took the Charlotte Symphony Orchestra twenty-eight minutes to play his arrangement of "John Henry." And he wanted the Briarhoppers ... to come down and do our version of "John Henry." The newspapers and radios — there wasn't no television then — the newspapers and radios played it up for a month before the night of the big performance, because they were wanting to raise some money for the Charlotte Symphony Orchestra. And they had to turn them [concertgoers] away that night. It took the Charlotte Symphony Orchestra twenty-eight minutes to play their version of "John Henry," and we did ours in about 45 seconds, our version of "John Henry."[144]

Grant remembered the times when the local restaurant owners would be watching for the WBT Briarhoppers to drive down the road. "I especially remember one place, Red Bridge's Barbeque, in Shelby, North Carolina. He would see us drive by and we would honk the horn to him. When we came back by after a show, he would not only have supper waiting for us, but he also put food in boxes for our families. That's how nice the folks were to the Briarhoppers."[145]

The WBT Briarhoppers were known for their practical jokes, and one was very memorable to those who worked in the Wilder Building:

We had a friend who lost both legs in World War II after he parachuted into what was called the tallest pine tree in Europe. He fell and lost his legs in the accident. Anyway, there were some foot doctors on the fourth floor of the Wilder Building, and we thought that it would be a good idea to wheel our friend into the doctors' waiting room. We got there and the room was filled with patients. We told them that if they followed what these doctors told them that they would end up like our friend here. Our friend threw off his blanket and there were two stubs where legs used to be. Everyone laughed so loud that the doctors came out. Thank goodness the doctors thought it was funny, too.[146]

Grammy-winning musician and storyteller David Holt was able to ask legendary picker Doc Watson some questions about the WBT Briarhoppers while Holt and Watson were traveling to New York for a series of concerts in the Summer of 2006. Doc Watson said:

I remember the Briarhoppers. Starting in 1938, when I was at the North Carolina School of the Blind, a lot of the boys would sneak in small electric radios with earphones and we would listen to the Briarhoppers. I remember Homer Briarhopper, Charles Crutchfield, Cecil Campbell, Whitey and Hogan, and many others. One song that I remember was one called, "Mama I'm Sick."

When the Briarhoppers were playing a show, I was sitting outside with my guitar and a cup trying to make some money. Whitey Grant came up and put 50 cents in the cup. Many years later [when Watson was famous], Whitey came up to me and asked if I remembered the time that he put the money in my cup. I told him that I remembered it and that I remembered it was him by the sound of his voice. I also asked him if he thought that the 50 cents was a good investment!

Roy "Whitey" Grant remembers the situation a little differently:

We were playing in Hickory or Morganton, North Carolina, and during intermission, I went outside. I saw this little boy playing a guitar and it was obvious that he was blind. I listened to him for a while and thought that he was quite good. I stepped up to him, told him how good I thought he was, and put a quarter in the cup.

Years later, after he got famous, we were playing at the same festival. Doc had told somebody that as soon as soon as we got to the festival, he wanted to see me. Well, a guy came up to me when I got there and said that Doc Watson wanted to see me right away. I told the guy, "What do you mean? He can't see me. Doc's blind." The guy told me that he was only repeating what Doc told him. He pointed me to the camper at the edge of the festival where Doc was staying. I knocked on the door and his son, Merle, opened the door. I told him that I was Whitey Grant and that Doc wanted to see me right away and that I did not know why. Merle told me that he knew what it was about, but he wanted his daddy to tell me. Sure enough, there was Doc and he knew me right away. He asked me if I remembered putting the quarter in his cup. I told him that I did, but how did he know that it was me? Doc said that his friend who was watching the cup at the time [so that no one would steal it] told him, "Do you know who that was? That was Whitey Briarhopper! Do you know how much he put in? A whole quarter!" In those days, a quarter meant something.

Anyway, Doc told me how much that meant to him and if he could do anything for me to let me know. I told him that he could do one thing for me and that would be to return that same quarter to me. Doc said, "Hell no, I will never give up that quarter." Apparently, he kept it.[147]

Doc Watson's other musical partner, Jack Lawrence, tells a story about his father, who, as a teenager, wanted to go to a Briarhopper show. "[H]e decided to hitchhike to a Briarhoppers show at a one-room schoolhouse near his home outside of Hamlet [North Carolina]. Just when he thought he'd never get a ride, a large Ford sedan stopped. To my father's surprise and delight, [Arval] Hogan leaned out the window and asked for directions to the schoolhouse. My father rode with them sitting on Whitey's lap and was given free admission to the show for directing them."[148]

During a WBT Briarhopper stage show, Curly Seckler remembered one tale that Grant used to tell to the audience. "Whitey would be up there and, sure enough, someone from the crowd would ask how many miles they traveled. Whitey had this answer that I remember to this day: 'Well, folks, you know that the Briarhoppers travel many miles to get to these shows. How we get here is easy. Our wives do the driving ... we only turn the steering wheel.'"[149]

Not all of the stories were funny. Grant remembered a day in the 1940s that still causes him to shutter:

A Briarhopper who will remain nameless at this time, he only spent a year or two with us, was known to have a problem with alcohol and drugs. We were always trying to help him and to try to get him off of that stuff. One time, me and Hogan and Fred Kirby and this person were at a restaurant and we started talking to him about what we could do to help his problem. He must have thought that we were trying to be a father to him, and he must not have liked it. While we were eating, he got really quiet. He then got up and went outside. We were afraid that he was going outside to tip a bottle or something. I went outside and I saw him in our car. He had one of Fred Kirby's cowboy pistols and he was putting bullets in it. I asked him, "What in the world are you doing?" He said, "I'm going to be on the front page of the *Charlotte Observer*." I asked, "What do you mean by that?" This person replied, "The headline will say how I killed off the Briarhoppers." I had to get rough with him and I wrestled the gun out of his hands. We immediately fired him. Many, many years later, this person showed up at my house, and he was friendly and all, but he still had the problem that cost him a job with the Briarhoppers and, eventually, a lucrative contract with a major recording label.[150]

Charlotte as a Country Music Mecca

WBT and the Charlotte community were a major country music recording and performance center long before Nashville's musical success and long before Charlotte's transformation into a major banking center.

Wade Mainer and his brother, J.E., had a band called Mainer's Mountaineers. They did a lot of shows on WBT. Wade told the authors in a telephone interview, "Boy, it was something playing on a 50,000-watt radio station. Me and J.E. played with the greats, including the Briarhoppers. I didn't get to know them as much as J.E. did, but I remember Hank Warren, Whitey & Hogan, Don White, Shannon Grayson, and Claude Casey. They were good Christian boys and had a great thing going. We didn't get together much beyond the radio station because we had places to play to make some money. We were never jealous of each other, we were really busy."

Wade Mainer continued. "WBT was strict about what you played. They wanted all of the approvals from whoever had the copyright or royalties before we played. It seemed that everyone was trying to catch us playing a song that we had not gotten permission to play."[151]

WBT was the last place where the Original Carter Family performed as a group. A *Charlotte Observer* listing for June 1939 indicates that the Carters were then broadcasting a "farm time " show with WBT announcer Grady Cole each weekday morning, and a second half-hour program every afternoon.[152] However, an earlier divorce of Sara and A.P. caused friction within the group, to the point where Sara wanted to stay away from the music business and stay in California with her new husband, Coy Bayes, A.P.'s cousin. Ralph Peer, a legend in the recording business, did everything possible to get the Carters, with A.P.'s sister-in-law, Maybelle Carter, to stay together and make records.

Sara was convinced to move to Charlotte and do a program on WBT. Historians report that the family returned in late 1941 or early 1942 for a final six months of work. It was here that A.P. and Sara parted company, bringing an end to the famed trio.[153]

"Maybelle Carter would sit with me and show me a thousand runs on the guitar," Grant said. "Old A.P., well, he would get nervous and have to walk around during a recording session. He would either flip a coin or would walk around until it was his time to sing. We never knew that he and Sara were going through a divorce. They kept that all to themselves."[154]

"A.P. hated performing.... He never said much, but once you got to know him, he'd talk the horns off of a billy goat."[155]

Janette Carter, daughter of A.P. and Sara Carter, remembered her time in Charlotte with WBT and the Briarhoppers in one of her last interviews. "I remember 'em [the Briarhoppers]. They were real popular in the Carolinas. Mom and Dad and Maybelle played on WBT and some with the Briarhoppers, but we never really socialized together outside of the station. Daddy really liked the Briarhoppers and so did Maybelle ... but momma didn't really care that much for it all. That was the time when Mom and Dad were divorced for good ... they didn't talk much about anything ... it was a sad time for us kids."[156]

When the Carters arrived in Charlotte, there was no house for them to rent. A.P., Sara, Maybelle, Ezra Carter (Maybelle's husband), and the children moved into the YMCA and then to the Roosevelt Hotel in Charlotte. Their radio show aired live Monday through Saturday from 5:15 A.M. to 6:15 A.M., to coincide with the farmers getting up and getting ready to start their day.[157]

Roy Grant remembered that June Carter, daughter of Maybelle Carter and future wife of Johnny Cash, used to entertain his daughters. "Our daughters would get bored at the radio station, and June Carter would take them to the elevator and would ride them up and down through the Wilder Building. Of course, everyone knew who June Carter was and it was a big thrill for the girls to be seen with her."[158]

Before coming to Charlotte, The Carter Family was on the waning side of the popularity that the group enjoyed in the 1930s. Even though divorced, A.P. thought that this Charlotte gig would bring them back to prominence. While in Charlotte, the Carters were notified that *Life* mag-

The Carter Family, 1941. Left to right: Joe Carter; Maybelle Carter; Anita Carter; A.P. Carter; Sara Carter; June Carter; Helen Carter. Courtesy Tom Hanchett.

azine would run a cover story on their career and music. The same week that *Life* was to run the Carters' picture on the cover in 1941, the Japanese bombed Pearl Harbor, knocking the Carters out of the lineup. Heartsick over knowing that was his last chance of bringing the Carter Family back to national attention, A.P. went back to Maces Spring, Virginia, and Sara moved back to California with her new husband, Coy.

According to Mark Zwonitzer, a young Earl Scruggs used to listen to the Carter Family on WBT when he was living in Flint Hill, North Carolina. "Maybelle just knocked me out," Scruggs was quoted as saying.[159] The authors contacted Earl Scruggs' management team to get any additional comments about the WBT Briarhoppers, but they declined to be interviewed.

The Monroe Brothers, Bill and Charlie, spent a lot of time in Charlotte. "When Bill was on WBT," Grant remembers, "he actually moved to Charlotte in a trailer park. Don White's mother-in-law rented the place to him. We would get together to pick and what-not." When asked about the fabled feud between the brothers, Grant would only say, "Bill and Charlie, when they were apart, they were very good people."[160]

Just before moving to WBT-Charlotte, a special, or more exactly, an unplanned event took place for Bill Monroe. According to Richard D. Smith's book, *Can't You Hear Me Callin': The Life of Bill Monroe*, "[S]omeone showed up whom Bill had known during his brief stay in Iowa.... It was Carolyn Minnie Brown. And she was very pregnant."[161]

Bill Monroe's daughter, Melissa Kathleen Monroe, was born in Charlotte, North Carolina.

After the Monroe Brothers broke up, Charlie Monroe started a band and wanted to play on WBT. Grant remembered that "Charlie would not join the musician's union, so he was not allowed to play his guitar on the air. The union told him that he would have to hire a union guitar player and have the player next to him on stage, whether he played or not, and he would have to pay him.... I was that guitar player," Grant said. "Every time that Charlie would see me, he would always ask me, 'Are you still my guitar player?'"[162]

Another version of this story comes from Curly Seckler. "I remember that incident.... The union in Charlotte was really tough to deal with, and they did not want Charlie to play his guitar ... just stand there with his hands at his sides and sing while a union guitar player played. Well, Whitey was asked to play the guitar. However, when we got into our quartet singing, Whitey did not play the guitar like Charlie did, and Charlie got mad, so mad that he threatened to pack up right then and there and leave WBT. An agreement was made that Charlie could play his guitar on these numbers, but Whitey had to sit in a chair beside them so that he could get paid. Every time I see Whitey now, we both laugh about it."[163]

"The Dixie Dewdrop," Uncle Dave Macon, recorded in Charlotte with his son, Dorris. A page from Macon's recording session on January 24, 1938, survives. He also came back to Charlotte during the 1940s. "Uncle Dave knew a thousand songs," Grant recalled, "and what he didn't know, me and Hogan knew. He was a sweet old man. He son, Dorris, watched over him like a hawk and took care of him and played a fine guitar behind Macon's banjo. He was a good son to his dad."[164]

In 1982, Hogan remembered the famous people on the Briarhoppers program:

> The Carter Family would be on our show occasionally. And then all of the musicians from Nashville and from Hollywood, or wherever, came through. All of them was delighted to be on the Briarhopper program, because it was so widely known, and they would get a plug for their appearances, see, which would mean a lot to them. We had Roy Acuff on our program, Eddy Arnold, Ernest Tubb, and just all the guys from Nashville. We worked show dates

with the majority of them.... They would come [to Charlotte] and stay a week, and we'd play jobs together. Bill Monroe would come [to Charlotte] and stay a week, and we'd play out with him and just such things as that, which made it enjoyable for us to get to play with the guys like that, see?[165]

The great violinist David Rubinoff appeared on the WBT Briarhopper radio show during the 1940s. "We had Rubinoff on the program one day," Grant told the authors, "and Crutchfield asked him if he would do a tune on the show. Rubinoff said that he would be glad to. I thought surely that he would play some opera stuff that would be way over our heads. Rubinoff looked me straight in the face and said, 'Do you know "Bile Them Cabbage Down"?' You could have knocked me over with a feather ... but he played it just like Fiddlin' Hank did. He had that Stradivarius fiddle, you know."[166]

In an interview with John Rumble, Grant remembered another non-country music star on the Briarhopper show. "Now, we had Jose Iturbi ... the great pianist came to Charlotte one time to do a concert, and he said, 'I want to be on the Briarhopper program....' I sat on the same bench as Jose Iturbi and did a duet with him. Of course, he played some fancy number, and I did [a two-finger-picking guitar rendition] of 'Coon Shine.'"[167]

Hogan added in the same interview, "We had Judy Canova on there.... Gene Autry was on the barn dance there with us and on the radio.... Jimmy Wakely ... Johnny Mack Brown ... all the greats, we had them."[168]

"The idea of the whole thing [Briarhoppers program]," Claude Casey told John Rumble, "was variety. That's what WBT always wanted, was variety. That's the reason there were so many people on the Briarhopper show. One would sing this type, and one would sing the other type, you see."[169] Claude Casey also commented on Judy Canova, saying that "Me and Judy would yodel together during programs."[170]

Even though WBT and Charlotte were enjoying the fruits of being one of the places professional musicians wanted to be seen and heard, it would not last for long. As Nashville continued the *Grand Ole Opry* on WSM, WBT failed to maintain a long-term country music show that could have secured Charlotte as a rival to Nashville.

WBT did not have only the Briarhoppers program. They had the *Carolina Hayride*, which had all of the WBT bands, including the Briarhoppers and the Tennessee Ramblers, which was held in the old Charlotte Armory and transcribed for network broadcast. *Carolina Calling* was a Sunday morning show, also transcribed for network broadcast. *The Dixie Jamboree* came on WBT daily at one o'clock in the afternoon. WBT was also a part of the *Dixie Network*, which was a music show that included many radio stations in the South. Many of the people either interviewed or researched clearly said that if WBT could have kept up any of these shows, the station could have rivaled or surpassed WSM and the *Grand Ole Opry*.

"Charlotte could have been Nashville," Wade Mainer said in a telephone interview on May 24, 2005. "Crutchfield told me that he let it all slip through his fingers. I don't think that he really liked our type of music, and that he thought that country music would never put Charlotte on the map. Crutchfield was wrong."

Crutchfield admitted in an April 1991 interview with Kevin O'Brien of the *Charlotte Observer*, "We certainly could have been the Nashville of the South. I just didn't realize that bluegrass and country music would become as popular as they did."[171] "This town was the center of it all. Charlotte was the place," Grant said in the same interview.

Cecil Campbell said in an interview with John Rumble, " ... [Y]ears ago, when they had the Crazy Water Barn Dance ... they had talent from the two Carolinas and some, I guess, from Virginia and maybe some from Georgia. They'd come here and be on that barn dance. WBT — gee whiz ... with the talent and a barn dance started here, if they'd just kept it going, this could have been the music capital of the world instead of Nashville."[172]

"Well," Campbell continued, "after the *Crazy Water Crystals Barn Dance* — it closed down.... It closed down about '36. I believe late '35 or '36. Then they started the *Carolina Hayride*. If they'd kept that thing going ... I think if they had kept the *Barn Dance* going, they [the recording companies] would have come in here with a studio. I think that RCA would have come in here with a studio, because this was the center of the two Carolinas."[173]

"What did it for Nashville was the *Grand Ole Opry* there. They didn't take it off the air; they kept it on there," Campbell concluded.[174]

Fred Kirby said in an interview with John Rumble, "If we had kept the *Carolina Hayride*, it would have been as equal as WSM at Nashville, but somehow or another, there's people in it that drifted and people that went someplace else, and, of course, for that reason, it finally left out."[175]

Former Briarhoppers

During this decade, Homer Briarhopper left Charlotte and moved to Raleigh, North Carolina, with his band, The Dixie Dudes. There he started a radio program on WPTF.[176]

Homer A. Briarhopper and His Dixie Dudes, mid 1940s. Homer Drye is third from the left with a cowboy hat. Other members are unknown. Courtesy Tim Drye.

According to Claude Casey in this chapter, Drye left with Johnny McAllister to go to Raleigh. Tim Drye, Homer Drye's son, says that he cannot remember his father talking about teaming with Johnny McAllister at WPTF. Therefore, the authors do not know if McAllister actually made it to Raleigh or if McAllister turned left and moved back to New York. A young fiddler, Paul Warren, worked for a few months with Drye. Warren would eventually join up with Lester Flatt and Earl Scruggs and the Foggy Mountain Boys. During the polio scare of 1947, crowds at musical venues dried up. Drye got a job with a bus company, where he received awards for driving millions of miles without an accident.

Billie Burton Daniel left Charlotte with her parents to move to Wilmington, North Carolina, where she began singing jazz at the Plantation Dinner Club with Jimmy Jett's Orchestra. She also sang at several jazz

Homer A. Briarhopper and His Dixie Dudes, late 1940s. Homer Drye is in the back row, second to the left, with a guitar. The banjo player is Rusty Scoggins. The other members are unknown. Courtesy Tim Drye.

clubs in San Francisco (the Savoy Club and Diamond Lil's, and at officers' clubs in the area). Legendary singer Billie Holliday "used to come and hear me sing in San Francisco," Daniel said in an email to this book's authors. Daniel also performed in Richmond, Virginia; Myrtle Beach, South Carolina; and Pinehurst, North Carolina.

During this time, Daniel remembered her troubles trying to marry. "We moved back to Charlotte in 1946 to work with Clarence Etters' orchestra for a brief time." She then moved to Fayetteville, North Carolina, where she married Bob Daniel. It was at this time when a falling-out occurred between Daniel and Etters. "He told me not to marry him, that I was throwing my future away. He thought that I'd grow up famous and marry a man with lots of money, but it didn't work out that way. He

[Etters] wanted to groom me for musical comedy, but I met Bob and married him. Clarence was adamant, he told me that if I married Bob we could no longer be friends, and he was good as his word."[177] Etters was so indignant about the marriage that he and several WBT employees "had a private detective accost Bob and tell him to go back to Texas, that he was not welcome in Charlotte...."[178]

The married couple moved to Houston and then back to San Francisco. The couple bore a daughter, Jennifer Kingsland Daniel, in 1948. Soon after, the couple divorced and mother and daughter moved back to Charlotte, North Carolina, Daniel singing at the Flamingo Club and with Ray Barrier's Orchestra. Daniel said, "When I came back to Charlotte with my little girl and we went to see Clarence. He was civil, but was not like he used to be at all. I started singing at the Flamingo Club and later with Ray Barrier's Orchestra. Sometimes we would play at the Myers Park Country Club in Charlotte and Clarence would be out there, and I'd just freeze up. I couldn't even sing. Ray Barrier didn't like to play out there just for that reason."[179]

Gibb Young was discharged from the Air Corps in the early 1940s. "Gibb Young was a good singer and a good guitar player. I corresponded with him when he was in the Army," Eleanor Fields said about Young.[180]

Billie Burton Daniel recalled, "Gibb was hurt badly while stationed in Denver, not in battle, but playing football. He almost died. He was honorably discharged. At this time I was singing at the Plantation Club in Wilmington [North Carolina] with Jimmy Jett's orchestra." Daniel continued in an email to the authors: "It was extremely difficult to find good musicians. Charlie Friar, who came to Charlotte as the piano man with the Rangers Quartet joined Jimmy's band. When we heard that Gibb had been discharged from the service, we suggested that Jimmy contact him. Then Gibb came to Wilmington and joined us. Gibb had lost weight and didn't look like he had before, but he was on the mend, we thought."[181]

Daniel recollected, "One night after work when we got to my house, Gibb got out of the car when I did and asked Jimmy [Jett] to wait, that he had something to tell me. He bowed and took my hand and kissed it and said, 'Little sister, I just want you to know how much I've enjoyed playing for you.' I just laughed and thanked him and went on into the house. The next morning I was still in bed and I heard Mama answer the phone, and I heard her say 'What? Gibb dead?' It was a horrible shock to us all. He was only 26 but he had suffered a heart attack, due we think, to his injuries in the service."[182]

"He had heart trouble," said Charlie Friar, a former musician who performed on WBT. "I was his roommate in Wilmington. He would not stop playing music and he would not take care of himself. I found him dead in his bed."[183]

"When I came back to the area, I was singing with Jimmy Jett's Orchestra," Daniel remembered. "Jimmy was from Charlotte and several times Jimmy and Charlie Friar and Gibb and I would go with Jimmy to Charlotte on our night off, and I would always stay with Curly [Don White] and Mary [his wife]."[184] According to Friar, Gibb had divorced before his death and knew of no family members remaining.

Thorpe Westerfield went into the air force during the war (where he played tuba in the air force band), and apparently never came back to WBT. According to his daughter, Terry, Westerfield came back from the war and began working at the family business, Carolina Wholesale Building Materials, in Charlotte.

Clarence Etters came back to WBT as its musical director after the war, where he was stationed at Fort Jackson in South Carolina.

Cecil Campbell, using the Tennessee Ramblers as a backup group, signed with RCA Victor in 1946, and made many recordings. In 1949, he recorded a country top ten hit, "Steel Guitar Ramble."[185]

Harry Blair stayed with the Tennessee Ramblers and the WBT Briarhoppers until 1943, when he went into the service. Blair returned to the band in 1945 while they were still in Charlotte. He also toured with the *Grand Ole Opry* tent shows during the decade and performed as a solo act in Virginia and Tennessee. In 1949, Blair married and moved to Columbus, Ohio, where the couple raised a family. It was here that Blair decided to quit the music business. He rejoined Wierton Steel, where he would work until retirement.[186]

Jack Gillette and Tex Martin continued their work with Campbell. After this point, we do not know what Gillette did or where he went. Martin was drafted in 1943 and did not return to WBT when he was discharged. He soon became a disc jockey in Cincinnati.

Charles Crutchfield became the general manager of WBT in 1945, becoming the youngest general manager of a 50,000-watt radio station in the United States. His new job would limit the time he could be with the Briarhopper radio show.

In a September 23, 1945, article in the *Charlotte Observer*, the announcement of Crutchfield's promotion mentioned the "world's best known artists" that received Crutchfield's encouragement and support. "He [Crutchfield] is credited with the starting of the meteoric rise of Dean Hudson and his orchestra. Johnny Long and John Scott Trotter began to gain national fame under his guidance and Lansing Hatfield of the Metropolitan Opera is another of his "finds," along with Fred Waring's personal announcer, Bill Bivens. He also discovered in Charlotte four African American lads who are the celebrated Golden Gate Quartet and, more recently, sent the local Southland Jubilee Singers, now the Four Knights, into New York, where they are being featured among the year's most promising discoveries."[187]

No information was found at the time of this book's publication regarding the whereabouts of Johnny McAllister, but there is evidence that he followed Homer Drye to the Raleigh area. A biography of McAllister can be found on the Iceberg Radio Website, written by Eugene Chadbourne from the All Music Guide, some of which is shown below; it is the last known biography on McAllister:

> Johnny Macalester [sic] may have called himself Pappy Briarhopper in order to establish that he was one of the first, if not the first, members of the Charlotte-based Appalachian musical institutional known as the Briarhoppers. Whether this is true or not is a difficult fact to establish, but at any rate the stage name did very little to help this artist in either his career or his place in Briarhopper history. Of all the early members of this group, he remains one of the least well-known.
>
> Of the two early members who nicked the group's name as a stage name for themselves, he had the least success; Homer Briarhoppper, on the other hand, made solo recordings for Bluebird and Decca and later hosted a long-running early morning Raleigh television show that featured a lot of live music. Macalester, whose name is also recorded as John McAllister, in some Briarhopper research projects, was certainly part of the early batch of string band performers hired by radio producer Charles H. Cruthfield to form the Briarhoppers group in the early '30s.... The group is not said to really hit its stride until the arrival of Whitey & Hogan.... They brought the excellent banjoist Shannon Grayson, himself a leader of the Golden Valley Boys, and presided over an influx of new players that included cowboy singer and guitarist Fred Kirby and bassist and singer Don White. Pappy Briarhopper was long gone by this time and the anti–Pappy faction in the Briarhoppers cult seem to feel it was the upgrade in musical ability represented by Whitey & Hogan that prompted his departure and nothing created in his pretty-much nonexistent solo career proves otherwise. Unlike Homer Briarhopper, he did not enjoy a later career as a charming older television cowboy, but shares the former artist's misfortune of having his stage name rendered as Brierhopper [sic] on a regular basis.[188]

In a 2006 interview with Newell Hathcock, briefly a fiddler for the WBT Briarhoppers and then with Homer Briarhopper and His Dixie

Dudes, Hathcock said that he left Charlotte with Drye and McAllister after accepting a job at WPTF in Raleigh. When the trio got there, McAllister received word that his father had died in New York. Hathcock continued to say that he drove McAllister to the bus station to get on a bus to New York. Hathcock told the authors that was the last time he was to see or hear from McAllister.

There is no further information on Jane Bartlett and Mildred and Floyd from this point forward. "Mildred and Floyd were after my time," Billie Burton Daniel told the authors, while Whitey Grant told the authors that "Mildred and Floyd were before my time.... I heard a lot about them, but I never met 'em. Don White could have told you about them."

The Storms Are on the Ocean

WBTV signed on for the first time, which marked the birth of television in the Charlotte market. Also, there was talk of playing records over the radio. As the 1950s rounded the corner, something Daniel said in her book draft would be the harbinger for the WBT Briarhoppers in the next decade: "I remember 'Dad' [Johnny McAllister] saying if radio stations were ever allowed to play records on the air, it would be the end of local [radio] shows. He was right."[189]

Timeline — 1940s

1940—The Johnson Family joined WBT. Minnie Pearl joined the Opry. Germany invaded Norway, Denmark, France, Holland, Belgium, and Luxembourg. Winston Churchill became the British prime minister.

1941—Whitey and Hogan joined the WBT Briarhoppers. The Carter Family joined WBT. Andy Griffith was not hired by WBT because he wanted too much money. Pearl Harbor was attacked by Japan, and Germany invaded the USSR. The USA declared war on Japan, Germany, and Italy. The Carter Family performed their last time as a group at WBT, with Sara Carter Coy moving to California with her new husband, Maybelle going on the road with her children, and A.P. returning to Maces Spring, Virginia.

1942—The Battle of Midway was fought. U.S. soldiers suffered in the Bataan Death March in the Philippines.

1943—Arthur Smith joined WBT. Ernest Tubb joined the Opry and the

Opry moved to the Ryman Auditorium. Italy surrendered to Germany. Churchill, FDR, and Stalin met in Tehran.

1944— WBT became the first 24-hour station in the Southeast. The D-Day landings took place in Normandy.

1945— WBT was sold to Jefferson Standard Life. The *Carolina Hayride* radio show began. Flatt & Scruggs joined Bill Monroe's Blue Grass Boys. FDR, Stalin, Churchill met in Yalta. FDR died and Truman took office. Hitler committed suicide and Mussolini was executed. Atomic bombs were dropped on Japan, and V-E Day marked the end of the war in Europe.

1946— Harry Von Tilzer, the composer of "Wait Till the Sun Shines, Nellie," who was born in 1872 died.

1947— WBT-FM signed on the air.

1948— Flatt & Scruggs formed the Foggy Mountain Boys. *Louisiana Hayride* began and Hank Williams joined the *Louisiana Hayride*. Mahatma Gandhi was assassinated.

1949— WBTV signed on the air. Hank Williams joined the Opry, and also had his first number one hit, "Lovesick Blues." The People's Republic of China was proclaimed under Mao Zedong.

America's Musical Taste:
The top song of this decade was Bing Crosby's "White Christmas."

The WBT Briarhoppers are still playing.

4

The 1950s: Elvis Who?

The beginning of the 1950s saw a continuation of the WBT Briarhoppers' fame and popularity. Grant remembers that the band backed former Louisiana governor Jimmie Davis when he sang the big hit he cowrote, "You Are My Sunshine."[1]

Early in 1950, the band had the opportunity to join the *Grand Ole Opry*. On the WBT Briarhopper shows, they would host many Opry stars, such as Ernest Tubb, Minnie Pearl, and Jimmy Dickens. "In those days and in this part of the country, we were as popular as the Beatles," Grant told Joe DePriest.[2]

"We had calls to join the Opry, but we had too good a setup in Charlotte. We could do our radio shows, go out and make personal appearances, and be back home in a day or two." Grant told this author, "Minnie Pearl, Ernest Tubb, and Red Foley advised us not to go to the Opry. The pay was bad and the time commitments were worse. I don't know if they didn't want the competition, but they told us that they envied the way that we could do our work and be home that night."[3]

But it all came crashing down in 1952, when WBT cancelled the Briarhoppers' radio show. When asked why the show was cancelled, Grant said one word: "Elvis," and then he continued: "We could see it coming. People had televisions. They wanted to separate themselves from old-time music. Elvis was just around the corner. WBT could not get enough sponsors to keep the show going."[4]

Grant had no ill words against Presley. "We actually enjoyed listening to him, and his people told us that he would listen to the Briarhopper radio show anytime that he could. He was a good man."

Stanley said in the video, *Ralph Stanley and the 5-String Banjo*, that he wrote the song "Hard Times" and recorded it in 1956, because it was hard times. "Crowds were not coming to the shows ... it was rock and roll that they were listening to. Many times we had to play the show before we could eat or get gas to get home ... hard times."[5]

Dewitt "Snuffy" Jenkins said it best: "We had to quit [the music business] because of our health.... We were starving to death."[6]

The narrator of *High Lonesome*, Mac Wiseman, said in the program, "Before rock and roll and music amplification, Western Swing, Cajun, Honky Tonk, and Bluegrass were thriving styles of country music. Musicians plugged into the pop music trends and the acoustic sound of bluegrass became obsolete."

The 1950s was a decade of change and national growth. Young people were getting interested in the new styles of music. Adults were changing their ways, watching television, purchasing new technological gadgets for their homes, trying, perhaps, to break away from the lives of their parents and grandparents, who were basically born at the turn of the century. Radio string bands became as out-of-date as Uncle Dave Macon must have felt when Earl Scruggs hit the *Grand Ole Opry* stage in 1945.

Charles Crutchfield talked about the end of the WBT Briarhoppers radio show in his interview with John Rumble of the Country Music Hall of Fame. "I was told (in all modesty) the reason it was cancelled was because I was no longer there [as the announcer, having been promoted to gen-

1950 Claude Casey and WBT Briarhopper advertisement. Courtesy Tom Hanchett.

eral manager]. [Also] the Briarhoppers sponsored by the company that had taken over the patent medicines was on the verge of going broke.... Drug Trade Products Company ... Radio became saturated with this type [of sponsorship] and maybe the public got wise to it."

Crutchfield continued, saying, "I think these products were good. They served their purpose. But I know we were advertising a hair dye called Kolor-bak. Many products came on the market like it, and that had something to do with the demise of that particular sponsor. There are cough medicines on the shelf in any drugstore that would do the same thing that Peruna did.... I guess it was competition that made it impossible for these people [patent medicine companies] to continue, but I had a good time with it. And I think the public must have enjoyed it."[7]

Grant thought the WBT Briarhopper program could weather the loss of the Drug Trade Company sponsorship, saying, "After the Drug Trade Company [ended its sponsorship], when the trend changed, we sold ourselves to Pilot Life Insurance Company. Crutch would say, 'Look, this insurance is really good stuff.... You ought to take advantage of this week's low funeral prices and just go ahead and die.' It went over like a house on fire, really. But we did sell a lot of life insurance for Pilot Life Insurance Company...."[8]

However, the program did not last. When the show was cancelled in 1951, Grant got a job driving a Charlotte city bus and Hogan ran a restaurant before they joined the U.S. Postal Service in Charlotte. White moved on to WLS in Chicago.[9] Grayson continued with his band, the Golden Valley Boys, and became an expert furniture builder. Warren continued working as a photographer for WBTV.

During the 1950s, the WBT Briarhoppers continued to make public appearances, but the venues began to shrink significantly. One memorable show was recounted by Grant:

We used to have an announcer who did some announcin', and his name was Lonzo Squires. He did a lot of late-night disc jockeyin' work, and he was blind. One night we went to a show in South Carolina. When we got there, Lonzo said "Whitey, let me hold your arm when we get in and you can find me a seat and I'll be okay." Well, I did that. It was at a schoolhouse that night and a storm came up. The power went off. It was dark as a dungeon and you could not see a foot in front of you. We called the program off. Hank said, "How are we gonna get out of here?" Lonzo yells out, "Where's Whitey?" I went to him and said, "Here I am." Lonzo told me to hold onto his coattail and have the other boys hang on to me and he would get us out of there. So the blind man led us out of the schoolhouse that night.[10]

Grant recounts another story that put the WBT Briarhoppers in Kentucky at a concert with the Delmore Brothers and Flatt & Scruggs:

Scruggs went over to the Delmore Brothers and told them, "If you want to know some stories, go over to Whitey over there.... He knows them all." We had never met the Delmore Brothers, me and Hogan, but they were our idols.... There were no others like them. We were at a hotel waiting for the show to start and two fellers got off the elevator and saw me and Hogan. I heard one of them say, "It's got to be them." So they kept coming closer to us while we were talking with Lester Flatt and Earl Scruggs. One of the boys asked us if we were Whitey and Hogan, and I said "Yes, we are." I asked them who they were and they said that they were Alton and Ray, the Delmore Brothers. I said, "Great day in the morning, we have always wanted to meet you because you are our idols and we wanted to sing like you and we have copied a lot of your songs. I hope that this doesn't make you mad." Alton said it was all right, and then he said that he and Ray "had every record that [we] had ever made and that they would never part with them because [they] idolized [us]!" That made us feel right proud.[11]

There are a few legends in the 1950s where the WBT Briarhoppers healed the sick. One story is found in Roy Blount, Jr.'s book, *Crackers*. He writes, "One night the Briarhoppers, a singing group from Charlotte, had a flat tire in front of our house, and they came in and sang for Nannie, our great-aunt, who had broken her hip and was in bed for ten years. There was a Baptist preacher's wife named Mrs. Cave who used to come in wearing a black cape and flap around the house and tell Nannie she could get up and walk if she wanted to. But the Briarhoppers did her a lot more good."[12]

In 1951, WBTV was growing in the television market. One television advertiser was not getting a lot of sales from commercials on WBTV. The sponsor turned to the WBT Briarhoppers.

According to Grant:

In about the early fifties, the Hotpoint branch of General Electric had a commercial program on WBTV, channel 3, here in Charlotte, North Carolina. They weren't getting too much response from this program for some reason or other. I don't know why, because the guys that were on it were good friends of ours. But they called us over one day to do an audition, and so the Briarhoppers with Fred Kirby, Claude Casey, the whole group, went over, and Whitey & Hogan, and we did an audition. Before we got through with the audition, they said, "Well, that's what we want. We want you guys to finish out our contract with WBTV."

So we did six or seven weeks for Hotpoint branch of General Electric here. I know on one particular program I remember, Hogan and I were introduced. "Well, here's Whitey and Hogan to do their number." But there was no Whitey and Hogan. When they found us, we were raising the lid on one of their freezers.... We were climbing out of the freezer.[13]

Fred Kirby, an off-and-on Briarhopper, started his television career on WBTV with the show *Junior Rancho* in 1951. Kirby began to develop a new fan base. Frank McGuirt, the Sheriff of Union County, North Carolina, remembered a parade he attended in Charlotte when he was an elementary school student in the early 1950s. The parade's grand marshal was William Boyd, who starred in television's *Hopalong Cassidy*, and who got a polite applause. "And then Fred [Kirby] came along and the crowd went wild." McGuirt never got to be on the *Junior Rancho* TV show, but he was a proud member of the show's club. He says, "Kirby aired a secret message, and you had to have the decoder [that went with the membership] to get the message. It was usually something about child safety or 'Do your homework.'"[14]

Doug Mayes, before he made his legacy in the television industry, began hosting a radio show on WBT called *Carolina Country Style*, where he would have guests on the show ranging from the Briarhoppers, to Bill Monroe, to Minnie Pearl, to Little Jimmy Dickens, and others. This radio show would run until the 1960s. Mayes' show was so influential and popular he was the first deejay invited to come backstage at the Ryman Auditorium in Nashville, Tennessee, on Saturday nights and tape interviews with the *Grand Ole Opry* stars.

Mayes, with his sister, was invited to play with a group on the *Grand Ole Opry* in 1939, which, in time, resulted in his joining country music pioneer Fiddlin' Arthur Smith [not Charlotte's Arthur Smith] for a year. This was where Mayes made his name at the Opry and gained the institution's trust.

During the 1940s, he was an emcee, bass player, and band leader, working out of WKPT in Kingsport, Tennessee. Returning from service in World War II, he took a job at the new WBTV television station in Charlotte, North Carolina.

It was during this time that he met and befriended the WBT Briarhoppers, and filled in on bass or guitar for the band as needed. The authors mention Doug Mayes due to his time working with the WBT Briarhoppers and the future accolades and commendations he would receive, many of those listed in later chapters of this book.

When asked about how he would describe his times with the WBT Briarhoppers, Mayes told the authors, "Just describe me as a huge fan and not as a sometimes-member of the band. I just helped out all that I could. They are the ones who did all of the work."[15]

The WBT Briarhoppers would continue to get together and play at special events, and they would never know who would be a part of the band. According to Grant, "It was always Whitey and Hogan, and usually Fiddlin' Hank. But sometimes we would have Claude Casey, Fred Kirby, Shannon Grayson, Big Bill Davis, or Don White. It was always a surprise."[16]

No matter who was playing with the Briarhoppers, the way they were paid, while on the road, remained the same. Grant remembered that " 'Fiddlin' Hank or Don White would collect the money that we were owed. While we slept in the hotel, they would slip the money in our shirt pockets."[17]

Former Briarhoppers

Homer Briarhopper Drye was maintaining a successful career in Raleigh, North Carolina, where he opened a club called the Carolina Pines Club. With his work in local radio, Drye was named Mr. Disc Jockey USA in 1954.[18] This award, and his radio work, also got Drye associated

Homer Drye (right) at WSM-Nashville's radio studio with Grant Turner, mid 1950s. Courtesy Tim Drye.

with Ernest Tubb, Eddy Arnold, Roy Acuff, and Ray Price, among others. Drye refused three offers to be a member of the *Grand Ole Opry*, wanting to remain in the Raleigh area with his wife and family. But it was in Raleigh's Memorial Auditorium where Drye's career went further than even

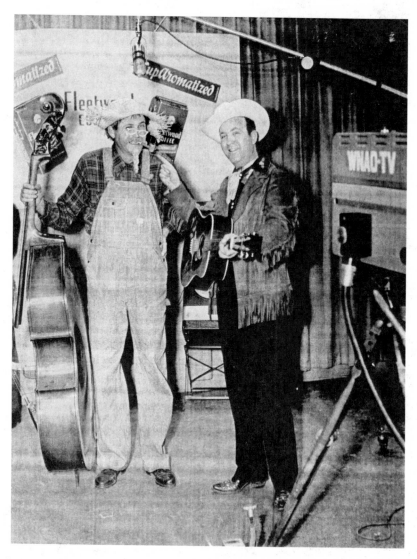

Homer Drye (right) with Granpappy Slim (Homer's brother, Crawford Drye) at WNAD-TV, Raleigh, NC, in the mid 1950s. Courtesy Tim Drye.

he could ever imagine. Grady Jefferys wrote in the Summer 1969 edition of *Raleigh Magazine* that Hank Snow came to town. Last on that bill was Elvis Presley. "Presley came on last," Drye said, "but he stopped the show." According to the article, Presley cancelled out on the Hank Snow tour and was given headline billing on his own show following the Raleigh performance. Elvis became, and remained, a close friend of Drye's from that point forward.

A young George Hamilton IV began his first recordings in the Raleigh/Durham area and performed at Drye's music hall. "Homer was an entrepreneur, an extrovert, a promoter, a musician, and a businessman," Hamilton IV said. "The name 'Briarhopper' was very catchy, and I grew up listening to them, but wondered if he was associated with the same group. Drye told me his name was from a radio show in Charlotte a long time ago, but he didn't elaborate any further. But he was successful at his business at a time when country music halls were falling by the wayside."[19]

Claude Casey moved to Augusta, Georgia, to work at radio station WGAC. Casey also made his last recording session for MGM records, with Fred Rose as producer and Chet Atkins as guitarist.[20]

Casey also continued playing music. "I played in Belk's Department Store [in Augusta] every Friday, and it was along about seven until eight.... Then from nine o'clock until twelve o'clock the same night, we played the Elks Club in Augusta, Georgia."[21]

Billie Burton Daniel moved with her daughter and parents to Richmond, Virginia, where she sang with a small band and worked at the Chef's Club to support her daughter.

Thorpe Westerfield continued to work at the family business, never keeping up with his old Briarhopper family.

Clarence Etters continued his work at WBT as the musical director. However, according to Doug Bell, a former announcer at WBT, Etters was arrested on West Trade Street in Charlotte, with "another man in his car.... It seemed that we did not know a lot about alternative lifestyles back then."[22] After the arrest, WBT fired Etters.

Eleanor Bryan Fields started a radio program on WGVR in Goldsboro, North Carolina. "I would sit on the piano, stretch my legs out, run the microphone down and play the guitar. It lasted a few years. I also got married again, to Mr. Fields. He ran the Red and White grocery store in town. He helped me raise Lew's kids and he was a wonderful man."[23]

Cecil Campbell signed with MGM during this decade, releasing several singles, some of which were deemed as "rockabilly."[24]

Harry Blair continued to work at Wierton Steel in Ohio.

Tex Martin (Martin Schopp) went under another name, Marty Roberts, and recorded under the name Marty Roberts and The (or His) Nightriders; and Marty Roberts and the Saxons. From 1954 through 1958, he recorded for Coral, Arc, and Flame record companies, which included a rockabilly hit, "Baby." During the mid–1950s, he was a deejay with Nelson King in Cincinnati. In 1959, Roberts became a disc jockey at WDZ in Illinois.[25]

Sam Poplin took several engineering jobs before he started in the clock business.

Charles Crutchfield, still the general manager at WBT/WBTV, was asked in 1951 by the U.S. State Department to travel to Greece to set up a broadcasting network. Crutchfield was also the only broadcaster in the nation to tour the Soviet Union in 1956, resulting in Radio Moscow.[26]

Billie Ann Newman Carson got married in 1948 and had a dance band in Charlotte until 1951, when her husband, who was a pilot for Eastern Airlines, was transferred to Atlanta, Georgia.

Carson said:

> We needed some money and I told my husband that I was going to go to WLWH in Atlanta and audition. They let me audition with the studio band, and as I was leaving the studio, the guy who had the radio show came to me and told me that I would be on this afternoon. This radio show host said, "Leave your name and number with me and if musicians call, I'll give 'em your number." I was on this guy's show from 2 to 3 P.M. five days a week. He had four children and he was making $95 per week. He asked for $125 per week and was fired, saying that he wasn't worth the $95 that they were paying him. That guy was Dick Van Dyke. He left and went to New Orleans, where he was spotted by a scout who encouraged him to try out for *Bye, Bye Birdie*. Thank God he got fired in Atlanta![27]

Buddy Holly recorded the song "Wait Till the Sun Shines, Nellie" in January 1959. Holly died in a plane crash in February 1959. The song was released a year or two after his death.

The authors found no records of Johnny McAllister, Jane Bartlett, Jack Gillette, Mildred and Floyd, Nat Richardson, or Homer Christopher from this point forward.

Timeline for the 1950s

1950 — The Korean War started.

1951 — WBT Briarhopper show was cancelled, but the WBT Briarhoppers continued to perform concerts.

1952 — Uncle Dave Macon died and Hank Williams was fired from the Opry.

1953 — Hank Williams died in his blue Cadillac. Eisenhower was elected president. Julius and Ethel Rosenburg were executed for espionage. The Korean War ended.

1954 — Elvis Presley appeared on the *Grand Ole Opry* for the first and only time. Elvis first recorded for Sun Records in Memphis. Segregated schools were ruled unconstitutional by the U.S. Supreme Court.

1955 — WBT moved from the Wilder Building to One Jefferson Place in Charlotte. The first McDonald's restaurant opened.

1956 — George D. Hay, "The Solemn Old Judge," retired from the Opry. Buddy Holly made his first recordings. The U.S. began training South Vietnam troops.

1957 — The first nuclear plant opened in Pennsylvania. The USSR was first in space with *Sputnik.*

1958 — First domestic airline service between New York City and Miami was established.

1959 — Radio Moscow debuted on WBT. Buddy Holly recorded "Wait Till the Sun Shines, Nellie" in his personal studio. Buddy Holly, Big Bopper, and others were killed in an Iowa plane crash.

America's Musical Taste:

The top song of this decade was Bill Haley's "Rock Around the Clock."

The WBT Briarhoppers are still playing!

5

The 1960s:
This Was a Time
for Rock and Roll

"The 1960s was a time for rock and roll," Grant said in a 2005 interview with this author. "It was also time for them to get jobs," Grant's wife, Polly, added. Whitey and Hogan got jobs with the U.S. Postal Service in Charlotte, North Carolina. "We would sing while we were a-sortin' mail," Grant said.[1]

Hank Warren remained at WBTV as a photographer. Shannon Grayson, when he was not playing with the Golden Valley Boys, made furniture. Don White got into sales.

Grant said, "We still played music together.... Me and Hogan and Don White would get together at small gatherings, basically to have fun and keep the Briarhopper name alive."[2] However, the places to play became scarce.

The Beatles began their invasion of America in the early 1960s, and gained popularity on the *Ed Sullivan Show*. Instead of cowboy outfits and close-cut haircuts, the boys from Liverpool had shaggy hair, collarless suits, and electric instruments. The children of country music lovers were screaming and crying for their new heroes.

Crutchfield saw the effect of the Beatles. "I think that the big change came about when the Beatles came," he said in an interview. "This was very obvious to me that they changed the beat, they changed the rhythm, they changed the type of program that the public went for."[3]

The Vietnam War was raging as was the anger of most of those who remained in the States, wondering why the country was sacrificing the lives of its best and brightest for a war no president could accurately explain. The music of Elvis was turning once more toward the Who, the Grateful Dead, and other rock bands who were known to play with passion, but also playing very, very loudly.

The early 1960s was almost the death knell of traditional country music and bluegrass music. Nashville, now the focal point of the country music universe, changed its format towards electrification and homogenization. Gone were the nasal, country voices that had graced the radio stations. Smooth singers, electric guitar riffs, and drums were added to appeal to a greater audience. Sonny Osborne remembers, "Nashville had the packaged country shows. They were electric and they were loud. That's where the money was ... so we would go to these shows [as the Osborne Brothers] and [we] couldn't be heard. By the time a person's ears got back to normal, we were off [the stage]."

WBTV, the television side of the WBT family, led the change in how people were entertained in the New South. From a Briarhopper standpoint, WBTV had a Sunday afternoon television show starring Fred Kirby. Kirby, with Jim Patterson posing as "Uncle Jim Mahaffey," sang cowboy songs in between the showing of *Little Rascals* and *Our Gang* episodes of the 1930s. Occasionally, Don White would come on the air and sing with his former partner from the WLW-Cincinnati and WLS-*National Barn Dance* days.

In the mid to late 1960s, the Folk Music Revival began to hit the college campuses and coffee houses from New York City to San Francisco. Bob Dylan performed Woody Guthrie songs and some of his own making, bringing acoustic music back to the young poets and music lovers. Movies like *Deliverance* and *Bonnie and Clyde* brought the sounds of the banjo and guitars and fiddles back to an audience who had either forgotten their existence or had never heard their sounds before. *The Beverly Hillbillies* television show catapulted Flatt & Scruggs to the top of the pop charts with the theme song, "The Ballad of Jed Clampett." Louise Scruggs, wife of Earl Scruggs and then–business manager for the Foggy Mountain Boys, worked relentlessly to convince the nation that bluegrass music was folk music, or as someone put it, "folk music in overdrive."

Bill Monroe was starting to see a rebirth of his career after the magazine, *Sing Out*, ran a story by Ralph Renzler that proclaimed Monroe as the "Father of Bluegrass Music."

Sonny Osborne said, "In the sixties, everybody in the world was tired of the synthetic, ridiculous things that was being forced onto them.... They wanted to get back to the earth, the basics, and bluegrass helped take them there."[4]

Bluegrass festivals, the brainchild of Carlton Haney, began to take root and flourish throughout the South and beyond. The first such festival was held in Fincastle, Virginia, in 1965. The yearning for the good old days was about to take hold.

Former Briarhoppers

Homer Briarhopper Drye continued his success in the Raleigh area with a music club and with his work in both radio and television. Homer's sister, Kate, taught country music star Randy Travis how to play the guitar during this decade.[5]

Billie Burton Daniel moved to Raleigh with her family. While she was working for a travel agency, she continued to travel to Myrtle Beach to perform at jazz clubs.

Thorpe Westerfield continued to work at the family business in Charlotte. As a member of the Musician's Union, he kept his hand in music by playing gigs during the holidays, according to his daughter, Terry Marshall, in an August 19, 2005, telephone interview.[6]

Cecil Campbell cut an all-original album for Starday in 1963, called *Steel Guitar Jamboree.*

Harry Blair retired from Wierton Steel in Ohio and moved to Myrtle Beach, South Carolina.

Sam Poplin continued working in the clock business.

Big Bill Davis lived in South Carolina in retirement but played with the WBT Briarhoppers when time allowed.

Clarence Etters died of cirrhosis of the liver. He had never married. Daniel remembers in an email to the authors, "I didn't go to the funeral. I wanted to, but just couldn't make it. I called his sister, Kitty, and she understood. It was very sad. I'll never forget what a good friend he was, how wise he was. I just wish we could have stayed friends."[7]

Charles Crutchfield became president of Jefferson Pilot, the owners of WBT and WBTV. In 1962, Crutchfield traveled to the Berlin Wall, where he stood as a bipartisan free enterpriser and Cold Warrior.[8]

In 1968, Crutchfield called for the firing of U.S. Attorney General Ramsey Clark for criticizing "police violence" at the Democratic convention in Chicago. He told Rumble, "When I was younger, I used to go right down the conservative line, no deviation whatsoever.... I've learned over the years that liberals are nice folks, too...."[9]

Eleanor Bryan Fields remained in Goldsboro and out of the music business.

Tex Martin continued to work as a deejay in the Cincinnati area.

Billie Ann Newman Carson was still in Atlanta and still singing at a few venues.

The Future

It would only be a matter of time until the WBT Briarhoppers would officially reform and play on Fred Kirby's TV show, and in all parts of the United States and Europe.

Timeline for the 1960s

1960 — Edward R. Murrow visited WBT. George Hamilton IV and Loretta Lynn joined the Opry. WLS canceled the WLS *Barn Dance*. A.P. Carter died in Maces Spring, Virginia. The Beatles began to play in England's pubs and music venues. Buddy Holly's recording of "Wait Till the Sun Shines, Nellie" was released.

1961 — Fred Rose, Jimmie Rodgers, and Hank Williams were the first to be inducted into the Country Music Hall of Fame. Alan Sheppard was the first U.S. astronaut in orbit around the earth

1962 — U.S. first used Agent Orange on North Vietnam. Roy Acuff was inducted into the Country Music Hall of Fame.

1963 — President Kennedy was assassinated and Lyndon Johnson became President. Oswald was shot and killed by Jack Ruby on national TV. Charles Crutchfield was named president of Jefferson Pilot Communications, which included WBT, WBT-FM, and WBTV. George Hamilton IV recorded one of his biggest hits, "Abilene."

1964 — The Beatles invaded the United States via the *Ed Sullivan Show*.

1967 — Country Music Hall of Fame and Museum opened and Red Foley was elected to the Country Music Hall of Fame

1968 — Red Foley died.

1969 — Richard Nixon was elected president. Neil Armstrong was the first man on the moon. The Beatles broke up as a group when John Lennon said that he "wanted a divorce." Flatt & Scruggs and the Foggy Mountain Boys ended their partnership after the inaugural parade of Richard Nixon.

America's Musical Taste:
The top song for this decade was Aretha Franklin's "Respect."

The WBT Briarhoppers are still playing, albeit rarely.

6

The 1970s:
The Phoenix Rises

Whitey and Hogan bought houses next to each other in the Plaza-Midwood section of Charlotte, near downtown, and they would be at each other's houses all the time. The Briarhopper wives, wanting their houses back, concocted a scheme to get the boys back together as a group. "Unknown to us, our wives got the idea of getting the group back together again," Grant said in 2005.[1] "We were tired of them being around the house all of the time," Polly Grant added during the same interview.

Grant continued, "We were invited to Hogan's house. Fiddlin' Hank, Don White, and Shannon Grayson came. Well, one of our wives asked us to play something. We didn't have our instruments. Hank said, 'I didn't bring my fiddle!' Hank's wife said, 'Yes you do, I put it in the car trunk.' All of the wives snuck out our instruments and brought them with us without us knowing it. Hank's fiddle was in pieces and we had to wait for him to put it together again. We started playing and found out that we could still carry a tune." Don White, who had customarily played an upright bass, began using a Gibson electric bass due to its being easier to carry around, "especially for a retired man," White would say in jest, according to Grant.[2]

Prior to this get-together, White recalled that getting Fiddlin' Hank to pick up a fiddle again was tough: "'He had lost his son ... so he hung up his fiddle and didn't play anymore, for many years.... I just happened to be over at his house one day, and his grandchildren were around. I suggested to him that he get his fiddle out and show his grandchildren how he used to play fiddle on the Briarhopper program." With White playing rhythm on a tenor banjo, Warren dug out his bow, dusted off his fiddle and started playing. "His eyes lit up, and he decided to play again."[3]

Word informally got out that the WBT Briarhoppers were playing again. Grant recalls: "Someone from Edwin Towers [a retirement home] asked us if we would come and play since we were the oldest band around and they were old people. We thought we would play for about an hour and then we would go home and put our guitars under the bed. A reporter from the *Charlotte Observer* got wind we were playing. They were there, taking pictures. The next thing we know, there are articles being printed that the Briarhoppers are back. It made the local TV news. We didn't get the chance to put our guitars under the bed."[4] Dot Jackson, now a nationally-known author, was the reporter who wrote about the rebirth of the Briarhoppers in the August 25, 1973, edition of the *Charlotte Observer*. She wrote:

> Fiddlin' Hank, Pappy [Don White], Whitey and Hogan got together Thursday night for the first time in two decades to play for a square dance at Edwin Towers. It was hard to say who had the best time…. The success of the reunion was so total that the Briarhoppers are going to play again, next for the Methodist Home on September 13…. Maybe Hank will play his saw again — music to bring tears to the eyes — No — it's lovely![5]

When asked how she knew about the Edwin Towers event, Dot Jackson told the authors in an email, "I think that Charlie Briarhopper [Charles Crutchfield] told me."[6]

Jackson also told the authors in a March 3, 2006, email that she was late in getting to know the importance of the WBT Briarhoppers:

> I came on the Charlotte scene in the mid–60s, when some of the Briarhoppers had played out and others got way-up-yonder rich and in high society, and what I saw of them were the reunions and gigs just for joy. Greatest bunch of guys going, at the time. I was very fond of Charlie Crutchfield; we knew where the other was coming from — straight out of the cornfield. No padding of resumes needed…. I'm not sure that his wife loved to hear him [being called] "Charlie Briarhopper," though. She probably figured he was due a lot more respect.
>
> I simply came too late [to recall Briarhopper stories]. What I can surely say is that I loved the little time that I got to spend with them, and loved their willingness to gather and go brighten spirits, which they did, wherever they played.[7]

The WBT Briarhoppers began working with school children in North Carolina. As part of the "Folk Arts in the Schools" program sponsored by the North Carolina Arts Council, students who would ordinarily listen

The WBT Briarhoppers in the 1970s. Back row left to right are Hank Warren and Don White. Front row left to right are Roy Grant and Arval Hogan. Courtesy Dwight Moody.

only to pop idols on AM radio were spellbound by the Briarhoppers' music and humor, and clamored for encores and autographs.

The 1970s marked the decade that the WBT Briarhoppers began a successful relationship with Bob Evans Farms, in Rio Grande, Ohio, where they played at their annual farm festival. According to Gale Leslie, assistant manager of events at Bob Evans Farm, "The Briarhoppers performed at the Bob Evans Farm Festival on the Homestead stage from 1979 to 2000."[8]

During this decade, the WBT Briarhoppers made several appearances on the Fred Kirby television show. Kirby, a former Briarhopper, had found new fame as the "Singing Cowboy at the Rocking K Ranch" on WBTV, channel 3 in Charlotte, where he would sing and show old *Little Rascals* shows. Emery Wister records the reactions of the Briarhoppers in the *Charlotte Observer*.

"Sure is nice to be back," Claude Casey shouted over the din when the first number had been completed. "Why, I haven't seen Bill Davis here since 1958."[9] "I thought it would be a good idea to get the gang back for a special show," said Kirby, 65, one of the original Briarhoppers. "I've been looking forward to this for a long time."[10]

The comedy, based on the age of the performers, was hot and heavy. According to Wister, "A camera operator asked if all the fellows could see the cue cards that provided guidance and instruction. 'See the cards?' asked one Briarhopper. 'I can't even see the fellow holding them.'"

Wister wrote that, during a commercial break, "One of the Briarhoppers shouted to a man in the studio audience, 'Hey, I can see the whiskers on your leg from here.'[11] The man in the audience shouted back, 'Why don't you fix it for me?'" According to Wister, the man "unstrapped an artificial leg and held it out to the Briarhoppers. No takes, but a lot of laughs."[12]

Charles Crutchfield declined to be on the reunion show. "The audience wouldn't relate. I'll leave that to the personalities," he said.[13]

Uncle Jim Mahaffey, who in real life was Jim Patterson, the first person to sign WBTV on the air in the 1950s, played the role of Charles Briarhopper Crutchfield as the announcer. Uncle Jim made up some commercials, one of which the author remembers when he saw the program as a young boy:

The Classic WBT Briarhoppers in the 1970s. Left to right: Hank Warren; Don White; Roy Grant; Arval Hogan; Shannon Grayson. Courtesy Dwight Moody.

Do you feel tired, bloated, ill-at-ease? Then what you need is Ruby's Random Rubbing Compound. Rub Ruby's Rubbing Compound on your brow and feel that cool, tingling relief in minutes.... Hey lady, would you quiet your baby, I'm trying to do a commercial.... Rub Ruby's Rubbing Compound on your brow and feel that cool, tingling relief in minutes. You won't have any eyebrows left, but who needs them.... Mix a little Ruby's Rubbing Compound with a little turpentine and "Wow!" Get Ruby's Random Rubbing Compound from your favorite store. You will appreciate it![14]

Another interesting thing about the show that day was when Fiddlin' Hank saw a patrolman in the audience: "Always a state cop around.... No matter where we'd go in the old days, we'd see one."[15] "He saw me," said the trooper, C.J. Roger of Charlotte. "I've been in Charlotte for 34 years now and always was a Briarhopper fan. I remember once I was riding a new patrolman around with me. He was still in training and when we stopped this car for going too fast, I sent the trainee to the car to talk to the drivers.... It was a car full of Briarhoppers and one of the fellows had

The WBT Briarhoppers on the *Fred Kirby Show*, WBTV, in Charlotte, NC, in 1976. Left to right: Jim Patterson; Hank Warren; Claude Casey; Shannon Grayson; Arval Hogan; Don White; Roy Grant; Bill Davis; Fred Kirby. Courtesy Dwight Moody.

a freckled face, red hair, and was wearing big red britches and red under-wear. It scared him so badly he almost quit."[16] (Refer to page 93 to read the Briarhoppers' memories of that night.)

George Hamilton IV moved back to Charlotte from Nashville espe-cially for Arthur Smith's local TV show. "Arthur and I used to go to places like the Mineral Springs [North Carolina] Music Barn and places like that just to hear bluegrass music. Several times, the WBT Briarhoppers were there and I got to 'rub shoulders' with them. They were all great guys and Arthur Smith always talked about the WBT Briarhoppers in glowing terms. I never got to know them personally during this time, however."[17]

Former Briarhoppers

Thorpe Westerfield died on May 5, 1972, at the VA Hospital in Sal-isbury, North Carolina, according to his daughter, Terry Marshall. "He was just 61 years old and he died of heart disease.... He was still working at the family business at his death. With the medicines of today, he would still be alive," she said.

Homer Briarhopper Drye continued his growing success in the Raleigh, North Carolina, region, spurning offers to join the *Grand Ole Opry*. Briarhopper began an hour-long television show on WRAL televi-sion in Raleigh.

Billie Burton Daniel began working with the Employment Security Commission in Raleigh, North Carolina.

Cecil Campbell started a record label in Charlotte and Winston-Salem, North Carolina.

Harry Blair remained at Myrtle Beach, South Carolina, in retire-ment.

Tex Martin continued his radio career throughout the Midwest.

Sam Poplin took several engineering jobs before he started in the clock business.

Bill Davis continued to play gigs with the WBT Briarhoppers when he could, but remained basically retired in South Carolina.

Claude Casey continued his radio station ownership in South Car-olina and played with the WBT Briarhoppers when his time allowed.

Charles Crutchfield retired from Jefferson Pilot as its president.

Eleanor Bryan Fields still lived in Goldsboro, North Carolina.

Billie Ann Newman Carson retired from the music business in 1971. "I left when I could still sing, but I could tell that I was losing it. I remem-ber hearing Rosemary Clooney on a record and I thought, 'God, she sounds terrible. She should have quit when she could still sing.' I wanted to leave it before somebody thought that about me."[18]

Carson moved to Fort Lauderdale, Florida, in 1971, and moved back to Charlotte in 1975.

Timeline for the 1970s

1970 — Ground was broken for Opryland in Nashville. The Environmental Protection Agency was formed.

1971 — WBT moved to a Top 40/adult music format. "The Pentagon Papers" were published in the *New York Times*. Bill Monroe was elected to the Country Music Hall of Fame.

1972 — Whitey and Hogan, Hank Warren, Don White, and Shannon Grayson reformed the group based upon trickery from their spouses. Nixon was reelected. Burglars were arrested at the Watergate Hotel.

1973 — *Charlotte Observer* reporter Dot Jackson reported in the paper that the WBT Briarhoppers were back (the news made the local TV news). *Roe vs. Wade* was decided in the U.S. Supreme Court. Native Americans protested at Wounded Knee, South Dakota.

1974 — Opryland opened and the Ryman Auditorium held its last *Grand Ole Opry* show, with Marty Robbins being the last performer. The *Grand Ole Opry* show moved to Opryland with Marty Robbins being the first act to perform. Nixon resigned the U.S. presidency due to pressures and possible impeachment regarding the Watergate investigation. Gerald R. Ford became president.

1975 — Patty Hearst was kidnapped. Communists took over Vietnam.

1976 — America celebrated its bicentennial. *Viking II* landed on Mars.

1977 — Jimmy Carter was elected president. The movie *Saturday Night Fever* ignited the disco craze.

1978 — WBT was named one of the top radio stations in the United States by Arbitron and was named Station of the Year by *Billboard Magazine*. Mother Maybelle Carter died.

1979 — Lester Flatt and Sara Carter died. The WBT Briarhoppers began a 21-year relationship with the Bob Evans Farm Festival in Ohio. The Three-Mile Island nuclear plant almost had a meltdown in Pennsylvania. The Soviets invaded Afghanistan.

America's Musical Taste:
The top song for this decade was Don McLean's "American Pie."
The WBT Briarhoppers are still playing!

7

The 1980s: The Charlotte Country Music Story

Whitey and Hogan of the WBT Briarhoppers were invited to play at the 1982 World's Fair in Knoxville. Grant remembers how they got to be in the World's Fair:

> We played in Johnson City, TN, and I noticed a fella in the front row with holes in his jeans, and no one seemed to be talking to him. After our show, I went over to talk to him and after asking him some questions, I knew that he was smart. The next show we did, he was right there and then he would talk to me ... not Hogan, but me. He told me his name but I forgot it.
>
> One morning, I got a call and the voice asked if this is Whitey of W&H and I said yes and I asked who this was and he said that would be covered in a minute. He asked if me and Hogan would be interested in doing the World's Fair in Knoxville, TN, for one week. I told him that we would love it but one obstacle could be money. He gave us a price and I thought that that would be agreeable. But I asked again who am I talking to? Mr. Avery, that was his name and he was the one who I took the time to talk to in Johnson City, TN. He was booking acts for the World's Fair and wanted Whitey and Hogan only. That's how we got to Knoxville.[1]

Eddie Stubbs, announcer for WSM, told the authors in an email that when he was with the bluegrass band the Johnson Mountain Boys, he got to know the WBT Briarhoppers, but more specifically Whitey & Hogan.

When asked whether or not he kept any memorabilia from the fair, he said he was sad that he did not keep anything "but good memories. Polly and Evelyn [Whitey and Hogan's wives, respectively] would be at every show. When we finished our last note, they would be out looking at the exhibits and talkin' to people."[2]

The 1980s also saw the WBT Briarhoppers on National Public Radio. Grant conveyed his story about being on Garrison Keillor's radio show on March 9, 1985:

Garrison Keillor wrote to us and asked if we wanted to be on his "Prairie Home Companion" radio show. After we confirmed on the telephone, I told Garrison, "You know, our wives like to travel with us. If it is all right with you, we will take what you are gonna give us for airfare and use the money to drive up there with our wives. Garrison said, "I don't care how you get here, just be here for the program." We took two cars and our wives. They took care of us so well. The snow was so high [in Minnesota, home to Prairie Home Companion] that they had to tunnel out, walk under the snow in the tunnel, to get to the street."[3]

In an interview with the *Shelby Star*, the local newspaper for Shelby, North Carolina, Grant told reporter Joe DePriest that as Keillor introduced the Briarhoppers Grant crossed his legs. "Now Whitey," Keillor said, "be calm, you'll get your chance to shine." The Briarhoppers performed the songs "Prisoner's Song," "Silver Haired Daddy of Mine," "Dear Old Dixie," and "Wreck of the Old 97."[4]

Grant continues:

We enjoyed doing the show with Garrison. He asked me a question on the air, "Whitey, how much mail did you get on WBT?" I told him that we got 10,000 letters in one day. Garrison asked me if there was something going on special. I told him that Hank's wife was havin' a baby and we were having a contest to see who in our audience would name the baby and win five dollars. Garrison asked me what the winning name was, and I said, "Larry." Well, Garrison had a fit, saying, "Out of all of that mail, the name 'Larry' was picked?" I said, "Yeah, and he still has the name."[5]

Grant remembers that the show was a sell-out. "The hall was packed and there were people outside in the snow waving signs that said, 'We need tickets.' People would follow us up there [in Minnesota] to hear us talk. Our Southern drawl they loved."[6] (The authors repeatedly contacted *Prairie Home Companion* officials regarding their memories of the show but received no response.)

Grant remembered one incident at a bluegrass festival where the WBT Briarhoppers were performing:

The makeup person for the *Andy Griffith Show* was Lee Greenway. Lee was a classmate of my wife Polly's brother and we all grew up together. One day, we were at a festival and Polly was helping sell our records. A Rolls Royce drove up, and out stepped Lee. I met him at the car and we said our hellos and such. He asked if we had any records to sell and I told him to go down to the table and if he would sweet-talk Polly, maybe she would give him a record.

Lee walked down to the table and started talking to Polly. He picked up a record, went to his wallet, and pulled out a hundred-dollar bill. Polly got a little flustered and told Lee that she did not have enough change to give him. Lee told her to keep the change and split it between the Briarhoppers.[7]

John Rumble, historian for the Country Music Hall of Fame in Nashville, Tennessee, began an Oral History project in which he interviewed old-time musicians and radio/record executives from the 1930s through the 1950s.

Rumble interviewed Whitey and Hogan, Fred Kirby, Claude Casey, Charles Crutchfield, and Cecil Campbell on a number of occasions for this project. Rumble also interviewed Thomas Jamison, record executive for Southern Record Company in Charlotte. The transcripts from the interviews are important because they captured the memories of people who have since died and the memories of the Golden Age of radio and of country music. Rumble provided the authors access to these records, which turned out to be an invaluable asset in the writing of this book.

An Old-Time Radio Reunion

Nineteen eighty-five was the year that "The Charlotte Country Music Story" occurred. With help from the Folk life Section of the North Carolina Arts Council and Charlotte's Spirit Square, a re-creation of the WBT Briarhoppers radio show was held with the WBT Briarhoppers, Snuffy Jenkins and Pappy Sherrill, Wade Mainer, Arthur Smith, Fred Kirby, Claude Casey, the Johnson Family, and Bill Monroe.

Charles Crutchfield and George Hamilton IV emceed the event at the NCNB Performance Place at Spirit Square. This was not only a concert, but also a multiday "classroom" tutorial of workshops about Charlotte's musical history, old-time music, culture and society in those days, mill hands and musicians, etc.

The schedule of events listed in the program that participants received, entitled "The Charlotte Country Music Story," were:

- Evening Concerts for Friday, October 25, 1985, 8:15 P.M.
- The Briarhopper Show featuring Charles Crutchfield, Announcer, Whitey & Hogan, Shannon Grayson, Hank Warren, Claude Casey, Fred Kirby, Betty Johnson, the Tennessee Ramblers with Cecil Campbell and Harry Blair, and the Johnson Family Singers
- Intermission
- George Hamilton IV, Emcee, Arthur Smith, Joe and Janette Carter, and the Red Clay Ramblers

Evening Concerts for Saturday, October 26, 1985, 8:15 P.M.:

- The Briarhopper Show featuring Charles Crutchfield, Announcer, Whitey & Hogan, Shannon Grayson, Hank Warren, Claude Casey, Fred Kirby, Betty Johnson, the Tennessee Ramblers with Cecil Campbell and Harry Blair, and the Johnson Family Singers
- Intermission
- George Hamilton IV, Emcee, Wade Mainer, Wiley and Zeke Morris, Snuffy Jenkins, Pappy Sherrill and the Hired Hands, and Bill Monroe and the Blue Grass Boys

Saturday Workshops:

- **The Piedmont in Transition, 1880–1940**, with Molly Davis, Glenn Hinson, James Eludes, Allen Tulles
- **Mill Hands and Musicians**: Country Music in the Piedmont, with Whitey & Hogan, and Pappy Sherrill
- **Kent Revisited**: Perspectives in Culture and Society in the Carolina Piedmont, with Hylan Lewis and John Kenneth Morland
- **Old-time Music in the Carolinas**, with Wade Mainer and Friends
- **Masters of the Banjo**, with Shannon Grayson, Snuffy Jenkins, and Wade Mainer
- **The Johnson Family Singers**, with Betty Johnson
- **It's Briarhopper Time**, with Shannon Grayson, Hank Warren, Don White, and Whitey & Hogan
- **Western Music Eastern Style**, with Claude Casey with Kelland Clark, the Tennessee Ramblers with Cecil Campbell and Harry Blair, Don White and Sam Poplin
- **Country Music and Comedy**, with Snuffy Jenkins, Pappy Sherrill and the Hired Hands
- **Country Music Comes of Age**, with Arthur Smith and Clay Smith, Tommy Faile, and Roy Lear
- **The Red Clay Ramblers**[8]

There were also exhibits in this program, including a photographic exhibit on the history of early country music radio and recording in Charlotte from the 1920s to the 1940s, entitled "The Country Music Story," and a photographic exhibit on textile mills and mill village life in the Charlotte area from the 1900s to the 1940s entitled "Weave and Spin."[9]

During this program, Grant remembered an instance involving Bill Monroe: "I was really tired because we had been practicing for this event all day. I was sitting in a chair, half-asleep, trying to take a nap. Bill

Monroe saw me and went back somewhere and got his mandolin out of its case. He came up right to my head and played a hard, loud chord in my ear! I said, 'Goodness sakes alive!' and Bill looked at me and said, 'Ain't that purdy?' I told him, 'No, not really!' Bill then took his mandolin back and put it in his case."[10]

This was also the time when George Hamilton IV began to understand the importance of the WBT Briarhoppers in country music. "It was maybe John Rumble [Country Music Hall of Fame] or George Holt [North Carolina Folklife Section], or maybe Arthur Smith who got me involved with this program," Hamilton IV said. "Through the Charlotte Country Music Story, I was able to learn how important that the WBT Briarhoppers were not only to Charlotte and the Carolinas, but to country music. I gained a great respect for them that weekend. Although I didn't know them personally, I was more of a fan because I was in awe of their tenure in music history."[11]

The original video tapes of these shows were found by WTVI's Regina Berry after the authors of this book inquired about them numerous times. For years, the tapes were thought lost; WTVI management was convinced the tapes were discarded. These tapes are now being copied into a digital format by WBTV for preservation and possible future use.

Whitey and Hogan were invited to perform at a month-long concert tour in Holland and West Germany. According to Joe DePriest, "Most of their shows will be in Holland, through the courtesy of A.G. and Kate Buening, Europe's most popular acoustic music duo and founders of the Little Grand Ole Opry."[12]

The "Little Grand Ole Opry" is located in Ryen, the Netherlands, and is a bastion of old-time country music in Europe.

The Buenings, mostly known to fans in Europe and North America as A.G. and Kate, perform prison ministry activities in the United States and Europe. According to Grant, A.G. and Kate heard Whitey and Hogan records and began to sing them overseas. They sang them so much that many people wanted to see Whitey and Hogan in person.

Grant said that a man and his wife rode bicycles 26 miles to and from one of the concerts.

Grant added some more information about the Holland trip in an interview in April 2005: "Hogan and I were touring Europe. We were in Holland at a U.S. Air Force Base. Our sponsors told the head of the base that we liked to sleep late in the mornings. The commander of the base had three fighter planes zoom over our rooms where me and Hogan and our wives were sleeping, and made all kinds of noise."[13]

Top: Whitey and Hogan performing with A.G. and Kate Buening in the Netherlands, 1984. Left to right: Kate Buening; Arval Hogan; Roy Grant; A.G. Buening. *Bottom:* Whitey and Hogan performing in 1984 at the Dutch Reformed Church in the Netherlands. Both photographs courtesy A.G. and Kate Buening.

The Grants and the Hogans at their hotel in the Netherlands, 1984. Courtesy A.G. and Kate Buening.

As most people who have been in Holland know, there are a lot of bicyclists in the Netherlands, and the bikers have the right-of-way on the road and in the bike lanes through the cities. The Grants got to know biking politics up close and personal. "When we walked around, all we could hear was the 'ching-ching' of the bells on the bikes. Well, Polly was in a bicycle path and we didn't hear the 'ching-ching.' A bicycle rider hit her.... He only grazed her but it scared him to death. He stopped, looked at us, and then rode away yelling in Dutch. We couldn't understand what he was yelling, but the only thing that we could understand was the word 'Dummy.'"[14]

Grant remembered that he and Hogan were to follow "the most famous bluegrass band in Holland. We were going on last in the show, and when they introduced the Holland band, the crowd started to yell, 'We want Whitey and Hogan.... We want Whitey and Hogan.' They kept up the chant until that band got finished. We were a little embarrassed."[15]

"During our show, we were playing a number, like 'Dust on the Bible,' or something similar," Grant remembered, "and we heard the crowd murmuring, and it got louder and louder. We thought that they did not like what we were playing, but we played on until the song was done. It was only later that one of our sponsors told us that the crowd was singing the song that we were playing, and they were singing in Dutch."[16]

During this decade, the place where the WBT Briarhoppers made their home for years, The Wilder Building, former home of WBT and its studios, was torn down for the sake of bringing modern buildings to the Charlotte scene. This practice would become a normal thing in the downtown area as Charlotte raced to get rid of vintage buildings so that the town could become a "world-class" city along the lines of Atlanta. The WBT Briarhoppers attended the demolition.

"When the Wilder Building was being torn down, I called the Charlotte Observer and told them that something was going on and that they needed to cover it," Grant said. "They asked what was I talking about, and I told them that they were tearing down the Home of the Briarhoppers. A reporter came down and took a picture of us at the building and did a story on it. She hopped right on it."[17]

The 1980s would be a fruitful decade for the WBT Briarhoppers as they seemed to be at every major music event in the region, or they were being celebrated as a Charlotte treasure. Every year during the 1980s, the WBT Briarhoppers were a featured group at the Bob Evans Farm Festival in Ohio.

This decade was also a time when a now-famous banjo player began her career on stage. Kristen Scott Benson, Hogan's granddaughter, took the stage several times, the first time being when she was seven years old. Benson, now a major banjoist in the bluegrass world, fondly remembered her grandfather in several emails to the authors.

Grant remembered that "Kristen, she would go out by herself with her mandolin and play in the stands or in the fairway if it was a fair.... The people who ran the stands would make sure that she had plenty of hotdogs and hamburgers and a nickel or dime. We would be playing on stage and she would come up to us Briarhoppers and ask if we were hungry because she had all of this food."[18]

Former Briarhoppers

Homer Briarhopper Drye died in May of 1983 after a long illness.

In his obituary in the *Charlotte Observer* on May 20, 1983, the Associated Press mentioned that Homer Drye:

performed with entertainers such as Eddy Arnold, Bill and Charlie Monroe, Roy Acuff, Loretta Lynn, and Elvis Pressley.... Drye played only for special occasions, against doctor's orders, since his retirement six years ago.... Charles

C-30:—THE WILDER BUILDING, CHARLOTTE, N. C.

A postcard of the Wilder Building in Charlotte, NC, unknown date. Courtesy Tom Hanchett.

The **WBT Briarhoppers witnessing the demolition of their home from the 1930s to the 1950s, the Wilder Building. Left to right: Shannon Grayson; Don White; Hank Warren; Roy Grant; Arval Hogan. Courtesy Dwight Moody.**

Crutchfield of Charlotte, who originated the Briarhopper radio show and hired Mr. Drye, remembered him fondly ..."He had a smile you couldn't forget ... [h]is face expressed sincerity. He was very intense, very likeable, and quite a good musician...." In 1971, Mr. Drye talked about country music's appeal. "It appeals to all people, although some won't admit it ... [w]e have a great following among city folks. And you take hillbilly — or country music—and put it on the Lawrence Welk show, and they'll admit they like it there."[19]

Billie Burton Daniel continued her work in Raleigh at the Employment Security Commission. In 1981, her former husband, Bob Daniel, died. In 1989, her daughter, Jennifer Kingsland Daniel, died. In a July 17, 2005, email to the authors, Daniel said that her daughter was the single most important person in her life.

Cecil Campbell and Harry Blair reunited for the "Charlotte Country Music Story" concert in 1985. Tex Martin was invited to attend but prior commitments prohibited him from joining his former band mates. Campbell worked with Claude Casey and Don White with the Western Film Festival in North Carolina a few years before his death in 1989.

Sam Poplin retired from the clock business in 1980, but continued to work on grandfather clocks. He continued to play his fiddle for his personal enjoyment. He participated in the "Charlotte Country Music Story" in 1985.

Fred Kirby was winding down his long and distinguished career as a television cowboy, but still made some personal appearances. In 1982, the movie *Atomic Café* used his songs in the movie and the soundtrack that was sold.

Big Bill Davis died during this decade. Davis was the longest-serving WBT Briarhopper. That mantle was left to Don White.

Tex Martin retired from radio and music and settled down in Illinois.

Eleanor Bryan Fields remained in Goldsboro in retirement.

Billie Ann Newman Carson continued to live in Charlotte in retirement.

Doug Mayes came out of retirement to coanchor WSOC *Eyewitness News* in Charlotte and was inducted into the North Carolina Broadcasters' Hall of Fame.

Timeline for the 1980s

1980—John Lennon was gunned down in New York City

1981—AIDS was first diagnosed. Ronald Reagan was elected president.

1982—WBT-AM was the first AM station to go to stereo in the Carolinas.

1983—Gaylord Broadcasting Company purchased WSM, Opryland, and Opryland Hotel. Nashville Network began on cable TV. Jimmy Dickens was elected to the Country Music Hall of Fame.

1984—Ernest Tubb died. TNN began on cable TV. WBT Briarhoppers performed at the World's Fair in Knoxville, Tennessee, and on NPR's *Prairie Home Companion* radio show. Geraldine Ferraro was nominated as the first female vice presidential candidate.

1985—*Grand Ole Opry* was on TV for the first time. President Reagan was reelected president.

1989— George Bush was elected president. The Berlin Wall fell. The *Exxon Valdez* spilled its oil load in Alaska's Prince William Sound.

America's Musical Taste:
The top song for this decade was Tina Turner's "What's Love Got to Do with It."

The WBT Briarhoppers are still playing!

8

The 1990s: Knockin' on Heaven's Door

For the first time in over fifty years, the rejuvenated WBT Briarhoppers had to think about succession planning.

Shannon Grayson, the banjo player for the group for over forty-six years, was developing Alzheimer's. At a performance at Mineral Springs Music Barn, Grayson told his band mates that they needed to find another banjo player, due to his health.[1] "We told him the he'd be first and foremost, our best banjo player," Whitey Grant said to Crystal Dempsey, staff writer for the *Charlotte Observer*.

Grayson died at age 76, on Monday, May 10, 1993. Grant said in Grayson's death announcement in the *Charlotte Observer*, "He was an all-around good musician. He loved to play and loved to meet people. He was a great talker."[2]

Grayson had already picked out the person to fill the Briarhoppers' banjo chair. David Deese, the banjo picker for Bill Monroe's Blue Grass Boys, Arthur Smith, the Jones Brothers and the Log Cabin Boys, and others, was the nominee.

David Deese

David Deese was born in Salisbury, North Carolina, on July 9, 1941. Tom Deese, David's father, who played guitar, and Burl Deese, David's grandfather who played banjo, influenced Deese's interest in music.

Deese has worked professionally with Arthur Smith, Bill Monroe and His Blue Grass Boys (which Deese played on the *Grand Ole Opry* many times), Red Smiley, the Jones Brothers and the Log Cabin Boys.

This banjo player's first "professional" gig was with J.E. Mainer, "back when he was getting popular again." Deese remembered there was a falling out between J.E.'s son and J.E.'s daughter:

> They hadn't heard from him [the son, who played banjo] in months, so I was called to play a date. I met J.E. while he was clearing brush at the church above his house.... That was how he made his money. I shook his hand and noticed his glasses. On one side, the arm of his glasses was normal, and on the other side, it was a piece of a clothes hanger connected to his glasses and going over his ear. Now, here was the famous J.E. Mainer, known throughout the world, and he made his money cleaning brush and had to wear broken glasses. I thought, "Is this what will happen to me after forty years in the music business?"
>
> We all went to wherever we played that day. Sure enough, J.E.'s son was in the audience. He came up on stage with his banjo and we played twin banjos. When it became time for a banjo solo, the son would nod to me to take it since I was hired to play banjo. It was a weird experience, but one that I would never want to forget.[3]

The first bluegrass festival was held at Fincastle, Virginia, in 1965, organized by Carlton Haney. Deese was present and played onstage with Red Smiley. On the fortieth anniversary of the event, Deese once again played onstage.

Deese discussed Shannon Grayson's banjo picking style, and how it was different from typical bluegrass-style picking. "Shannon played either two-finger or three-finger. It depended on the song and how fast the tempo was. But Shannon did not have what we call now a banjo roll. He played in 'phrases,' or, he did not play a whole roll. There really was no connective tissue between four notes and the next four notes ... sorta like a gallop. Snuffy [Jenkins] was a little like that, but he learned to put in that extra note to make it sound like a banjo roll. It was old sounding, choppy, and purely Shannon. The Briarhoppers had to adjust a little when they hired me to play banjo."[4]

A Vietnam veteran, Deese became a Briarhopper in 1991. "Shannon got to the point where he just couldn't go to where the Briarhoppers were scheduled to play. That is when he called me and I became a Briarhopper."[5] Dreese continued, "I called Whitey and asked when we were going to practice, and he told me to meet them at Berea College in Kentucky because we had a gig. That was Whitey's idea of practice."[6]

Deese also is an active Mason, Scottish Rite, and Shriner, Past Patron of the Eastern Star, a Blue Grass Boy, a Kentucky Colonel [Kentucky's highest award that was given to all of Bill Monroe's Blue Grass Boys], and is an accountant by trade. He is married to Barbara and they reside in Salisbury, North Carolina, with Deese working as a tax preparation professional by day, legendary banjo player by night.

With the help of the Matthews–Mint Hill, North Carolina, Rotary Club, the WBT Briarhoppers started the Briarhopper Fest in 1996, which ran for a few years in the Charlotte area.

Hank Warren died on December 16, 1993. Warren's obituary was in the December 18, 1993, edition of the *Charlotte Observer,* written by Tonya Jameson. Jameson reported that Whitey Grant said at the time of Warren's death, "Hank is the best comic fiddler that any of us have ever seen."[7] Bob Inman, former news anchor for WBTV, and currently a best-selling novelist and screenwriter, wrote an article on Shannon Grayson's and Hank Warren's deaths in the *Charlotte Observer,* part of which is shown below:

If you are listening to the wind moaning at the eaves or sighing through the branches of a tall pine and imagine you hear the faint strains of a fiddle, don't worry. It's Fiddlin' Hank. You might hear the ringing of a banjo, too. That's Shannon. And that tapping sound? That's God's foot, keeping time to a little bluegrass, thanks to a couple of old Briarhoppers.

Hank Warren, one of the finest fiddlers and nicest people to come out of the Carolinas in many a year, passed away back in December at the age of 88. He was preceded by Shannon Grayson, who could make the banjo talk. They were both original members of the Briarhoppers, a legendary string band with its roots deep in Carolina soil and its music a testament to what happens when talent meets heart....

So give an ear to the wind. If you listen carefully, you'll hear Hank and Shannon, playing at the heavenly hoedown.

Hank Warren clowning around at the doctor's office during the 1990s while directing Jim "Fiddlin' Scanc" Scancarelli on how to take the picture. Courtesy Jim Scancarelli.

Then go listen to the present-day Briarhoppers at a venue near you. You'll find yourself part of a big, enthusiastic audience, young and old, who are drawn to their music. Some folks say it's all about nostalgia. Heck no. It's because these guys are just plain good.[8]

Warren fell ill about four years before, and had to miss numerous events. South Carolina fiddler Homer "Pappy" Sherrill filled in as the Briarhopper fiddler.

Pappy Sherrill

Homer "Pappy" Sherrill began his fiddling in 1922 when his father bought him a Sears and Roebuck tin fiddle for Christmas. Sherrill took lessons from Dad Williams in Mooresville, North Carolina. His professional career began at the age of seven, when he played for his father at farmer's markets, selling watermelons.[9] By 1935, Sherrill was working for Bill and Earl Bolick (who later became the Blue Sky Boys) in Asheville, North Carolina, where they were sponsored by JFG Coffee and were known as the Good Coffee Boys—John, Frank, and George.[10]

In 1938, Sherrill learned "The Orange Blossom Special" from its co-composer, Ervin Rouse. Sherrill is credited with making the song popular in the two Carolinas.[11]

Sherrill joined Bryon Parker and his Mountaineers in 1938/1939, which included banjoist DeWitt "Snuffy" Jenkins. When Bryon Parker died, Sherrill and Jenkins formed the Hired Hands in 1948, in honor of Parker's nickname, the Old Hired Hand.[12] During the 1990s, Hank Warren began to miss shows due to illness. Whitey and Hogan contacted Sherrill, who agreed to play for the Briarhoppers when he could, outside of the Hired Hands.

Dwight Moody

Even though Sherrill filled in during Warren's illness, Warren had another fiddler in mind to take his chair in the group—Dwight Moody. Warren had approached Moody, owner of Lamon Records, to record some Briarhopper songs for a new album in the early 1990s.

Moody was born in LaCrosse, Virginia, on December 26, 1929. He learned to play the fiddle, guitar, and mandolin through the influence of his aunt and uncle.

He formed his first real band, the Virginia Playboys, in 1946, and had Curly Lambert on mandolin. Lambert would make his name immortal in music through his work with the Stanley Brothers, and his mandolin introduction to the Stanley Brother's classic song, "Angel Band," played on the now-influential and famous movie *Oh Brother, Where Art Thou?*

From 1947 through 1951, Moody played for the Wheeler Brothers, the Sunshine Rangers, and Clyde Moody and the Carolina Woodchoppers (with whom Moody made many appearances on the *Grand Ole Opry*). Moody also worked with Roy Acuff at Acuff's Dunbar Cave in Centerville, Tennessee, playing fiddle with Acuff, Red Foley, Bill Monroe, Clyde Moody, and others. He also spent two years in the Army with the 101st Airborne and the 5th Regimental Combat Team in Korea, receiving three Battle Stars while with the 5th.

Moody married Cathy Little, who was with the group the Sunrise Rangers, led by Little's brother, Tommy. Moody and family moved to the Charlotte area in the 1960s and had a television show. He also played with Clyde Moody and Homer Briarhopper in Briarhopper's band.[13]

Moody is in possession of one of the greatest fiddles in the musical world: the fiddle that Chubby Wise used when he first recorded "Orange Blossom Special." Moody sent the authors an email telling the story of how he came to possess this wonderful instrument:

> In 1948, I was working over at radio station WHIT-AM in Durham, North Carolina, with Cathy's [Moody's wife] brother, Tommie Little & the Sunrise Rangers. Clyde Moody (no relation) and the Carolina Woodchoppers moved from Washington, DC, to Durham and started playing dates in the Carolinas. He had been working on the *Connie B. Gay Show* at Constitution Hall for a few years and felt it was time to make a move, so he chose Durham. I met Clyde in the early 1940s while I was in high school, when he was with Bill Monroe. He came to South Hill High School with Bill and played with the black baseball team that afternoon after the show.
>
> Clyde wanted to use twin fiddles so he hired me to twin with Chubby [Wise] in April of 1949. We toured the eastern states on through that summer. Chubby left for a while and later returned, in late summer, and we made dates up in Virginia and Maryland. On returning to Raleigh, North Carolina, Chubby had a telegram from his wife in Lake City, Florida, that he must come home. He needed money for a train ticket so he offered to sell me his fiddle, the one he said that he had recorded the famous "Orange Blossom Special" in 1939, if I'm not mistaken, this is the date he told me and Billy Grammer at the train station where I carried him to catch the train.
>
> I was with him again in Raleigh a few years later and offered to sell the fiddle back to him and this time he told me to just hold on to it. Cathy and I met him again at the Charlotte Coliseum in 1962, when he was with Hank Snow, and I offered to sell it back to him again and his very words were, "Dwight, as long as I know you have it, it will be safe." That's the last time that I offered to sell it back.

The fiddle became a part of my style of fiddling, the touch was right, the sound was mellow, and the action was perfect. I have had the bridge replaced a few times, but always went back to the one that was on it when I first bought it. The fiddle had been touched by the master's hand — Chubby Wise — and I did not want to part with it.[14]

Moody is an ordained Methodist minister, and even he was surprised with what happened when he played Wise's fiddle at a certain concert. "I remember the first time that I played Chubby Wise's fiddle with Clyde Moody's son, who was playing his father's guitar," Moody reflected. "When we hit the first notes, it was apparent that the fiddle recognized the guitar. Both had been on many Bill Monroe records. For that entire night, the instruments were talking to each other and having a family reunion. I am an ordained Methodist minister, and the hair stood up on my arms, it was so intense."[15]

Moody also remembered when he almost became a member of the Stanley Brothers:

One of the important aspects of my career was when I was asked by Ralph Stanley to join his band as fiddle player. There was Curly Lambert, my old student, playing mandolin, and he was really hoping that I would join up. I had to tell Ralph that I wished I could accept his offer, but I had a family and I could not envision traveling all over the world, at that point, and leave Cathy with the kids.... My family was, and still is, most important to me. I still remember the look on Curly Lambert's face when he realized that I was not going to be part of Ralph Stanley's group."[16]

In 1985, Moody and his three sons, Trent, David, and Carlton (professionally known as the Moody Brothers), were nominated for a Grammy in 1985 for their instrumental, "Cotton Eyed Joe," and a second nomination in 1989 for "The Great Train Medley."

Moody joined the Briarhoppers in 1993. As the remaining Briarhoppers got older, the band members used it to their advantage onstage. Many times, Whitey Grant would say to the audience:

"We're so old that it takes us an hour and a half to watch *60 Minutes*."

"Santa Claus came down the chimney at one church we were playing.... He saw us and said, 'Hey, I remember the Briarhoppers when I was a boy!'"

"I just got married again. We spent our honeymoon getting out of the car."

In 1994, the Western Film Festival, a North Carolina–based festival honoring vintage Western films and their stars, started the Ernest Tubb Award, which was given to individuals who had made significant contributions through their work in movies, television, recordings, and personal appearances. Justin Tubb, son of Ernest Tubb, with the festival, was a driving force in helping select the honoree.

WBT Briarhopper Don White won the award in 1999 and was presented with it in Charlotte, North Carolina, at that year's festival. Other winners of this award include Justin Tubb, Sheb Wooley, Patsy Montana, Stonewall Jackson, Johnny Western, Hank Thompson, Tommy Overstreet, George Hamilton IV, Freddie Hart, Rose Lee Maphis, and the Statler Brothers.

In 1991, Garrison Keillor wrote a book, *WLT — A Radio Romance*. The book appears to be telling a story with WBT radio, the WBT Briarhoppers, and the WBT radio shows of the 1940s, including *Carolina Calling* and *The Dixie Jamboree*, in mind. The story occurs in Minnesota. The authors tried to contact Keillor but did not get a response.

A collection of essays entitled *New Magics*, contained a short story written by Andy Duncan called "Liza and the Crazy Water Man," which is set around the WBT Briarhopper radio show of the late 1930s and is complete with a description of the WBT Briarhopper radio show and the products that were advertised on the show. Cameo appearances in the short story include those of Charles Crutchfield, then–Charlotte Mayor Douglas, Mr. Tate the barber, and Kokenes Family at the Star Lunch, and the staff of the *Charlotte News*.

Duncan shared with this book's authors about why he chose WBT and the WBT Briarhoppers radio show as the focal point of his short story:

"Liza and the Crazy Water Man" was originally published in the World Fantasy Award-winning anthology, *Starlight 1*, edited by Patrick Nielsen Hayden, and published in 1996. I wrote "Liza" in 1994, when I was in graduate school at North Carolina State in Raleigh [North Carolina], though I actually wrote the bulk of it in a dormitory at Seattle University in Washington State.

My research for this story was easy, because I had a very specific time and place in mind. The North Carolina Division of Cultural Resources [in 1985] had sponsored a celebration in Charlotte of the city's nearly-forgotten country music heritage, reuniting many old-time performers for whom Charlotte had been a home base.... I hadn't attended [the celebration] but my friend Barry Johnson had, and told me all about it. I also had a copy of *The Charlotte Country Music Story*, a wonderful historical booklet, rich with text and illustrations, that [the North Carolina] Cultural Resources had published in commemoration of the event.

[From all of this] I settled on 1936 for various reasons.... With the place and date decided, I went through every illustrated book of Charlotte history that I could lay my hands on.... I believe that everything I knew of the Briarhoppers at the time I wrote the story came from *The Charlotte Country Music Story*.[17]

In 1998, the Levine Museum of the New South created an exhibit called "Don't Touch That Dial: Carolina Radio Since the 1920s." Pamela Grundy was guest curator and Jean Johnson was executive curator. The WBT Briarhoppers' music was a major part of the exhibit.

Former Briarhoppers

Charles Crutchfield died on August 19, 1998. His obituary in the *Charlotte Observer* stated his accomplishments: "Charter Member of the Broadcasting Hall of Fame; Chamber of Commerce President; U.S. Chamber Board of Directors; Broadcasters Precept Award; Distinguished Citizen Award, Civitan Club; Chairman of the Board, Charlotte Salvation Army; NC Association of Broadcasters' Distinguished Service Award; Chairman of the Board of NC Agency for Public Telecommunications; Director of CBS Advisory Board; Honorary Doctorate from Belmont Abbey and Appalachian State University."[18]

Roy Grant said, "He [Crutch] depended on Whitey and Hogan more than anyone realized. He relied on us to keep the show going. He was a great man and he was really good to all of us Briarhoppers."[19] Grant also remembered that when Charles Crutchfield died, the WBT Briarhoppers were asked to play at the funeral. WBT radio personality Henry (Hello Henry) Boggan came in and sat behind the wives of the Briarhoppers in the church. One of the wives turned around to talk to Boggan. The Briarhopper wife said, "Henry, you know that the Briarhoppers are playing here today?" Boggan, a long-time friend and fan of the Briarhoppers, said, "I know, but I came anyway."[20]

Claude Casey died on July 24, 1999, in Edgefield, South Carolina, at the age of 86. His obituary in the *Charlotte Observer* noted that Casey was a member of the Screen Actors Guild and the American Society of Composers and Authors.[21]

Children aged 5 to 95 cried when Fred Kirby, "The Singing Cowboy" and "The Victory Cowboy," died at his home in Indian Trail, North Carolina, on April 22, 1996, at the age of 86.

Prior to his death, punk music musicians Jello Biafra and Mojo Nixon recorded Kirby's song, "Atomic Power." After Kirby's death, PBS produced a documentary, *Race for the Superbomb*, and used Kirby's recording of "When the Hellbomb Falls."[22]

In retirement, Tex Martin began to perform at retirement centers and assisted-living centers in Illinois.

Eleanor Bryan Fields continued to live in Goldsboro, North Carolina.

Billie Burton Daniel (center) with family members, mid 1990s. Courtesy Billie Burton Daniel.

Billie Ann Newman Carson continued to live in retirement in Charlotte, North Carolina.

Billie Burton Daniel retired from the Raleigh Employment Security Commission in 1990 and moved back to Wilmington, North Carolina, where her sisters and other family members live.

Even in retirement, Mayes formed Doug Mayes and Company, which concentrated on training executives in media relations. Mayes also coauthored with Nancy Stanfield a pictorial history of Charlotte entitled *Charlotte: Nothing Could Be Finer.*

Timeline for 1990s

1991— WBT added *The Rush Limbaugh Show.* The Soviet Union collapsed. Bill Clinton was elected president.

1992— Gaylord Broadcasting began renovations on the Ryman. Roy Acuff died. Race riots occurred in Los Angeles.

1993— Janet Reno was the first female U.S. Attorney General and the FBI attacked the Branch Davidians in Waco, Texas. The Whitewater investigation began.

1994— WBT was named the Flagship Station for Charlotte's new NFL team, the Carolina Panthers. The Ryman opened again for bluegrass music. The O.J. Simpson murder trial began.

1995 — O.J. Simpson was found not guilty of the murder of his wife and Ron Goldman in Los Angeles.

1996 — Bill Monroe and Minnie Pearl died.

1997 — Pathfinder sent back pictures from Mars. Dolly the sheep was cloned in England.

1998 — The Monica Lewinsky/Bill Clinton stain-on-a-dress scandal hit the fan and the president was eventually impeached.

America's Musical Taste:
The top song for this decade was Nirvana's "Smells Like Teen Spirit."

The WBT Briarhoppers are still playing!

9

The 2000s: The WBT Briarhoppers at Twilight

This chapter title is taken directly from Joe DePriest, a writer for the *Charlotte Observer*, who chronicled the antics of the WBT Briarhoppers for years.

The WBT Briarhoppers continued to do concerts as this decade began. In 2000, the band was invited to perform at the Public Library Association's 8th National Conference. The WBT Briarhoppers rubbed elbows with librarians from North America and Europe, as well as special speakers Michael Gelb, children's writer Paula Danziger, poet Robert Morgan, and National Public Radio's Bailey White and Baxter Black.

The group was also honored as a recipient of the North Carolina Folk Heritage Award. The Folk Heritage Award was created in 1989 to recognize outstanding traditional artists with a lifetime achievement award.

In 2002, the WBT Briarhoppers were presented the Brown-Hudson Award from the North Carolina Folklore Society in Raleigh, North Carolina. The other winners that year were gospel singer Reverend Dready Manning of Halifax [N.C.], fiddler Oscar "Red" Wilson of Bakersville, potters Neolia Cole Womack and Celia Cole Perkinson of Sanford, wheelwright Emmett Parker Jones of Tyner, and master of Cherokee traditions Jerry Wolfe of Cherokee.

In the official announcement, the North Carolina Folklore Society cited the merits of the WBT Briarhoppers' award:

Since 1935, Roy Grant, Arval Hogan, Don White, Dwight Moody, David Deese, and other "Briarhoppers" have regaled audiences throughout the South with the fiddle breakdowns, gospel tunes, lively waltzes and sweet love ballads that they had learned while growing up amid the rich musical culture of the rural and small-town South. With their regular radio broadcasts on Charlotte's WBT, and with thousands of personal appearances, the Briarhoppers helped keep their listeners connected to the songs and sentiments of North Carolina's cultural heritage, even as the state's residents faced many changes sparked by rapid industrialization. Nashville's Grand Ole Opry, with its nationally celebrated array of star performers, came to North Carolina once a week through WBT's 50,000-watt signal; however, every day but Sunday was "Briarhopper Time." A 2002 Brown-Hudson Award from the North Carolina Folklore Society recognized their musical contributions.[1]

"We're thrilled to death," Roy Grant told *Charlotte Observer* reporter Joe DePriest. "We never thought we'd be recognized like this. Old-time music is coming back with a bang. That's the only kind we ever played. We've seen a lot of musical styles stay hot and then fade away, but the Briarhoppers are still in there pitching."[2]

John Rumble, of the Country Music Hall of Fame in Nashville, Tennessee, said, "The Briarhoppers represents the fundamental qualities of country music that made it successful in the first place ... things like artistry, authenticity, and the ability to communicate emotions openly and honestly.... North Carolina has a rich country music heritage and acts like the Briarhoppers are living treasures. Acts like this come around once in a lifetime."[3]

The WBT Briarhoppers continued to perform about five to ten times a month during the early part of this decade, and they really wanted to play in front of children at schools. Grant remembered a show at a Winston-Salem high school, and the principal was worried that the kids would not relate or appreciate the Briarhoppers. "I told him if we didn't entertain the kids, we wanted them to boo us off the stage.... After the second number, we had them eating out of our hands. They sat and watched and didn't make a sound except to applaud.... We just had something that clicked."[4]

One of the last times that Whitey and Hogan performed as a duo was at "Bluegrass Thursday Night©" in York County, South Carolina.

Arval Hogan died on September 12, 2003, in Charlotte. This was a sad event not only for the Hogan family and the Briarhoppers, but also for Roy Grant, who says, "He was my partner for over 60 years.... We were known as Whitey & Hogan since the 1930s. I doubted that I would ever play on a stage again."[5]

Grant was at Hogan's house the Wednesday before Hogan died. "[Hogan] said, 'Whitey, if I keep on feeling better like this, bring your guitar over tomorrow and we'll pick a tune.'"[6]

Musician David Holt said in the same article mentioned above, "If you are a musician in North Carolina, you have been influenced by Whitey and Hogan through their radio work, their songs, their professionalism and their gracious personalities."[7]

Grant said, in an interview with the authors, "A while back (before Hogan's death), Hogan called me over to his house and he wanted me to hear something. He played 'The Old Rugged Cross' and then wanted me to get my guitar so that we could record it together. Well, we did. At his funeral, that recording was played, as per his wishes. He never told me, but he wanted that song recorded so that it could be played at his funeral, the rascal."[8]

The Briarhoppers regrouped with another concert at "Bluegrass Thursday Night," founded by the authors. "That was the hardest time I have ever had," Whitey Grant remembered in an April 2005 interview. "That was the first time in over sixty years that I did not have Hogan singin' with me. I didn't think that I could do it."[9]

Dwight Moody confirmed this. "We knew that the future of the Briarhoppers rested with your concert in York, South Carolina. We were worried that Whitey couldn't pull it off. But he is a professional. He got through it. We knew that the Briarhoppers would be around a little bit longer."[10]

Although Hogan died, his granddaughter continues his legacy in the music business. Kristen Scott Benson recorded a CD entitled *Straight Paths* on the Pinecastle record label. Benson mentions her grandfather several times

in the liner notes of the CD. "I remember my grandfather singing this tune ['Just Because'] when he would come visit us. I would usually wake up to him playing his mandolin when they were at our house, but never before 9 A.M., per my request." She also said for the song "Put Me on the Trail to Carolina": "This is another tune that my grandfather taught me. I was about eight years old when he showed it to me on the mandolin and I can remember it seeming like it had a 1,000 chords!"[11] Benson continues to perform in Nashville and at bluegrass festivals throughout the United States.

Fiddlin' Dwight Moody, 2003. Courtesy Tom and Lucy Warlick.

Don White died at his home after a short illness. Many people who knew him personally said that he could not live without his wife, Mary, who died earlier in the year.

Wanting to keep the tradition alive, Briarhoppers III was formed in 2005, comprised of Whitey Grant, David Deese, and Dwight Moody, with David Moody playing bass on occasion. "We don't do a lot of school concerts anymore since Don White died. But we do a few," Grant said. "You know, whenever we do a show, we allot a little time so that the audience can ask us questions. When we are playing in front of children, they will usually ask these two questions: are you married and where did that funny name 'Briarhopper' come from?"[12]

The Western Film Fair invited the WBT Briarhoppers and the Jones Brothers and the Log Cabin Boys to play for its BBQ luncheon in Wadesboro, North Carolina, in May 2005. Tom Warlick, coauthor of this book, was honored to play banjo and dobjo (part Dobro and part banjo) with the WBT Briarhoppers III.

In an interview on December 13, 2005, Grant still remembers the time that the Briarhopper show came on. "Everyday, at 4:30 in the morning and 4:30 in the afternoon, I think about the Briarhoppers and the fans who enjoyed our music. If it wasn't for them, you would not be writing about us ... there wouldn't be any 'us.'"[13]

We asked Grant a simple question that he had never been asked: "When you are gone, do you want the Briarhopper name to continue?"

The legendary WBT Briarhoppers. Left to right: Dwight Moody; David Deese; Roy Grant; Arval Hogan; Don White. Courtesy Dwight Moody.

He thought long and hard, and tears came to his eyes. "No, I would hope that the boys would retire the name. I would like to leave it with Hogan and Fiddlin' Hank, Shannon Grayson, Don White, Charles Crutchfield, me, and the rest who have gone on. We can be the Briarhoppers in heaven with the rest who are up there."[14]

The WBT Briarhoppers on Record Again!

The WBT Briarhoppers were surprised to be on a newly released CD by Cattle Records out of Europe in 2006. The CD, *The Carolina Playboys Play and Sing Country Music,* were from recordings made by Sonora records in the 1940s.

Roy "Whitey" Grant remembers when those recordings were made:

> Me and Hogan and Don White, Fred Kirby, Claude Casey, Nat Richardson, Dewey Price, got the itch one day and we wanted to record some songs. A good friend of ours ... I forget his name, now ... was an engineer at WBT and lived off of Park Road in Charlotte. We told him that we wanted to do some recordings and he told us that he could record us at his house.
> We wanted to do something under another name since we had done everything under the "Briarhopper" name, so we came up with the name "The Carolina Playboys." We did a whole bunch of songs that day, with me and Hogan and Dewey Price doing the singing, and Fred and Don did some, and it really came out nice. I thought that was the end of it until somebody, possibly Fred Kirby or Claude Casey, sent the tapes to Sonora Records and, all of the sudden, there were records out under the name "The Carolina Playboys." Didn't make a dime off of it. Now you tell me that it is on a CD from Europe. I am 90 years old now. I can tell my friends and neighbors that I just put out a new CD although it was recorded in the 1940s.[15]

Former Briarhoppers

Billie Burton Daniel, living in Wilmington, North Carolina, started work at the Boutique at Stein Mart and began writing her book, "Whatever Happened to Billie Briarhopper." She relayed to the authors via an email dated July 17, 2005, "I cannot believe that next year it will be 70 years since I started being Billie Briarhopper."

Roy and Polly Grant ran into Eleanor Bryan Fields for the first time in a very long time at a show near Raleigh, North Carolina, in the year 2000. Polly wrote down Fields' telephone number, but they never kept in touch. In 2005, the Grants gave the authors the telephone number, which was for a residence in Goldsboro, North Carolina. When we tried dialing the telephone number, an automated message said that the number was

Top: The WBT Briarhoppers, winners of the 2002 Brown-Hudson Award from the North Carolina Folklore Society, 2002. Left to right: Don White; Dwight Moody; Roy Grant; Arval Hogan; David Deese. Courtesy Dwight Moody. *Bottom:* The WBT Briarhoppers at Bluegrass Thursday Night; York, South Carolina, 2003. Left to right: Dwight Moody; David Deese; Roy Grant; Arval Hogan; Don White. Courtesy Tom and Lucy Warlick.

no longer in service. When using the Internet, a search site showed her name, her address, and the same telephone number that the authors used.

The authors called every Fields in the Goldsboro telephone directory until one person knew where Fields had moved and knew her new telephone number. We called Fields the day after Christmas 2005 and surprised her with the announcement that a book was being written on the WBT Briarhoppers, that she would be in it, and that we had Whitey and Polly Grant's telephone number.

Fields commented that she used to have scrapbooks with decades of memories and photographs, but they were lost over the years. When asked if WBT had the files, we had to inform her that most of the files were destroyed during the move to WBT's current location. "It's crazy that no one would have kept those records at WBT. I guess, in later years, WBT didn't like country music anymore," she said.

Fields said during the interview that she does not perform anymore, except for her children. When asked if she had ever kept up with any of the WBT Briarhoppers, she said that she never did: "Isn't it bad that you spend time with people and then you lose touch and don't know what happened to them?"[16]

The WBT Briarhoppers at Don White's memorial, 2005. Left to right: Dwight Moody; Roy Grant; David Deese. Courtesy Tom and Lucy Warlick.

Billie Ann Newman Carson celebrated her 80th birthday with a party at her house in Charlotte. "My children put together a collection of my recordings and old pictures. I loved it very much. Whitey and Polly [Grant] came to my party, too!"[17]

Nobody had heard from Johnny McAllister since the 1930s. Many had assumed that he went back to New York, based on interviews with Billie Burton Daniel and written interviews with Charles Crutchfield. Some articles said that McAllister left with Homer Drye from Charlotte to Raleigh. McAllister's name barely shows up in any databases. Everyone thought he died a while ago.

While using a "people search" Website, the authors found a Johnny McAllister, age 106, living in New York City. The authors called information for his telephone number, and the operator confirmed the name but said that the telephone number was unlisted.

The authors contacted Daniel to determine how old McAllister would be now. She said that he was the same age as her mother was, and that her mother would be 106 years old today.

A letter was sent to this Johnny McAllister, asking him if he was the

The WBT Briarhoppers III, 2005. Left to right are Dwight Moody, Roy Grant, David Deese. Courtesy Tom and Lucy Warlick.

same McAllister who was on the WBT Briarhopper Show. As of the date of this book's publication, the authors have not heard back from this Johnny McAllister.

It would have been the crown jewel of this project to have located Johnny McAllister.

Timeline — 2000s

2000 — George W. Bush was elected president without getting the majority of the American votes. "Hanging Chad" became the phrase of the year.

2001 — The World Trade Centers in New York City were attacked by Osama bin Laden's al Qaeda and fell to the ground, killing thousands.

2002 — WBT went to a news/talk format. America invaded Afghanistan to get bin Laden, and leaders made the case that Iraq has weapons of mass destruction and warned the public of "mushroom clouds" from Iraq.

2003 — WBT Briarhoppers won the North Carolina Folk Heritage Award. WBT Briarhoppers performed one of their last concerts with the duo of Whitey and Hogan. Arval Hogan died. America invaded Iraq. June Carter Cash and Johnny Cash died. George Harrison died.

2004 — Don White died. George W. Bush was reelected U.S. president.

2005 — Lamon Records won Dove Awards for gospel recordings. Briarhoppers III was formed with Roy "Whitey" Grant, Dwight Moody, and David Deese, with David Moody playing bass at times. Joe Carter (son of A.P. and Sara Carter) died.

2006 — Janette Carter (daughter of A.P. and Sara Carter) died. NASA retrieved a space craft it had launched in 1997 which contained captured comet dust. NASA launched a space craft to study Pluto and beyond. Louise Scruggs, wife of Earl Scruggs, Ruby Mayes, wife of Doug Mayes, and Evelyn Hogan, wife of the late Arval Hogan, died.

And the WBT Briarhoppers are still playing!

Afterword

In 2003, my wife and I pulled into the parking lot of Allison Creek Presbyterian Church in York, South Carolina, the site of Bluegrass Thursday Night, one of the Carolinas' largest ongoing bluegrass jams that we started a few years ago. A single van was parked in the lot. All of the men in the van had on red shirts, dark pants, and white ties. All of the women in the van were straightening the men's ties. Out of the van came 87-year-old "Whitey" Grant, 91-year-old Arval Hogan, and 93-year-old Don White. The WBT Briarhoppers arrived one hour early to perform to what would be a packed house. I had already booked a group, the South Fork Boys, as the featured act that night. However, writer Joe DePriest, who wrote an article in the April 20, 2003, *Charlotte Observer* entitled "Briarhoppers at twilight," gave me the Briarhoppers' telephone number and said that they were looking for places to play. So, for this night, we had two featured acts.

"We've only missed one concert in our career.... It was when FDR died ... and nobody showed up to open the door for us, so it wasn't our fault!" said Grant, as he extended his hand to mine.

Dwight Moody, who replaced the late Fiddlin' Hank Warren, and David Deese, a former Blue Grass Boy who replaced the late Shannon Grayson, grabbed the equipment out of another vehicle. The band members' wives got out of the van, and we led them gently into the building.

The Briarhoppers thought that they were playing for a church function. They had no idea that 450 people would eventually line up at the door to get in and see the recent recipients of the 2003 North Carolina Arts Council's Folk Heritage Award.

My father arrived earlier than normal, driving the 28 miles from Lincolnton, North Carolina, to York, South Carolina. "He has been excited all week about this thing," said his companion, Faye. "It has been all that he has been talking about," she said of the 70-year-old man.

We set up the sound equipment. People begin to compare "Briarhopper" stories.

To check the sound, the host band that I play for, the Clover Feed & Seed Bluegrass Band, usually play "Roll in My Sweet Baby's Arms." As I started it out on the banjo, the Briarhoppers surrounded me quickly to play backup. We switched to an extended version of the song. My wife, Lucy, was quick to capture the moment with a camera.

I asked the band to modify their opening line by including my father's name. Sure enough, Hogan bent down towards the microphone and asked, "Bill, do you know whut hit is?" Dad dry mouthed, "Hit's Briarhopper Time!"

The band began to play. Well, some of them did. The others started about two seconds later. We forgot to raise the volume for musicians older than we were, and they couldn't hear each other. Once that got fixed, it was a night full of memories relived for the majority of our fans. The songs were clear and filled with the essence that I can only imagine young Bill and Charlie Monroe felt when they heard the Briarhoppers at WBT.

They played gospel songs and "country" songs, and did recitations. Don White, now playing an electric bass instead of an upright, sang a Spanish song and never missed a lick on the bass.

Each band member took time out to describe the various instruments they were playing. Hogan described his 1940 Gibson mandolin and Grant talked about his 1944 Martin Guitar. "I paid on a monthly basis to get this thing ... $125 total. I put about another $125 into it for a case and other things ... but I bet you that I would not sell it for $250 today!" Deese described a time when he played with Bill Monroe at a drive-in theater that was apparently only several miles away from the church where we were playing. Grant put one hand on Don White's shoulder and the other hand on Arval Hogan's shoulder and proudly told the audience that they "had been together as a group for nearly 63 years." DePriest's article mentioned earlier quoted Tom Hanchett, historian at the Levine Museum of the New South, as saying that the Briarhoppers "is the longest-running band to come out of the Great Depression era celebrated in the movie *O Brother, Where Art Thou?*"

At the side of the stage, the Briarhopper women sat around a table with a tablecloth that had the word "Briarhoppers" sewn on it, selling the various tapes and CDs for the band and talking to whoever came by.

The Briarhoppers ended their performance after 50 minutes, to a

Roy "Whitey" Grant remembering his old friends, 2005. Courtesy Tom and Lucy Warlick.

standing ovation. A mass of people lined up where the Briarhoppers were putting away their instruments. Comments ranged from "I remember when you guys came to play at my school in the 1940s," to "What was it like to play music with Mother Maybelle Carter?" My barber, Duke, brought an old Briarhoppers vinyl record for the band to sign, telling Don White as he signed it, "I saw you boys fifty years ago when I was in elementary school in Clover." Pickles, one of our most ardent fans, came up and said, "Tom, I heard these guys on the radio when I was a little boy. I am 72 years old. I never thought that I would see them in person. I feel like a kid again." My dad clutched an autographed photo that I had the band sign before they took the stage. The past was alive for many people that night, and we were glad to give it back to them if only for a few hours.

The next band to take the stage was the South Fork Boys, a trio consisting of a 15-year-old banjo player, a 15-year-old mandolin player, and the banjo player's father on bass. Although they have been together for a short time, I think that if anyone from our area makes it big, it will be these boys. These guys are so young that they consider me old. When they kicked into their second song, Dwight Moody grabbed his fiddle and played the set with them. Everyone could tell that he was having a ball playing with young musicians. Afterwards, Dwight Moody put his arm around my shoulder and said, "You really have something here. I have been to the [Grand Ole] Opry, and I have never seen anything like this, especially in this part of the world." The rest of the Briarhoppers were shaking the hands of the young boys who had just completed their set. Then Don White came up to me and said, "I really enjoyed your work.... You play like Snuffy [Jenkins] and hold a crowd together like Bryon Parker did in the '30s. I believe that you will keep this music alive when we are gone."

I don't know if the South Fork Boys understood the significance of this. I surely did. Realistically, the WBT Briarhoppers are at the twilight of their careers, to quote Mr. DePriest. To watch the musical stars of the 1930s interact musically with what is the future of bluegrass was moving. I hope that the South Fork Boys appreciated the passing of the torch, so to speak. I know that two grown-up boys from Lincolnton felt good about it.

Appendix A: Letters to the Briarhopper Fans

(Presented as written by its author)

December 12, 2005
Dear Folks out there in Radio Land:

I doubt if many of you are still around who remember the little girl who used to be me, the little girl who, more than anything, loved to sing. I was so lucky, because back then, there were so many of you who wrote to me, and wrote to Radio Station WBT and requested songs for me to sing, for Homer to sing, for Dad to sing, for all my "big brothers" to play and sing; it was because of you that Drug Trade Products continued to sponsor our show, and enabled us to perform for you, for the five long years that I was on the show. I say five LONG years, because when you're very young, five years seems like almost forever. Those five years when I was Little Billie Briarhopper were a wonderful part of my life.

I want to thank you all for the cards and letters and telegrams and packages, for the delicious cookies, for the candy, for the daffodils that came in the mail every March, for everything. And for you "shut-ins" who were out there in Radio Land, I thank you for asking me to dedicate my songs to you. That was a privilege. And for you, Father Rayfield and Father Girard over at Belmont Abbey, you were always so nice to me. All those telegrams and letters you sent. I loved singing those songs for you. I wonder if you really knew how much you meant to me. I thank you, Mayor Ben Douglas, for the ice cream cones you brought me. And for all of you who would come out of your stores and service stations, when I walked by, to tell me how much you enjoyed my songs that day. I can still hear you now.

I want to thank you, too, Mr. Crutchfield, for all of the nice things you said about me. They tell me that you were my biggest fan, and I want you to know the feeling was mutual. And for you, Mr. Kirby (Lee Kirby), I loved it when you announced the show. And Mr. J.B. Clark, I thought that you were the funniest man in the world. And Bill Bivens, what can I say? You just teased me to death about that little page boy that liked me that I did not WANT to like me. I was nearly always mad with you (but I couldn't help liking you).

Yes, I want to thank you all, though I realize that most of you have left this world and are now in a better place. Maybe, somehow, you'll see this letter anyway.

I'm the last, you know, the last of "Dad Briarhopper's original Briarhoppers." There's nobody left to "remember with." How wonderful it would be if I could go back to then, to just one more time hear Mr. Crutchfield say, "Hey, Pappy, what time is it?" and to hear Dad answer, "Why, Crutch, hit's Briarhopper time!!!!!"

Sincerely,
Billie Burton Daniel

Dear Fans:

As I am the last one of the Briarhoppers, I thought I would write you a sort of thank you note. You fans were and are the biggest things in the life of the Briarhoppers. If it weren't for you loyal fans there would be no Briarhoppers. You have stood in the cold and rain for hours waiting to buy a ticket to see us. Please don't think we don't appreciate this, we do. Also, you young fans, who would hurry home from school to listen to us on the radio. we also want to thank you wonderful fans for buying the products we sold on the radio.

Each time the clock says 4:30, whether it's a.m. or p.m., I think of you loyal fans again. I will say thanks to you, for if it weren't for you there would be no Briarhoppers. We thank you from the bottom of our hearts. we love you, just as much as you love us.

Thanks!
Roy "Whitey" Grant

Appendix B: Partial Discography of the WBT Briarhoppers

(Album/CD titles and Individual Band Members are in italics. Single records are not in italics)

The WBT Briarhoppers
Old Homestead Records

- *Early Radio—1977*
- *Whitey & Hogan with The Briarhoppers Volume 1—1981*
- *Whitey & Hogan with The Briarhoppers, Volume 2—1984*

Rounder

- *Early Days of Bluegrass, Vol. 1,* unknown date

Lamon Records

- *Hit's Briarhopper Time—1980*
- *Hit's Briarhopper Time, Again—1983*
- *Hit's Briarhopper Hymn Time—1988*
- *The Legendary Briarhoppers—1996*
- *The WBT Briarhoppers: Winners of the 2003 NC Folk Heritage Award—* 2003

Cattle Records

- *The Carolina Playboys Play and Sing Country Music*— 2003

INDIVIDUAL/DUO RECORDINGS:

Whitey & Hogan

- Decca Records
  Sunny Side of Life —1939
  You'll Be My Closest Neighbor —1939
  Gosh I Miss You All the Time —1939
  It's Alcatraz for Me —1939
  I've Changed My Mind —1939
  Ridin' On My Savior's Train —1939
  Turn Your Radio On —1939
  Tell Mother I'll Meet Her —1939
  Don't Be Knockin' —1939
  I Can Tell You the Time —1939
  Watching You —1939
  That's a Way with a Broken Heart —1939
  Answer to Budding Roses —1939
  Old Log Cabin for Sale —1939
  I'll Meet You in the Morning —1939
  Let Me Travel Along —1939

Don White

- Bluebird Records
  My Old Saddle Horse Is Missing (with Fred Kirby)—1936
- Decca Records
  Deep Sea Blues (with Fred Kirby)—1938

Shannon Grayson

- RCA Victor
  Roses and Thorns — unknown date
  Work Is All I Have — unknown date

Fred Kirby

- Decca Records
  Cathedral in the Pines —1938

Every Day Is Mother's Day — 1938
You're the Only Star — 1938
Calling Ole Faithful — 1938
Birmingham Jail — 1938
Columbus Stockade Blues — 1938
God's Love Will Shine — 1938
Precious Jesus I'll Be There — 1938
My Carolina Home — 1938
Prayer Meeting Time — 1938
Life's Railway to Heaven — 1938
Find My Precious Home — 1938
Bury Me Beneath the Roses — 1938
Deep Sea Blues — 1938

- Bluebird Records
    Get Along Old Paint — 1936
    Where the Longhorn Cattle Roam — 1936
    Night Time on the Prairie — 1937
    Home (Answer to Home on the Range) — 1937
    Hello My Baby — 1936
    I've Got a Red Hot Mama — 1936
    My Mother Comes from Ireland — unknown date
    My Sweet Mother on the Range — unknown date
    I'm Roughest and Toughest — unknown date
    Underneath Texas Moonlight — unknown date
    My Man — 1936
    My Heavenly Sweetheart — 1936
    Wagon Train Keeps Rolling Along — 1936
    Song of the Golden West — 1936

- Gennett Records
    Just a Little Bit of Driftwood — unknown date
    Get Out and Under the Moon — unknown date

- Sonora Records
    Atomic Power — 1946
    Honey Be My Honey Bee — unknown date
    My War-Torn Heart — unknown date
    The Wreck of the Old 97 — unknown date
    Deep in the Bottom of the Sea — unknown date
    Boogie Woogie Farmer — unknown date

My Little Boy Blue — unknown date
Casey Jones — unknown date
It's the Beginning of the End — unknown date
That's How Much I Love You — unknown date
After All These Years — unknown date
Downright Lonely, Downright Blue — unknown date
I Can't Tell That Lie to My Heart — unknown date
I've Been a Too Often and Too Long — unknown date
Somewhere a Heart Is Breaking — unknown date
Hang Your Head in Shame — unknown date
Our Hearts Beat Together — unknown date
Please Don't Take My Baby — unknown date

- Columbia Records
   The Old Country Preacher — 1952 (?)
   When the Hell Bomb Falls — 1952 (?)
   My Red Hot Potato — 1952 (?)
   My Zig Zaggin' Baby — 1952 (?)
   Lost — 1952
   Out of My Mind — 1952
   My Soul Is Not For Sale — 1952
   When It's Reveille Time in Heaven — 1952
   When the Devil Sends His Calling Card — 1952
   Crossroads to Eternity — 1952

- MGM Records
   My Little Dog Loves Your Little Dog — unknown date
   Jukebox Jackson from Jacksonville — unknown date

- Super Disk Records
   God Made This Country — unknown date
   The Almighty Dollar — unknown date
   I Thank My Lucky Star — unknown date
   A Greater Power — unknown date

- Cattle Compact
   The Original Atomic Power CD — unknown date

Fred Kirby and Bob Phillips

- Bluebird Records
   My Carolina Sweetheart — 1936
   My Darling Nell — 1936

Fred Kirby and Cliff Carlisle

- Bluebird
    That Good Old Utah Trail — 1936

Claude Casey / Claude Casey and the Pine State Playboys

- RCA Records
    Journey's End — possibly 1946
    Look in the Looking Glass — possibly 1946
    The Days Are Long and the Nights Are Lonely — possibly 1946
    I Wish I Had Kissed You — possibly 1946
    Two Little Girls With Golden Curls — 1946
    My Little Tootsie — 1946
    I Wish I'd Never Met You — 1946
    Family Reunion in Heaven — 1946

- Super Disk Records
    Juke Box Gal — 1946
    Carolina Waltz — 1946
    It's Hard To Lose These Lonesome Blues — 1946
    Living In Dreams — 1946

- Bluebird Records
    I'll Always Love You — possibly 1941
    You're Gonna Be Sorry — possibly 1941
    My Heart's in the Heart of the Blue Ridge — possibly 1941
    Lonesome as Can Be — possibly 1941
    It Doesn't Matter — possibly 1941
    What's Wrong with Me Now — possibly 1941
    Little Girl Go Ask Your Mother — possibly 1941
    When I First Met You — possibly 1941
    Hottest Little Baby in Town — possibly 1941
    Swinging with Gilbert — possibly 1941
    All I Do Is Dream — 1938
    Pine State Honky Tonk — 1938
    Don't Say Goodbye if You Love Me — 1938
    Boy from North Carolina — 1938
    Why Don't You Come Back to Me — 1938
    The Installment Song — 1938
    You're the Only Star in the Blue Sky — 1938

My Memory Lane —1938
My Heart Was Stamped with Your Name —1938
Kinston Blues —1938
Old Missouri Moon —1938
I'm So Lonesome Tonight —1938
Keep Praying —1938
Road Weary Hobo —1938
Happy Cowboy —1938

- Dot's Music Roundup
  History of Country Music —1928–1951—unknown

- Krazy Kat Records
  Dough Boys, Playboys, and Cowboys— 2003
  Farewell Blues— 2003

- Old Homestead
  Pine State Honky Tonk —unknown date

Homer Christopher and Wife

- OKEH Records
  After the Ball —1926
  Southern Railroad —1926

Homer Christopher and R. Van Link

- OKEH Records
  Lost Mama Blues —1927
  Red Wing —1927
  Going Slow —1927
  Spartanburg Blues —1927
  Alabama Jubilee —1927
  Hilo March —1927
  Honky Tonk Rag —1927
  Drifting Back to Dreamland —1927
  Sleep Baby Sleep —1927
  Old Fashioned Waltz —1927
  March in D —1927
  Farewell to Thee —1927

The Tennessee Ramblers either with Dick Hartman or Cecil Campbell

- Brunswick Records
  Cacklin' Pullet — 1928
  Arkansas Traveler — 1928
  Fiddlers Contest — 1928
  Preacher Got Drunk — 1928
  Medley of Mountain Songs — 1928
  Satisfied — 1938

- Bluebird Records
  How Beautiful Heaven Must Be — 1935
  My Little Hut in Carolina — 1935
  How Do You Do — 1935
  Dese Bones Gonna Rise Again — 1935
  Mountain Dew Blues — 1935
  Back to the Old Smoky Mountains — 1935
  Kentucky Jig — 1935
  Pennsylvania Hop — 1935
  Going Down the Road — 1935
  Dis Train — 1935
  New River Train — 1935
  New Red River Valley — 1935
  Birmingham Jail — 1935
  Who Broke the Lock — 1935
  Little Green Valley — 1935
  Sweetheart of the Mountain — 1935
  Dick's Hoedown — 1935
  Memories of the Old Hoedowns — 1935
  Leechburg Polka — 1935
  Rambler Bag — 1935
  Neath Hawaiian Palms — 1940
  All My Natural Life — 1940
  Blue Eyed Baby — 1940
  Grab Your Saddlehorn — 1940
  Don't You Sometimes Dream of Me — 1940
  Sweet Mama — 1940
  Steel Guitar Swing — 1940
  Come Swing with Me — 1940
  The Beach at Waikiki — 1940

I'm Through Wishing on Stars —1940
You Certainly Said It —1940
New Red River Valley —1940
Oh Mary Don't You Weep —1940
I Love Hawaii —1940
Why Should I Be Blue —1940
You're Always on My Mind —1940
Trumpet Talking Blues —1940
I'll Keep on Loving You —1939
Don't Put a Tax on That Beautiful Girl —1939
Over the Santa Fe Trail —1939
There's a Blue Sky —1939
Carry Me Back to Carolina —1939
Tonight You Belong to Me —1939
Hootchie Kootchie Koo —1939
Four or Five Times —1939
Out on the Lone Prairie —1939
Steel Guitar Blues —1939
Doug Ain't Doing the Jitterbug —1939
The Washboard Man —1939
I Like It That Way —1940
Coquette —1940
I'll Never Let You Cry —1940
Hard Hearted Love —1940
I Don't Know Why I Should Cry Over You —1940
I'd Love to Be a Cowboy —1940

- RCA Victor
    Chant of Hawaii — unknown date
    Campbell's Steel Guitar —1945
    I Trusted You —1945
    Last Night I Cried — unknown date
    Little Hula Shack — unknown date
    She's Got the Cutest Eyes — unknown date
    Steel Guitar Hop — unknown date
    It's Gonna Come Home to You — unknown date
    Hawaiian Moon — unknown date
    Talk, Talk, Talk — unknown date
    Hawaiian Dream — unknown date
    Please Dad, Don't Drink Any More — unknown date
    Time Will Tell — unknown date

I'm a Henpecked Man — unknown date
Midnight Boogie — unknown date
Hawaiian Skies — unknown date
Carolina Steel Guitar — unknown date
No Wedding — unknown date

- Jasmine Records
  Steel Guitar Swing— 2004
  Appalachian Stomp Down— 2006

- Krazy Kat Records
  Farewell Blues— 2003

- County Records
  Rural String Bands of Tennessee—1987
  Steel Guitar Swing—2004

- Buster Bronco
  Cecil Campbell and His Tennessee Ramblers— 2003

- Bear Family
  That'll Flat Git It—1996

- Big Tone BT
  MGM Rockabillies, Vol. 2 —1993

- Chief CCD
  Ultra Rare Rockabilly's Vol. 10—1993

- MGM Records
  MGM Rockabilly Collection Vols. 1 & 2—1997

- Winston Label
  Steel Guitar Jamboree — unknown date
  Lonesome at Twilight — unknown date

- Super Disk
  Each Night at Nine — unknown date
  Please Come Back — unknown date

Homer Briarhopper Drye

- Bluebird Records/Montgomery Ward (possibly with Johnny McAllister — spelled "Macalester" in the notes — and Big Bill Davis)
  Bill Bailey —1937
  If You Had the Blues —1937
  Lights in the Valley Outshine the Sun —1937
  Beautiful Home Sweet Home —1937
  Roses Bloom Again —1937
  Shall Not Be Moved —1937
  Mr. McKinley —1938
  I Am Just What I Am —1938
  Little Lulie —1938
  We Parted at the Gate —1939

- BACM Records
  BACM CDs 70–100 — unknown date

- Mercury Records
  Fifty Years of Country Music from Mercury —1995

- Lamon Records
  Chicken —1964
  What Did the Deep Blue Sea Say? —1964

Dwight Moody

- Numerous radio transcriptions

- Lamon Records
  Dwight Moody: Plays Fiddle with Family and Friends —2000

The Moody Brothers (with Dwight, David, Trent, and Carlton Moody)

- Lamon Records
  Cotton-Eyed Joe —1985 (Grammy nomination)
  Friends —1988 (Gold Record Award)
  Great Train Song Medley —1989 (Lamon/Supraphone) (Grammy nomination)
  The Moody Brothers —1989 (Lamon/Magnum Force — UK)
  Brother to Brother —1990
  Christmas with The Moody Brothers —1991

Guitar Boogie—1994
On a Blue Ridge Sunday: George Hamilton IV with the Moody Brothers—2004 (Dove Award nomination)

- Conifer Records — UK
  American Country Gothic (George Hamilton IV and the Moody Brothers)—1992

- Disney Records — Sony/France
  Disney's Country Music For Families—1995

- Supraphon Records — Czech Republic
  Country Express—1995

- Virgin/Sound & Media — UK
  The Moody Brothers Boxed Set—1998
  The Moody Brothers Line Dance Album—1998 (Gold Record)
  The Moody Brothers Line Dance Album II—1998 (Gold Record)

- Word Records — UK
  Streets of London—1999 (selected tracks featuring George Hamilton IV and the Moody Brothers)

David Moody

- Lamon Records
  I Will Follow You—2000
  Chet Atkins Tribute: Will The Circle Be Unbroken—2001
  Blinded—2002
  Right Where I Belong—2005

David Deese

- Session work for many acts, total number unknown

- Several albums with Red Smiley

- Several albums with the Jones Brothers and the Log Cabin Boys

- Deese Records (David Deese with Dixie Bluegrass)
  I'm Branching Out—1992
  I'm Just a Stranger Here—1993

Pappy Sherrill (With the Hired Hands)

- Numerous radio transcriptions

- Arhoolie
  Snuffy Jenkins — Pioneer of the Bluegrass Banjo —1998
  Carolina Bluegrass—1962

- Rounder
  33 Years of Pickin' and Pluckin'—1971
  Crazy Water Barn Dance—1976

Appendix C: WBT Briarhopper Comings and Goings

This listing is based on this book's research; the authors can be off by a few years for any person. Since this is the first time such a listing has been compiled, there will be some mistakes that will be corrected in future reprintings.

Please keep in mind that many of the artists listed below were WBT employees prior to becoming WBT Briarhoppers. The dates given reflect only their time with the WBT Briarhoppers, and not with their time with WBT radio or WBTV television.

- Charles Crutchfield starts the WBT Briarhoppers in 1934 and becomes the first WBT Briarhopper.
- Johnny McAllister gathers some hillbilly musicians — 1934
- Bill Davis joins in 1934
- Don White joins in 1934
- Jane Bartlett joins in 1934
- Thorpe Westerfield joins in 1934
- Clarence Etters joins in 1934
- Homer Drye joins in 1936
- Billie Burton Daniel joins in 1936
    - Jane Bartlett leaves in 1937
    - Don White leaves in 1938
- Charlie and Roger Davis join in 1938
- Hank Warren joins in 1938
- Gibb Young joins in 1938
    - Bill Davis and sons Charlie and Roger leave in 1938

- The Tennessee Ramblers join in 1938/1939
- Newell Hathcock joins briefly in 1940
    Johnny McAllister, Newell Hathcock, and Homer Drye leave
        in 1940
- Bill Davis returns in 1940 after McAllister leaves
- Fred Kirby joins in 1940
    Clarence Etters and Thorpe Westerfield leave in 1940
    Fred Kirby leaves briefly in 1940
- Floyd and Mildred join in 1940
- The Oklahoma Sweethearts join in 1940
    Billie Burton Daniel leaves in 1941
    The Oklahoma Sweethearts leave in 1941
    Floyd and Mildred leave in 1941
- Fred Kirby rejoins in 1941
- Claude Casey joins in 1941
- Dewey Price joins in 1941
    Dewey Price leaves in 1941
- Eleanor Bryan Fields joins in 1941
- Whitey & Hogan join in 1941
- Shannon Grayson joins in 1942
- Homer Christopher joins in 1942
- Don White returns in 1942
    Eleanor Bryan Fields leaves in 1942
    Gibb Young leaves in 1942
- Martin Schopp (Tex Martin of the Tennessee Ramblers) is drafted,
    leaves, and never returns as a WBT musician
- Charles Crutchfield becomes the station manager in 1945 and leaves
    the role of Charlie Briarhopper
    Fred Kirby and Don White leave in 1946
- Sam Poplin joins in 1946
- Nat Richardson joins in 1949
    Tennessee Ramblers leave in 1949
    Nat Richardson leaves in 1949
    Homer Christopher leaves in 1949
    Sam Poplin leaves in 1950

When the WBT Briarhopper show ended in 1951, the members were
Whitey and Hogan, Shannon Grayson, Hank Warren, Bill Davis, and
Claude Casey.

During the 1950s and 1960s, the WBT Briarhoppers performed in
various combinations that included one or more of the following in

each individual band setup: Whitey and Hogan; Don White; Hank Warren; Bill Davis; Shannon Grayson. WBTV newsman Doug Mayes performed at times with the WBT Briarhoppers either on guitar or on upright bass.

In the 1970s, the WBT Briarhoppers were the subjects of Dot Jackson's news article about their return to the music business. The group included Whitey & Hogan, Hank Warren, and Don White, with Doug Mayes and Jim Scancarelli either filling in or joining. With the amount of work done with the WBT Briarhoppers, these men are considered members of the group.

Performing on the televised *Fred Kirby Show*, the WBT Briarhoppers consisted of Whitey and Hogan, Don White, Bill Davis, Fred Kirby, Claude Casey, Hank Warren, and Shannon Grayson.

During the 1980s, the group was comprised of Whitey and Hogan, Don White, Hank Warren, and Shannon Grayson, with Bill Davis performing at times. The 1985 "Charlotte Country Music Story" included the WBT Briarhoppers comprised of Whitey and Hogan, Shannon Grayson, Hank Warren, Don White, Claude Casey, and Fred Kirby.

Big Bill Davis and Homer Drye died in the 1980s.

In the 1990s and 2000s:

- Whitey & Hogan were still performing
- Shannon Grayson was performing
    Shannon Grayson died in 1993
- David Deese joined the WBT Briarhoppers in 1991
- Hank Warren performed in the early 1990s, but retired due to illness
- Homer "Pappy" Sherrill took over temporarily for Hank Warren in 1992
- Fred Kirby died in 1996
- Hank Warren died in 1997
- Homer Sherrill stopped filling in for Warren in 1993
- Charles Crutchfield died in 1998
- Dwight Moody joined in 1993
- David Moody substituted for White during White's occasional illnesses in the 1990s
- Arval Hogan died in 2003
- Don White died in 2004
- Tom Warlick joined in 2007

In 2004, The WBT Briarhoppers III were formed with Whitey Grant,

David Deese, Dwight Moody, and David Moody on bass when needed. Billie Burton Daniel and Martin Schopp (Tex Martin) were the only pre–1940 Briarhopper Family members still alive in 2006; Eleanor Bryan Fields and Roy "Whitey" Grant were the remaining 1941 WBT Briarhopper string band members still alive in 2006. As of this writing, Grant has been performing as a Briarhopper for 66 years.

Notes

Chapter 1

1. Vincent J. Roscigno and William F. Danaher, *The Voice of Southern Labor: Radio, Music and Textile Strikes, 1929–34* [*VOSL*] (Minneapolis: University of Minnesota Press, 2004), 27.

2. Roscigno and Danaher, *VOSL*, 27.

3. McCloud, Barry. *Definitive Country: The Ultimate Encyclopedia of Country Music and Its Performers* (New York: Berkley Publishing Group, 1995), 335.

4. Roscigno and Danaher, *VOSL*, 21.

5. http://www.wbt.com/.

6. Ibid.

7. Ibid.

8. Ibid.

9. Ibid.

10. Roscigno and Danaher, *VOSL*, 28.

11. Pam Grundy, "From 'Il Trovatore' to the Crazy Mountaineers: The Rise and Fall of Elevated Culture on WBT-Charlotte, 1922–1930," *Southern Cultures* [*SC*] 1, no. 1 (Fall 1994), 52.

12. Barry McCloud, *Definitive Country: The Ultimate Encyclopedia of Country Music and Its Performers* (New York: Berkley Publishing Group, 1995), 97–98.

13. Lew Powell, *Charlotte Observer* [*COB*], July 7, 1982, 1F.

Chapter 2

1. Grundy, "From 'Il Trovatore' to the Crazy Mountaineers," *Southern Cultures*, 68.

2. Pam Grundy, "'We Always Tried To Be Good People': Respectability, Crazy Water Crystals, and Hillbilly Music on the Air, 1933–1935," *Journal of American History* [*JAH*] (March 1995), 1597.

3. Grundy, *JAH*, 1597.

4. Grundy, *JAH*, 1620.

5. Grundy, *SC*, 68.

6. Fred Kirby, interviewed by John Rumble, First Archive, Country Music Foundation Oral History Project (November 24, 1982), 16.

7. David Perlmutt, *Charlotte Observer*, May 23, 1999, [Perlmutt], 6z.

8. Bob Inman, *A Biography of Charles Crutchfield* (Self-published for the Crutchfield retirement party, June 1997), 3.

9. Joe DePriest, *Charlotte Observer*, April 20, 2003, 8.

10. Ivan Tribe, *Bluegrass Unlimited* (March 1978), 31.

11. George Holt, *The Charlotte Country Music Story Program* (Charlotte and Raleigh: Spirit Square Art Center and the North Carolina Arts Council, 1985), 17.

12. Holt, 17.

13. Barry W. Willis, *America's Music Bluegrass: A History of Bluegrass Music in the Words of Its Pioneers* (Franktown, CO: Pine Valley Music, 1989), 84.

14. Willis, 84.

15. Claude Casey, interviewed by John Rumble, First Archive, Country Music Foundation Oral History Project (October 14, 1983), 35.

16. Ibid.

17. Billie Burton Daniel, email to the authors (January 21, 2006).

18. McCloud, *Definitive Country*, 96.

19. *Charlotte Observer*, report on Crutchfield's death, unknown date.

20. Charles Crutchfield, interviewed by John Rumble, First Archive, Country Music Foundation (September 7, 1982), 18.

21. "The Crutchfield Chronicle" (internal handout distributed at Crutchfield's retirement, December 2, 1977), 3.

22. Charles Crutchfield, interviewed by John Rumble, First Archive, Country Music Foundation Oral History Project (November 23, 1982), 13.

23. http://www.btmemories.com/.

24. *Charlotte Observer*, December 19, 1977, section A.

25. Charles Crutchfield, interviewed by John Rumble, First Archive, Country Music Foundation Oral History Project (September 7, 1982), 2.

26. Billie Burton Daniel, interviewed by the authors (June 26, 2005).

27. Charles Crutchfield, interviewed by John Rumble, First Archive, County Music Foundation Oral History Project (September 7, 1982), 16.

28. Charles Crutchfield, interviewed by John Rumble, First Archive, Country Music Foundal Oral History Project (November 23, 1982), 20.

29. Newell Hathcock, interviewed by the authors (March 5, 2006).

30. Kate Mangum, telephone interview by the authors (October 31, 2005).

31. A.C. Snow, *Raleigh Times*, October 30, 1971, p. 5.

32. Whitey Grant, interviewed by the authors (April 15, 2005).

33. Mangum, October 31, 2005.

34. Billie Burton Daniel, "Whatever Happened to Billie Briarhopper?" (unpublished manuscript, not paginated as of this writing).

35. Kingsland Loughlin, telephone interview by the authors, February 28, 2006.

36. Daniel, email to the authors (June 26, 2005).

37. Daniel, "Whatever Happened to Billie Briarhopper?"

38. Ibid.

39. Ibid.

40. Ibid.

41. Ibid.

42. Ibid.

43. Ibid.

44. Terry Marshall, email to the authors (June 26, 2005).

45. Daniel, email to the authors (August 11, 2005).

46. Billie Ann Newman Carson, telephone interview by the authors (December 15, 2005).

47. Marshall, email to the authors (June 26, 2005).

48. Carson, telephone interview by the authors (July 10, 2005).

49. Ibid.

50. http://www.btmemories.com/.

51. Holt, 17.

52. Ibid.

53. Tom Hanchett, interviewed by the authors (February 28, 2006).

54. Daniel, email to the authors (July 9, 2005).

55. Ivan Tribe, "The Briarhoppers: Carolina Musicians," *Bluegrass Unlimited* (March 1978), 34.

56. Ray Thigpen, "The WBT Briarhoppers," *Bluegrass Unlimited* (May 1989), 50.

57. Holt, 18.

58. Daniel, email to the authors (December 11, 2005).

59. Pat Borden Gubbins, with Joe DePriest, Kay McFadden and Tony Brown, Fred Kirby Obituary, *Charlotte Observer*, April 23, 1996, 1A.

60. Fred Kirby, interviewed by John Rumble, First Archive, Country Music Foundation Oral History Project (November 24, 1982).

61. Taped conversation with Fred Kirby, made sometime in the 1980s with Claude Casey and Whitey & Hogan, courtesy of Leslie Crutchfield Tompkins.

62. Fred Kirby, interviewed by John Rumble, First Archive, Country Music Foundation Oral History Project (November 24, 1982).

63. Ibid

64. Holt, 18.

65. Gubbins, 1A.

66. Ibid.

67. Ibid.

68. Ibid.

69. Ray Thigpen, *Carolina Bluegrass Review* [*CBR*], date unknown, 5.

70. Fred Kirby, interviewed by John Rumble, First Archive, Country Music Foundation Oral History Project (November 24, 1982).

71. Taped conversation with Fred Kirby, Claude Casey, and Whitey & Hogan, 1980s, courtesy of Leslie Crutchfield Tompkins.

72. Thigpen, *Bluegrass Unlimited*, 51.

73. Holt, 18.

74. Ibid.

75. Thigpen, *Carolina Bluegrass Review*, 5.

76. Grant, interview with the authors (December 13, 2005).

77. *WBT Briarhopper Family Album*, compiled by WBT in 1948, 5.

78. *Ibid.*

79. Grant, interview with the authors (April 15, 2005).

80. *WBT Briarhopper Family Album*, 5.

81. Grant, interview with the authors (April 15, 2005).

82. Holt, 18.

83. Claude Casey, interviewed by John Rumble, First Archive, Country Music Foundation Oral History Project (November 22, 1982), 7.

84. Holt, 30.

85. McCloud, 797.

86. Holt, 30.

87. Ibid.

88. Cecil Campbell, interviewed by John Rumble, First Archive, Country Music Foundation Oral History Project (September 7, 1982), 1–2.

89. Holt, 30.

90. Cecil Campbell, interviewed by John Rumble, First Archive, Country Music Foundation Oral History Project (September 7, 1982), 3.

91. Grundy, *Journal of American History*, 1604.

92. Ibid.

93. Cecil Campbell, interviewed by John Rumble, First Archive, Country Music Foundation Oral History Project (September 7, 1982), 4.

94. Holt, *Charlotte Country Music Story*, 30.

95. Cecil Campbell, interviewed by John Rumble, First Archive, Country Music Foundation Oral History Project (September 7, 1982), 3.

96. http://www.hillbilly-music.com/.

97. Martin Schopp, Telephone interview by the authors (August 15, 2006).

98. Daniel, email to the authors (January 21, 2006).

99. Ibid.

100. Ibid.

101. Kingsland Loughlin, telephone interview by the authors (February 28, 2006).

102. Daniel, email to the authors (January 21, 2006).

103. Ibid.

104. Kingsland Loughlin, telephone interview with the authors (February 28, 2006).

105. Daniel, email to the authors (February 21, 2006).

106. Ibid.

107. Kingsland Loughlin, telephone interview with the authors (February 28, 2006).

108. Daniel, email to the authors (August 15, 2005).

109. Ibid.

110. Daniel, email to the authors (August 13, 2005).

111. Ibid

112. Daniel, email to the authors (December 11, 2005).

113. Perlmutt, *Charlotte Observer*, 6z.

114. Grundy, *Southern Cultures*, 68.

115. Perlmutt, *Charlotte Observer*, 7z.

116. Kevin O'Brien, "Music Archives Show City's Wealth Not All in Banks," *Charlotte Observer*, April 8, 1991.

117. Holt, *Charlotte Country Music Story*, 14.

118. Lew Powell, *Charlotte Observer*, 3F.

119. Perlmutt, 6z.

120. Cameron Shipp, *Charlotte News*, January 26, 1938.

121. O'Brien, 1B.

122. Ibid

123. Grundy, *SC*, 69.

124. Daniel, email to the authors (September 8, 2005).

Chapter 3

1. Daniel, "Whatever Happened to Billie Briarhopper?"

2. Daniel, email to the authors (September 8, 2005).

3. Carson, telephone interview with the authors (July 10, 2005).

4. Holt, 20.

5. Ibid.

6. Ibid.

7. Ibid.

8. Claude Casey, interviewed by John Rumble, First Archive, Country Music Foundation Oral History Project (October 4, 1983), 15.

9. Ibid.

10. Claude Casey, interviewed by John Rumble, First Archive, Country Music Foundation Oral History Project (October 4, 1983), 41.

11. Ibid, 13.

12. Claude Casey, interviewed by John Rumble, First Archive, Country Music Foundation Oral History Project (October 4, 1983), 13.

13. Ibid.

14. Holt, 20.

15. Carson telephone interview with the authors (December 15, 2005).

16. Ibid.

17. Briarhoppers Press Sheet, date unknown.

18. Grant, interview with the authors (April 15, 2005).

19. Ibid.

20. Thigpen, *Bluegrass Unlimited*, 51.

21. DePriest, *COB*, May 8, 1991.

22. Thigpen, *BU*, 51.

23. Kathy Haight, *"Getting Back to the Country,"* *COB*, October 25, 1985, 1C.

24. Grant, interview with the authors (April 15, 2005).

25. Haight, *COB*, 1C.

26. Thigpen, *BU*, 51.

27. Grant, interview with the authors (April 15, 2005).

28. Roscigno and Danaher, *VOSL*, 48.

29. Grant, interview with the authors (April 15, 2005).

30. Ibid

31. Thigpen, *BU*, 51.

32. Grant, interview with the authors (April 15, 2005).

33. Thigpen, *BU*, 51.

34. Grant, interview with the authors (April 15, 2005).

35. Ibid.

36. Ibid.

37. Ibid.

38. Ibid.

39. Ibid.

40. Ibid.

41. George Holt, *Charlotte Country Music Story*, 28.

42. Grant, interview with the authors (December 13, 2005).

43. Carson telephone interview with the authors (December 15, 2005).

44. Thomas Warlick, "Two Fast Finger: Wade Mainer," *Banjo Newsletter* (February 2003), 24.

45. Thigpen, *CBR*, date unknown.

46. Grant, interview with the authors (April 15, 2005).

47. David Holt, email to the authors (July 16, 2006).

48. Gina Robinson, email to the authors (February 7, 2006).

49. Thigpen, *BU*, 52.

50. Holt, 18.

51. Thigpen, *BU*, 52.

52. Robinson, email to the authors (February 7, 2006).

53. Grant, interview with the authors (April 14, 2005).

54. Ibid.

55. Ibid.

56. Mainer, telephone interview with the authors (May 25, 2005).

57. Grant, interview with the authors (April 15, 2005).

58. Holt, 11.

59. http://www.music.com/.

60. Crystal Dempsey, "Briarhoppers Banjo Player Shannon Grayson Dies at 76," *COB*, May 13, 1993, 1C.

61. http://www.music.com/.

62. Robinson, email to the authors (February 7, 2006).

63. Charles Wolfe and James Akinson, *Country Music Goes to War*, 107.

64. Wolfe, 108.

65. Ibid., 108–109.

66. Wolfe, 108.

67. Wolfe, 114–115.

68. Whitey & Hogan, interviewed by John Rumble, First Archive, Country Music Foundation Oral History Project (November 24, 1982), 39.

69. Grant, interview with the authors (December 13, 2006).

70. Eleanor Bryan Fields, telephone interview by the authors (December 26, 2005).

71. Ibid.

72. Eleanor Bryan Fields, telephone interview by the authors (December 26, 2005).

73. Ibid.

74. Ibid.

75. Grant, interview with the authors (December 13, 2006).

76. Ibid.

77. Daniel, telephone interview by the authors (June 12, 2005).

78. InfoWrangler Wikipedia Snapshot on the Internet.

79. Daniel, email to the authors (December 14, 2005).

80. 1940 Briarhopper radio script from Charles Crutchfield's files, copies of which are at the University of North Carolina Chapel Hill Library.

81. 1940 Briarhopper radio script from Charles Crutchfield's files, copies of which are at the UNC Chapel Hill Library.

82. Hogan, interviewed by John Rumble (interview with Whitey and Hogan), First Archive, Country Music Foundation Oral History Project (November 24, 1982), 20–21.

83. Charles Crutchfield, interviewed by John Rumble, First Archive, Country Music Foundation Oral History Project (November 23, 1982), 12.

84. Warlick family discussion, July 12, 2005.

85. Jack Lawrence, letter to the editor, "2 Fallen Country Stars Left Enduring Mark," *COB,* September 28, 2003.

86. Warlick family conversation, July 12, 2005.

87. Joe Kiser (NC Representative), telephone interview by the authors (March 8, 2006).

88. *Our State* (January 2003), 59.

89. Curly Seckler, telephone interview by the authors (February 25, 2006).

90. Kuralt and McGlohan, *North Carolina Is My Home,* 80.

91. Gubbins, *COB,* 1A.

92. Grant, interview with the authors (April 2005).

93. Whitey and Hogan interview, interviewed by John Rumble, First Archive, Country Music Foundation Oral History Project (November 24, 1982), 5.

94. Grant, interview with the authors (April 15, 2005).

95. Ibid., (December 13, 2005).

96. Whitey and Hogan, interviewed by John Rumble, First Archive, Country Music Foundation Oral History Project (November 5, 1982), 39.

97. Grant, interview with the authors (April 15, 2005).

98. Whitey and Hogan, interviewed by John Rumble, First Archive, Country Music Foundation Oral History Project (November 24, 1982), 3.

99. Charles Crutchfield, interviewed by John Rumble, First Archive, Country Music Foundation Oral History Project (November 23, 1982), 19.

100. Warlick family discussion, July 12, 2005.

101. From a script found in Charles Crutchfield's files, now stored at the University of North Carolina-Chapel Hill.

102. Charles Crutchfield, interviewed by John Rumble, First Archive, Country Music Foundation Oral History Project (September 7, 1982), 26.

103. Ibid., (November 23, 1982), 21.

104. Charles Crutchfield, interviewed by John Rumble, First Archive, Country Music Foundation Oral History Project (November 23, 1982), 7.

105. Ibid., 21.

106. Whitey and Hogan, interviewed by John Rumble, First Archive, Country Music Foundation Oral History Project (November 5, 1982), 43.

107. Ibid.

108. Grant, interview, December 13, 2005.

109. Bob Inman, *COB,* date unknown.

110. Whitey and Hogan, interviewed by John Rumble, First Archive, Country Music Foundation Oral History Project (November 5, 1982), 48–49.

111. Ibid., 49–50.

112. Grant, interview with the authors (December 15, 2005).

113. Whitey and Hogan, interviewed by John Rumble, First Archive, Country

Music Foundation Oral History Project (November 24, 1982), 9–10.

114. Ibid., 9–10.

115. Whitey and Hogan, interviewed by John Rumble, First Archive, Country Music Foundation Oral History Project (November 24, 1982), 12.

116. Ibid., 22.

117. Whitey and Hogan, interviewed by John Rumble, First Archive, Country Music Foundation Oral History Project (November 24, 1982), 22–23.

118. Ibid., 14–15.

119. Whitey and Hogan, interviewed by John Rumble, First Archive, Country Music Foundation Oral History Project (November 24, 1982), 15.

120. Grant, interview with the authors (December 12, 2005).

121. Seckler, telephone interview by the authors (February 25, 2006).

122. Grant, telephone interview by the authors (April 15, 2005).

123. John Rumble, "Country Music and the Rural South: Reminiscing with Whitey and Hogan," *Journal of Country Music* (October 1985).

124. Holt, 18.

125. Grant, interview, April 15, 2005.

126. Jon Ostendorff, Claude Casey obituary, *COB,* date unknown.

127. Grant, interview with the authors (December 13, 2005).

128. Ibid., (April 15, 2005).

129. Larry Warren, telephone interview by the authors (April 14, 2005).

130. Grant, interview with the authors (April 15, 2005).

131. Whitey and Hogan, interviewed by John Rumble, First Archive, Country Music Foundation Oral History Project (November 5, 1982), 6.

132. Ibid., 54.

133. Whitey and Hogan, interviewed by John Rumble, First Archive, Country Music Foundation Oral History Project (November 5, 1982), 54.

134. Ibid., 21.

135. Whitey and Hogan, interviewed by John Rumble, First Archive, Country Music Foundation Oral History Project (November 5, 1982), 26–27.

136. Ibid., 27.

137. Grant, interview with the authors (April 15, 2005).

138. Whitey and Hogan, interviewed by John Rumble, First Archive, Country Music Foundation Oral History Project (November 24, 1982), 5–6.

139. Grant, interview with the authors (May 10, 2005).

140. Whitey and Hogan, interviewed by John Rumble, First Archive, Country Music Foundation Oral History Project (November 5, 1982), 25.

141. Roscigno and Danaher, 54.

142. Grant, interview with the authors (May 10, 2005).

143. Ibid., (April 15, 2005).

144. Whitey and Hogan, interviewed by John Rumble, First Archive, Country Music Foundation Oral History Project (November 5, 1982), 35.

145. Grant, interview with the authors (April 15, 2005).

146. Ibid.

147. Doc Watson interview with David Holt (June 1, 2006).

148. Lawrence, *COB,* September 28, 2003.

149. Seckler, telephone interview by the authors (February 25, 2006).

150. Grant, interview with the authors (April 15, 2005).

151. Wade Mainer, telephone interview by the authors (May 23, 2005).

152. Holt, 19.

153. Ibid

154. Grant, interview with the authors (April 15, 2005).

155. DePriest, "Revival of Roots Music," *COB,* March 22, 2002, 1L.

156. Janette Carter, telephone interview with the authors (May 25, 2005).

157. Mark Zwonitzer and Charles Hirshberg, *Will You Miss Me When I'm Gone: The Carter Family & Their Legacy in American Music* (New York: Simon & Schuster, 2002), 248.

158. Grant, interview with the authors (April 15, 2005).

159. Zwonitzer & Hirshberg, 338.

160. Grant, interview with the authors (April 15, 2005).

161. Richard Smith, *Can't You Hear Me Callin': The Life of Bill Monroe, Father of*

Bluegrass (New York and London: Little, Brown, 2000), 40.

162. Grant, interview with the authors (April 15, 2005).

163. Seckler, telephone interview with the authors (February 25, 2006).

164. Grant, interview with the authors (April 15, 2005).

165. Whitey and Hogan, interviewed by John Rumble, First Archive, Country Music Foundation Oral History Project (November 11, 1982), 30.

166. Grant, interview with the authors (April 15, 2005).

167. Whitey and Hogan, interviewed by John Rumble, First Archive, Country Music Foundation Oral History Project (November 5, 1982), 36.

168. Ibid., 37–38.

169. Claude Casey, interviewed by John Rumble, First Archive, Country Music Foundation Oral History Project (October 4, 1982), 8.

170. Ibid., 34.

171. Kevin O'Brien, "Music Archives Show City's Wealth Not All in Banks," *COB*, April 8, 1991, 1B.

172. Cecil Campbell, interviewed by John Rumble, First Archive, Country Music Foundation Oral History Project (September 7, 1982), 19.

173. Ibid., 20.

174. Cecil Campbell, interviewed by John Rumble, First Archive, Country Music Foundation Oral History Project (September 7, 1982), 21.

175. Fred Kirby, interviewed by John Rumble, First Archive, Country Music Foundation Oral History Project (November 24, 1982), 14.

176. Grady Jefferys, "A Musician Who Is All Heart and Soul," *Raleigh Magazine*, Summer 1969.

177. Daniel, email to the authors (July 10, 2005).

178. Daniel, "Whatever Happened to Billie Briarhopper?"

179. Daniel, email to the authors (July 10, 2005).

180. Fields, telephone interview with the authors (December 26, 2005).

181. Daniel, email to the authors (July 9, 2005).

182. Ibid.

183. Charlie Friar, telephone interview with the authors (July 9, 2005).

184. Daniel, email to the authors (December 11, 2005).

185. McCloud, 798.

186. Holt, 30.

187. *Charlotte Observer,* September 13, 1945, 1

188. http://www.icebergradio.com/artist/533270/pappy_briarhopper.html.

189. Daniel, "Whatever Happened to Billie Briarhopper?"

Chapter 4

1. DePriest, *COB*, March 22, 2002, 1L.

2. DePriest, *COB* article, May 8, 1991, page unknown.

3. Grant, interview with the authors (December 13, 2005).

4. Ibid.

5. *The Banjo of Ralph Stanley,* Homespun Videos, Woodstock, NY.

6. Tony Trischka, "'Snuffy' Jenkins," *Bluegrass Unlimited* (October 1977), 21.

7. Charles Crutchfield, interview ed by John Rumble, First Archive, Country Music Foundation Oral History Project (November 23, 1982), 6–7.

8. Grant, interview with the authors (December 13, 2005).

9. *COB,* May 20, 1983, 7C.

10. Grant, interview with the authors (April 15, 2005).

11. Ibid.

12. Roy Blount, Jr., *Crackers,* 145.

13. Grant, interview with the authors (April 15, 2005).

14. Gubbins, *COB,* April 23, 1996, pg. 1A.

15. Doug Mayes, interview by the authors (May 23, 2005).

16. Grant, interview with the authors (April 15, 2005).

17. Ibid.

18. Melanie Sill, "Briarhoppers to bring old-time radio sound to Raleigh," *Raleigh News and Observer,* September 14, 1985.

19. George Hamilton, telephone interview by the authors (June 1, 2006).

20. http://www.chronicle.augusta.com/.

21. Claude Casey, interviewed by John Rumble, First Archive, Country Music Foundation Oral History Project (October 4, 1985), 17.

22. Doug Bell, telephone interview by the authors (August 19, 2005).

23. Eleanor Bryant Fields, telephone interview by the authors (December 26, 2005).

24. McCloud, 127.

25. http://www.rcs.law.emory.edu/.

26. *Crutchfield Chronicle,* December 2, 1977.

27. Carson, interview with the authors (December 15, 2005).

Chapter 5

1. Grant, interview with the authors (April 15, 2005).

2. Ibid.

3. Charles Crutchfield, interviewed by John Rumble, First Archive, Country Music Foundation Oral History Project (November 1982).

4. "High Lonesome: The Story of Bluegrass Music." Rachel Liebling, Director. DVD. Newton, NJ: Shanachie Entertainment, 1994.

5. Kate Mangum, telephone interview with the authors (October 31, 2005).

6. Terry Marshall, interview with the authors (August 19, 2005).

7. Daniel, email interview with the authors (July 10, 2005).

8. Powell, *COB,* December 19 1977 section A.

9. Ibid.

Chapter 6

1. Grant, interview with the authors (April 15, 2005).

2. Ibid.

3. Melanie Sill, "Briarhoppers to Bring Old-time Radio Sound to Raleigh," *Raleigh News and Observer,* September 14, 1985. Grant, interview with the authors (April 15, 2005).

4. Grant, interview with the authors (April 15, 2005).

5. Dot Jackson, *COB,* August 25, 1973, 1C.

6. Dot Jackson, email interview with the authors (February 9, 2006).

7. Ibid., (March 3, 2006).

8. Gale Leslie, letter to the authors (August 18, 2005).

9. Wister, *COB,* May 17, 1976, 1B.

10. Wister, 1B.

11. Ibid.

12. Ibid.

13. Ibid.

14. Authors' tape recording of the event, 1976.

15. Wister, 1B.

16. Ibid.

17. George Hamilton IV interview with the authors (January 23, 2006).

18. Carson, telephone interview with the authors (December 15, 2005).

Chapter 7

1. Grant, interview with the authors (April 15, 2005).

2. Ibid.

3. Ibid.

4. Ibid.

5. Ibid.

6. Grant, interview with the authors (December 13, 2005).

7. Ibid.

8. Holt, 31.

9. Ibid.

10. Grant, interview with the authors (December 13, 2005).

11. Hamilton, interview with the authors (June 1, 2006).

12. Joe DePriest, *Shelby Star,* July 2, 1986, 12.

13. Grant, interview with the authors (April 15, 2005).

14. Ibid.

15. Ibid.

16. Ibid.

17. Ibid.

18. Ibid.

19. Associated Press, *COB,* May 20, 1983, 7C.

Chapter 8

1. Dempsey, *COB,* May 13, 1993, 1C.

2. Ibid.

3. David Deese, interview by the authors (November 12, 2005).

4. Ibid.

5. Ibid.

6. Ibid.

7. Jameson, *COB,* December 18, 1997, 4C.

8. Bob Inman, *COB,* unknown date and page.

9. Barry R. Willis, *America's Bluegrass: A History of Bluegrass Music in the Words of Its Pioneers* [*AB*], 26.

10. Willis, *AB,* 27.

11. Willis, *AB,* 27.

12. Willis, *AB,* 28.

13. Dwight L. Moody, Jr., *The Life of Dwight L. Moody, Jr.: Autobiography of a North Carolina Fiddler, 1929–2001* (Charlotte: Laymond Publishing, 2001), 68.

14. Moody, email to the authors (January 4, 2006).

15. Dwight Moody, interview by the authors (March 15, 2005).

16. Moody, 52–53.

17. Andy Duncan, interview by the authors (March 12, 2006).

18. *COB,* page and date unknown.

19. Grant, interview with the authors (December 13, 2005).

20. Ibid.

21. *COB,* July 25, 1999, obituary section.

22. http://www.music.com/person/fred_kirby, /1.

Chapter 9

1. Wayne Martin, North Carolina Folk Heritage Award program, 1.

2. DePriest, *COB,* April 4, 2005, 1L.

3. Ibid.

4. Ibid.

5. Grant, interview with the authors (April 15, 2005).

6. DePriest, *"Country Legend Dead at 92,"* *COB,* September 13, 2003, 5B

7. DePriest, *COB,* September 13, 2003, 5B.

8. Grant, interview with the authors (May 10, 2005).

9. Ibid.

10. Moody, interview with the authors (June 6, 2005).

11. Liner notes to "Straight Paths," Kristen Scott Benson, Pine Castle Records

12. Grant, interview with the authors (May 13, 2005).

13. Grant, interview with the authors (May 10, 2005).

14. Ibid.

15. Grant, interview with the authors (June 1 2006).

16. Fields interview with the authors (December 26, 2005).

17. Carson, interview with the authors (December 15, 2005).

Bibliography

Books and Articles

Ahrens, Pat. *"Snuffy" Jenkins and "Pappy" Sherrill: The Hired Hands.* Columbia, SC: Self Published, 2002.

Blount, Roy, Jr. *Crackers.* Athens: University of Georgia Press, 1980.

Bluegrass Unlimited (magazine). Edited by Peter V. Kuykendall. Warrenton, VA: Bluegrass Unlimited.

Carlin, Bob. *String Bands in the North Carolina Piedmont.* Jefferson, NC: McFarland & Company, 2005.

Charlotte News. Charlotte, NC, various years.

Charlotte Observer. Charlotte, NC: Knight-Ridder, various years.

Daniel, Billie Burton. "Whatever Happened to Billie Briarhopper?" Unpublished manuscript. Wilmington, NC, 2005.

Eades, David. *The History of WBT/WBTV.* Charlotte, NC: WBTV (a Jefferson Pilot Company), 2002.

Grundy, Pam. "We Always Tried to Be Good People: Respectability, Crazy Water Crystals, and Hillbilly Music on the Air, 1933–1935." *Journal of American History* (1995).

_____. "From 'Il Trovatore' to the Crazy Mountaineers: The Rise and Fall of Elevated Culture on WBT-Charlotte, 1922–1930." *Southern Cultures* 1, no. 1 (Fall 1994).

Holt, George. *The Charlotte Country Music Story Program.* Charlotte and Raleigh: Spirit Square Art Center and the North Carolina Arts Council, 1985.

Jefferys, Grady. "A Musician Who Is All Heart and Soul." *Raleigh Magazine,* Summer 1969.

Kingsbury, Paul. *The Grand Ole Opry History of Country Music.* New York: Villard Books, 1995.

Kuralt, Charles, and Loonis McGlohan. *North Carolina Is My Home.* Old Saybrook, CT: Globe Pequot Press, 1998.

Liebling, Rachel, director. "High Lonesome: A Story of Bluegrass Music." DVD. Shanachie Entertainment, Newton, New Jersey. 1994.

McCloud, Barry. *Definitive Country: The Ultimate Encyclopedia of Country Music and Its Performers.* New York: Berkley Publishing Group, 1995.

Moody, Dwight L., Jr. *The Life of Dwight L. Moody, Jr.: Autobiography of a North Carolina Fiddler, 1929–2001.* Charlotte: Laymond Publishing, 2001.

Nitchie, Hub, and Nancy Nitchie, eds. *Banjo Newsletter.* Annapolis, MD: Banjo Newsletter.

North Carolina Arts Council and Spirit Square Art Center. *The Charlotte Country Music Story Proposal*. Raleigh and Charlotte, NC, 1984.

Raleigh News and Observer. Raleigh, NC: Knight-Ridder, various years.

Roscigno, Vincent J., and William F. Danaher. *The Voice of Southern Labor: Radio, Music, and Textile Strikes, 1929–1934*. Minneapolis: University of Minnesota Press, 2004.

Rosenberg, Neil V. *Bluegrass: A History*. Chicago: University of Illinois Press, 1993.

Rumble, John. "Oral Histories." The Oral History Project. Nashville, TN: Country Music Hall of Fame, various years.

Shelby Star. Shelby, NC: Freedom Communications Company, various years.

Smith, Richard D. *Can't You Hear Me Callin': The Life of Bill Monroe, Father of Bluegrass*. New York and London: Little, Brown and Company, 2000.

Thigpen, Ray. "The WBT Briarhoppers." *Bluegrass Unlimited* (May 1989).

Tribe, Ivan. "The Briarhoppers: Carolina Musicians." *Bluegrass Unlimited* (March 1978).

Trischka, Tony, and Pete Wernick. *Masters of the 5-String Banjo*. New York: Oak Publications, 1988.

Willis, Barry W. *America's Music Bluegrass: A History of Bluegrass Music in the Words of Its Pioneers*. Franktown, CO: Pine Valley Music, 1989.

Wolfe, Charles K., and James E. Akinson, eds. *Country Music Goes to War*. Lexington: University of Kentucky Press, 2005.

Wright, John. *Traveling the High Way Home: Ralph Stanley and the World of Traditional Bluegrass Music*. Chicago: University of Illinois Press, 1993.

Zwonitzer, Mark, and Charles Hirshberg. *Will You Miss Me When I'm Gone: The Carter Family and Their Legacy in American Music*. New York: Simon and Schuster, 2002.

Websites

http://www.btmemories.com/ (for fans of WBT radio).

http://www.countryworks.com/ (includes a section called "The Century of Country").

http://www.hillbilly-music.com/.

http://www.levinemuseum.com/ (Levine Museum of the New South, Charlotte, North Carolina).

http://www.mmguide.musicmatch.com/ (contains a great deal of information on old-time musical acts).

http://www.music.com/ (music and musicians, past and present).

http://www.nationmaster.com/ (an encyclopedia).

http://www.ncarts.org/ (North Carolina Arts Council).

http://www.nydailynews.com/ (*New York Daily News*).

http://www.oldandsold.com/ (contains data on patent medicines).

http://www.settlet.feedback.com/ (online discography of recordings made on 78 records from RCA Victor and other recording companies).

http://www.surfnetinc.com/ (information on cowboy movies and related items).

http://www.tcmradio.com/ (for traditional country music).

http://www.wbt.com/ (for both WBT and WBT).

http://www.westernfilmfair.tripod.com/ (for the Western Film Fair held in Charlotte, North Carolina).

Interviews

Warlick, Thomas, and Lucy Warlick. Interview with Roy "Whitey" Grant and Polly Grant, at the Grant Home, on April 15, 2005, and December 13, 2005.

_____. Interview with Roy "Whitey" Grant at the Western Film Fair BBQ in Wadesboro, NC, for the Western Film Festival, 2005.

_____. Interview with Doug Bell, via telephone, 2005.

_____. Many Interviews with Billie Burton Daniel from her home in Wilmington, NC, 2005–2006.

_____. Telephone interview with Billie Ann Newman Carson on December 15, 2005.

_____. Many Interviews with Betty Johnson of the Johnson Family Singers, via email, 2005.

_____. Telephone interview with Homer Briarhopper Drye's sister, Kate Mangum, on October 31, 2005.

_____. Many interviews with Tim Drye, son of Homer Briarhopper Drye, 2005–2006.

_____. Interview with David Deese, November 12, 2005.

_____. Telephone interview with Eleanor Bryan Fields on December 26, 2005.

_____. Telephone interview with George Hamilton IV on January 23, 2006.

_____. Telephone interview with Curly Seckler on February 25, 2006.

_____. Telephone interview with Kingsland Loughlin on March 1, 2006.

_____. Interview with Tom Hanchett, on March 2, 2006, at the Levine Museum of the New South.

_____. Telephone interview with Newell Hathcock, March 5, 2006.

_____. Interview with David Holt, via email, July 16, 2006.

_____. Telephone interviews with Martin Schopp (Tex Martin), August 15 and 30, 2006.

Libraries, Museums and Personal Materials

Charlotte-Mecklenburg Public Library, "Carolina Room," Charlotte, North Carolina.

Country Music Hall of Fame and Museum, Nashville, Tennessee.

The files of Charles Crutchfield, Charlotte, North Carolina.

The files of Dwight Moody, Indian Trail, North Carolina.

The files of Don White, Roy Grant et al., Charlotte, North Carolina.

Levine Museum of the New South, Charlotte, North Carolina.

North Carolina Folk Heritage Offices, Raleigh, North Carolina.

University of North Carolina at Charlotte Library, Charlotte, North Carolina.

University of North Carolina Library, Chapel Hill, North Carolina.

Index